Hans Dieter Betz is Professor of New
Testament at The Divinity School,
University of Chicago, Chicago, Illinois.
He is the author of the Hermeneia com-
mentary on Galatians, and forthcoming
commentaries for the same series on the
Sermon on the Mount and Second Cor-
inthians 8 and 9.

Essays on the
Sermon on the Mount

HANS DIETER BETZ

Essays on the
Sermon on the Mount

Translations by L. L. Welborn

FORTRESS PRESS   PHILADELPHIA

When indicated, biblical quotations are from the Revised Standard
Version of the Bible, copyright 1946, 1952, ©1971, 1973 by the
Division of Christian Education of the National Council of the
Churches of Christ in the U.S.A. and are used by permission.

Library of Congress Cataloging in Publication Data

Betz, Hans Dieter.
  Essays on the Sermon on the mount.

  Includes indexes.
  1. Sermon on the mount—Addresses, essays, lectures.
I. Title.
BT380.2.B48 1984   226'.906   84-47910
ISBN 0-8006-0726-0

K896D84   Printed in the United States of America 1-726

Gerhard Ebeling
In Friendship

"Laereren er da Guden selv, der virkende som Anledning foranlediger, at den Laerende mindes om, at han er Usandheden, og er det ved egen Skyld."

Søren Kierkegaard, *Philosophiske Smuler eller En Smule Philosophi, af Johannes Climacus, Samlede Vaerker* 4 (Copenhagen: C. A. Reitzel, 1844), 209

"The Teacher is then the God himself, who in acting as an occasion prompts the learner to recall that he is in Error, and that by reason of his own guilt."

Translated by D. S. Swenson, in S. Kierkegaard, *Philosophical Fragments or A Fragment of Philosophy, by Johannes Climacus*, 2d ed. (Princeton, N. J.: Princeton University Press, 1962), 19

Contents

CONTENTS

Preface

The Sermon on the Mount transmitted by the evangelist Matthew (5:3–7:27) is an unusual, not to say uncanny, text in many respects. It impresses one first of all by its simplicity and straightforwardness; it addresses its readers, even the non-Christian, immediately and compels them to take a stand. Yet this dimension of the text could prove misleading were one to conclude that the simple, practical, uncompromising message of Jesus was first to be found here, a message not yet burdened with the technical theological language that makes access to the Gospel writers and Paul so difficult. In reality, the Sermon on the Mount is the New Testament text most remote from modern men and women. It would be a grave misunderstanding to persist in the view that this text is attractive only because it presents, in a strange, exotic, fascinating manner, an alternative view of the world which promises—in apparent opposition to modern Western civilization—a better world.

Only the superficial reader can find a text such as the Sermon on the Mount simple, practical, and untheological. As one penetrates more deeply into the work—a task to which specialized knowledge in the areas of philology, form and redaction criticism, literary criticism, history of religions, and New Testament theology necessarily applies —a theological problematic becomes increasingly more evident, found in highly compressed form in the Sermon on the Mount. One can understand, therefore, why New Testament scholarship up to the present has offered no satisfactory explanation of this vitally important text. Scholarship still finds itself in the process of unraveling this apparently confused and opaque body of teaching, while at the same time an enormous number of popular books, pamphlets, and journal articles flood the marketplace and purport in ever new ways to be able to disclose what is found in this text, what it means, and what conclusions are to be drawn from it.

The author of the present collection of essays once belonged, more or less, to those who had resigned themselves to the present state of research on the Sermon on the Mount. More intensive preoccupation with the Sermon on the Mount only began during preparation of the Galatians commentary, as the extraordinarily intimate, more precisely adversarial, relationship of the Epistle to the Galatians and the Sermon on the Mount continued to force itself upon me.

The essays republished here, some of which are translations from the German, represent investigations undertaken during the years 1974 to 1983. They bear witness to a progressively deeper penetration of the fundamental problems of the Sermon on the Mount. Out of these studies the hypothesis arose that the Sermon on the Mount was a pre-Matthean source composed by a redactor. This source presents us with an early form—deriving from Jewish Christianity—of the Christian faith as a whole, which had direct links to the teaching of the historical Jesus and thus constituted an alternative to Gentile Christianity as known above all from the letters of Paul and the Gospels, as well as later writings of the New Testament.

Thus behind the Sermon on the Mount the problem of the teaching of the historical Jesus emerges once again. If the Jewish-Christian Sermon on the Mount represents a response to the teaching of Jesus of Nazareth critical of that of Gentile Christianity, then it serves unmistakably to underline the well-known fact, frequently forgotten today, of how little we know of Jesus and his teaching. The reasons for our lack of knowledge are of a hermeneutical sort, and cannot be overcome by an excess of good will. The Gentile-Christian authors of the Gospels transmitted to us only that part of the teaching of Jesus that they themselves understood; they handed on only that which they were able to translate into the thought categories of Gentile Christianity, and which they judged worthy of transmission. This process of selection and revision is familiar to anyone who has been deeply occupied with the history of the Gospel traditions.

By contrast, the Sermon on the Mount stands nearer to the Jewish thought of Jesus of Nazareth, and manifests its characteristic affinity and distance over against later Christianity. Our current dilemma in regard to Jesus of Nazareth resembles that of the historical Socrates: on the one hand we know too little, and on the other hand we know too much to be able to agree quite simply with the different interpretations or to forgo them completely. Access to the historical Jesus of Nazareth is obstructed for us by the debates that his teaching called into existence. The record of these discussions, embedded in the fragments of the teaching of Jesus himself, lies before us in the texts of the New Testament. Yet from these texts his original teaching can neither be reconstructed nor abstracted in its entirety. But much will already have been achieved if the alternative theological positions called forth by his teaching can be brought into relation to one another. As Ernst Käsemann intimated in his address to the old Marburgers,* it is by pursuing the connections and tensions between the teaching of Jesus and that of the early Christian communities that the problem of the historical Jesus can be taken up anew.

The essays published here in no way presuppose that the far-reaching hypothesis mentioned above has already been established, or could be easily proven. Rather, each of the essays presents evidence for the fact that there are sufficient grounds for the formation of such a hypothesis. Needless to say, a scientific hypothesis is not to be confused with a mere whim or a fleeting inspiration. Only further investigations which carry forward the work begun here can furnish proof of the hypothesis as a whole. That proof is yet lacking and will finally be supplied by the detailed commentary to appear in the Hermeneia series.

Thus the present essays represent preliminary studies with a view to the commentary now underway. They are published together here because repeated reference will be made to them in the commentary,

---

*E. Käsemann, in the lecture originally delivered thirty years ago at the reunion of former Marburg students and colleagues on 20 October 1953, in Jugenheim. First published in *ZThK* 51 (1954): 125–53. Eng. trans.: "The Problem of the Historical Jesus," in *Essays on New Testament Themes* (Philadelphia: Fortress Press, 1982), 15–47, esp. 46: "The solution of this problem cannot, however, if our findings are right, be approached with any hope of success along the line of supposed historical *bruta facta* but only along the line of the connection and tension between the preaching of Jesus and that of his community. The question of the historical Jesus is, in its legitimate form, the question of the continuity of the Gospel within the discontinuity of the times and within the variation of the kerygma."

and as a means of stimulating discussion before that work appears. In this way, a certain impatience on the part of the author may be bridged, an impatience created by the text itself. For the Sermon on the Mount demands of the scholar not a little care, a great deal of time, and a considerable degree of intellectual abstinence.

More than he is aware, the author is indebted to a large number of colleagues, students, and friends who have over the years helped by thinking things through with him and by making stimulating or critical suggestions. To all of them, too many to be named here individually, I wish to express my sincere gratitude. Some persons, however, must be mentioned by name. Gerhard Ebeling, to whom the volume is dedicated, has been a friend and wise counselor during the years when the essays were worked out. Norman Hjelm, director of Fortress Press, has been an enthusiastic supporter of the present project. Laurence Welborn has made the translation of the German articles a pleasant experience for the author, something not to be taken for granted. Mr. Welborn also compiled the indices. Marjorie Menaul and Martha Morrow-Vojacek prepared the final typescript.

H. D. Betz
October 1984

Acknowledgments

The author thanks the original publishers for permission to republish his papers in this book.

1. "The Sermon on the Mount: Its Literary Genre and Function," *JR* 59 (1979): 285–97.
2. "Die Makarismen der Bergpredigt (Matthäus 5, 3–12). Beobachtungen zur literarischen Form und theologischen Bedeutung," *ZThK* 75 (1978): 3–19.
3. "Die hermeneutischen Prinzipien in der Bergpredigt (Mt 5, 17–20)," in *Verifikationen, Festschrift für Gerhard Ebeling zum 70. Geburtstag,* ed. Eberhard Jüngel, Johannes Wallmann, Wilfrid Werbeck (Tübingen: J. C. B. Mohr [Paul Siebeck], 1982), 27–41. "The Hermeneutical Principles of the Sermon on the Mount (Mt. 5:17–20)," *Journal of Theology for Southern Africa* 42 (1983): 17–28.
4. "Eine judenchristliche Kult-Didache in Matthäus 6, 1–18," in *Jesus Christus in Historie und Theologie, Neutestamentliche Festschrift für Hans Conzelmann zum 60. Geburtstag,* ed. Georg Strecker (Tübingen: J. C. B. Mohr [Paul Siebeck], 1975), 445–57.
5. "Matthew vi.22f. and Greek Theories of Vision," in *Text and Interpretation: Studies in the New Testament Presented to Matthew Black,* ed. by Ernest Best and Robert McL. Wilson (Cambridge: At the University Press, 1979), 43–56.
6. "Kosmogonie und Ethik in der Bergpredigt," *ZThK* 81 (1984): 139–71.
7. "Eine Episode im Jüngsten Gericht (Mt 7, 21–23)," *ZThK* 78 (1981): 1–30.

Abbreviations

	of the Old Testament. 2 vols. Oxford: At the Clarendon Press, 1912.
Diels-Kranz	H. Diels and W. Kranz. *Die Fragmente der Vorsokratiker.* 6th ed. Berlin: Weidmann, 1964.
EWNT	*Exegetisches Wörterbuch zum Neuen Testament.*
FRLANT	Forschungen zur Religion und Literatur des Alten und Neuen Testaments.
HNT	Handbuch zum Neuen Testament.
HSW, *NT Apocrypha*	E. Hennecke. *New Testament Apocrypha.* Edited by W. Schneemelcher, trans. R. McL. Wilson, 2 vols. Philadelphia: Westminster Press, 1963–65.
HThR	*Harvard Theological Review.*
HTS	*Harvard Theological Studies.*
IDB	*Interpreter's Dictionary of the Bible.*
JBL	*Journal of Biblical Literature.*
JR	*Journal of Religion.*
LCL	The Loeb Classical Library.
LXX	Septuaginta.
MH	*Museum Helveticum.*
NT	*Novum Testamentum.*
NTD	Das Neue Testament Deutsch.
NTS	*New Testament Studies.*
par.	parallel(s)
PGM	*Papyri Graecae Magicae.*
P.Oxy.	*Oxyrhynchus Papyri.*
PRE	Pauly-Wissowa, *Real-Encyclopädie der classischen Altertumswissenschaft.*
RAC	*Reallexikon für Antike und Christentum.*
RVV	Religionsgeschichtliche Versuche und Vorarbeiten.
SBLDS	Society of Biblical Literature, Dissertation Series.
SBS	Stuttgarter Bibelstudien.
SCHNT	Studia ad Corpus Hellenisticum Novi Testamenti.
SCSt	Septuagint and Cognate Studies.
SEÅ	*Svensk Exegetisk Årsbok.*

SM   Sermon on the Mount.
SPAW.PH   *Sitzungsberichte der preussischen Akademie der Wissenschaften,* philosophisch-historische Klasse.
TDNT   *Theological Dictionary of the New Testament.*
TDOT   *Theological Dictionary of the Old Testament.*
ThLZ   *Theologische Literaturzeitung.*
VetChr   *Vetera Christianorum.*
VF   *Verkündigung und Forschung.*
VigChr   *Vigiliae Christianae.*
WUNT   Wissenschaftliche Untersuchungen zum Neuen Testament.
WZ[L].GS *Wissenschaftliche Zeitschrift der Karl-Marx-Universität Leipzig,* gesellschafts- und sprachwissenschaftliche Reihe.
ZNW   *Zeitschrift für die neutestamentliche Wissenschaft und die Kunde der älteren Kirche.*
ZPE   *Zeitschrift für Papyrologie und Epigraphik.*
ZThK   *Zeitschrift für Theologie und Kirche.*

1

The Sermon on the Mount (Matt. 5:3–7:27): Its Literary Genre and Function[1]

In his presidential address before the Studiorum Novi Testamentum Societas annual meeting of 1977,[2] Professor Günther Bornkamm raises the problem of the literary *Gattung* of the Sermon on the Mount (henceforth abbreviated SM). It is certainly appropriate to address this problem because the literary *Gattung* needs identification[3] regardless of whether the SM is a composition of the Gospel writer, as Bornkamm maintains, or a pre-Matthean composition, as I

---

1. Inaugural Lecture given at the University of Chicago 16 October 1978.
2. G. Bornkamm, "Der Aufbau der Bergpredigt," *NTS* 24 (1978): 419–32. Cf. his earlier discussion of the "Aufbau" in G. Bornkamm, G. Barth, and H. J. Held, *Überlieferung und Auslegung im Matthäusevangelium* (Neukirchen: Neukirchener Verlag, 1960), 14–15. Bornkamm to a large degree agrees with M. Dibelius, "Die Bergpredigt," in his *Botschaft und Geschichte* (Tübingen: J. C. B. Mohr [Paul Siebeck], 1953), vol. 1, 79–174. In this Shaffer Lecture of 1937, Dibelius, in an intuitive way, has expressed a number of very important ideas, although he does not consider their literary implications. See, for example, 92–93: "... können wir feststellen, dass die Bergpredigt eine Zusammenstellung verschiedenartiger Sprüche ist. Aber der Evangelist fügte diese Sprüche und Spruchgruppen aneinander, um eine charakteristische Übersicht über Jesu Predigt zu geben." To be noted is the term "Zusammenfassung" (97): "Die ersten Gemeinden, sagen wir um 50 n. Chr., verlangten eine Zusammenfassung der Lehre des Herrn, um ein Gesetz für ihre Lebensführung zu haben." Cf. also 98, 141–42.
3. Cf. C. Burchard, "Versuch, das Thema der Bergpredigt zu finden," in *Jesus Christus in Historie und Theologie, Festschrift für H. Conzelmann,* ed. G. Strecker (Tübingen: J. C. B. Mohr [Paul Siebeck], 1975), 409–32 (Eng. trans.: "The Theme of the Sermon on the Mount," in *Essays on the Love Command,* ed. R. H. Fuller [Philadelphia: Fortress Press, 1978], 57–91). Burchard does not discuss the genre problem, but searches for a thematic unity of the SM.

1

have suggested.[4] Bornkamm immediately states his conclusion: that he does not see any real analogy to the literary *Gattung* of the SM in either the primitive Christian or Jewish literature.[5] This conclusion, however, raises a number of questions. Even if it is true that there is no formal analogy to be found in primitive Christian and Jewish literature, does this situation render the problem insoluble? Have form-critical and redactional studies reached a point where all conceivable literary forms have been discovered? Is the search for literary analogues necessarily limited to primitive Christian or Jewish writings? One need only state these questions in order to realize that there must be other possibilities not yet investigated and that the question of the literary genre of the SM cannot be declared insoluble.

In the following paper, therefore, an attempt will be made to determine the literary genre of the SM by searching for clues to the literary form and function in the SM itself (section I); by interpreting these clues in terms of Hellenistic rhetoric and ethic (section II); by relating these findings to the proper literary genre (section III); and by stating a hypothesis (section IV).

I

In spite of the indisputable dearth of evidence, the SM itself provides at least some clues to the question of its literary genre. At the beginning of the eschatological section, the motif of the Two Ways is employed:

Enter by the narrow gate!
For the [one] gate is wide and the way is spacious that leads to destruction, and those who enter by it are many.

4. See H. D. Betz, "Die Makarismen der Bergpredigt (Matthäus 5,3–12). Beobachtungen zur literarischen Form und theologischen Bedeutung," *ZThK* 75 (1978): 3–19, esp. 4 (in this volume, 17–36).
5. Bornkamm, "Der Aufbau der Bergpredigt," 432: "Sehe ich recht, so gibt es für sie keine wirkliche Analogie." Bornkamm considers from Qumran 1QS, 1QSa, and the Damascus document; then *Abot*. But these, he says, are structured differently. Admittedly the *Didache* is a church order ("Kirchenordnung"), but the SM and *Didache* agree in the first section (*Did.* 1–6), while only the later sections make it the church order. The question is whether these differences in structure and content necessarily rule out a common genre.

[But] how narrow is the [other] gate and [how] confined is the way that leads to life, and those who find it are few.[6]

Actually, two traditional motifs are combined in this passage, in order to create the image of the Two Ways leading to two gates, the wide gate representing the gate to hell and the narrow gate the gate to the heavenly Jerusalem which for the SM is identical with "the kingdom of the Heavens."[7]

For the question of the literary genre, however, the motif of the Two Ways contains important clues. Due to the traditional function of this motif in the context of teaching,[8] other literary elements enter the area of consideration. That in the SM the Two Ways serves as an image is indicated by the phrases "leading to the [eschatological] destruction" ($\epsilon i\varsigma \tau\dot{\eta}\nu \dot{\alpha}\pi\dot{\omega}\lambda\epsilon\iota\alpha\nu$) and "leading to the [eternal] life" ($\epsilon i\varsigma \tau\dot{\eta}\nu \zeta\omega\dot{\eta}\nu$). In the concluding section of the SM (7:24–27) we learn that the "confined way" is to be identified with the sayings ($\lambda\dot{o}\gamma o\iota$) of Jesus as they are contained in the SM.[9] In other words, the SM in its entirety is to be regarded as "the way to eternal life," whereas "the way to destruction" consists of the doctrines and practices explicitly or implicitly rejected by the SM. Matthew's Gospel is no doubt correct when it concludes that the sayings of Jesus constitute his "teaching" ($\delta\iota\delta\alpha\chi\dot{\eta}$: 7:28–29; cf. 5:2), particularly because this external description is internally confirmed by the SM itself and its remark about "teaching" ($\delta\iota\delta\dot{\alpha}\sigma\kappa\epsilon\iota\nu$) in 5:19.

What then is to be done with these sayings of Jesus? In the program-

---

6. Matt. 7:13–14. The translation, which is mine, attempts to preserve the *parallelismus membrorum* and the Semitism in v. 14. For the textual problems, see Th. Zahn, *Das Evangelium des Matthäus*, 4th ed. (Leipzig: Deichert, 1922), 312 n. 33; J. Jeremias, *TDNT* 6, 922–23; B. Metzger, *A Textual Commentary on the Greek New Testament* (New York and London: United Bible Societies, 1971), 19. On the Semitism in the exclamative $\tau\dot{\iota}$ in v. 14, see BDR, section 299, 4; Bauer, *Lexicon*, s.v. "$\tau\dot{\iota}\varsigma$," 3b.

7. I follow at this point the interpretation by J. Jeremias, *TDNT* 6, 922ff. Cf. W. Grundmann, *Das Evangelium des Matthäus*, 2d ed. (Berlin: Evangelische Verlagsanstalt, 1971), 230ff. See also Matt. 5:3, 10, 19, 20; 6:10, 13, 33; 7:21.

8. See Jan Bergman, "Zum$_o$ Zwei-Wege-Motiv. Religionsgeschichtliche und exegetische Bemerkungen," *SEÅ* 41–42 (1976–77): 27–56, with further bibliography.

9. Matt. 7:24, 26: ". . . these my words" ($\mu o\upsilon \tau o\dot{\upsilon}\varsigma \lambda\dot{o}\gamma o\upsilon\varsigma \tau o\dot{\upsilon}\tau o\upsilon\varsigma$). Cf. the formulaic "truly I say to you," $\dot{\alpha}\mu\dot{\eta}\nu \lambda\dot{\epsilon}\gamma\omega \dot{\upsilon}\mu\dot{\iota}\nu$ (5:18, 26; 6:2, 5, 16) and "but I say to you," $\dot{\epsilon}\gamma\dot{\omega} \delta\dot{\epsilon} \lambda\dot{\epsilon}\gamma\omega \dot{\upsilon}\mu\dot{\iota}\nu$ (5:22, 32, 34, 39, 44; cf. "I say to you," $\lambda\dot{\epsilon}\gamma\omega \dot{\upsilon}\mu\dot{\iota}\nu$, 5:20; 6:25, 29).

matic conclusion in 7:24–27 we are told that the proper reaction to these sayings is "hearing and doing." This pair of terms is of course also traditional. Apart from the SM, where it occurs only here in 7:24 and 26, the word-pair is widely attested in early Christian literature.[10] But the primary question is what do these terms mean in the SM?

"Hearing" (ἀκούειν) refers not only to the physiological act of hearing but also to the wide range of notions describing the understanding of what one has heard. "He who has ears to hear, let him hear!" This saying does not occur in the SM,[11] but the intellectual process presupposed in it is certainly intended in the SM as well. More specifically, in the SM "hearing" designates the appropriation of tradition, that is, didactic activities in the wider sense of the term. Thus the stereotyped formula introducing the so-called antitheses "You have heard that it was said . . ."[12] designates what in the view of the SM is the uncritical acceptance of false teaching about the meaning of the Torah.

Rather than mere physical hearing, the SM emphasizes the comprehension of what has been perceived physically. This theoretical presupposition shows up in the form of characteristic indicators, such as the typical exhortations προσέχετε ("pay attention!")[13] and καταμάθετε ("observe, notice, learn!").[14] It is characteristic for the SM that the whole field of terms dealing with observation by vision is carefully worked out.[15] Included in this field is not only visual observation of the self-evident[16] but also visualization of mythical events, such as the scene of the last judgment (7:21–23), and the imaginative perception of the paradoxical as it is necessary for the understanding of the often hyperbolic imagery in the SM.[17] This emphasis upon vision is by no means accidental or merely proverbial, but, as I have shown in my

10. See esp. Luke 6:47, 49; John 13:17; Rom. 2:13; James 1:22, 23, 25. For a discussion see M. Dibelius, *James* (Philadelphia: Fortress Press, 1976), 114.
11. Matt. 11:15; cf. 13:9, 43; Mark 4:9, 23; 7:16; 8:18; Luke 8:8; 14:35, etc.
12. Matt. 5:21, 27, 33, 38, 43 (RSV).
13. Matt. 6:1; 7:15.
14. Matt. 6:28.
15. See the use of the terms βλέπειν, "see" (Matt. 5:28; 6:4, 6, 18; 7:3); διαβλέπειν, "see clearly" (7:5); ἐμβλέπειν, "observe" (6:26); ὁρᾶν, "see" (5:8); ὀφθαλμός, "eye" (5:29, 38 [Exod. 21:24]; 6:22–23; 7:3, 4, 5).
16. See, for example, 6:26.
17. See esp. 7:3–5.

analysis of the section "On Vision" (Matt. 6:22–23), it is based upon a serious philosophical and theological theory of vision.[18]

From sense-perception to "knowledge" is a small but significant step. A few occurrences of terms related to γινώσκειν show that "knowledge" is the expected result of sense-perception. The "false prophets" of the section 7:15–20 are to be "recognized [ἐπιγινώσκειν] by their fruits," we are told twice.[19] A programmatic passage is 5:16, where the community of the SM is exhorted: "Let your light shine in such a way before the people, that they may see [ἴδωσιν] your good works and praise your Father who is in heaven."

The term εἶδον includes both sense-perception (βλέπειν, ὁρᾶν) and understanding (εἰδέναι).[20] Simple conclusions must, however, be avoided at this point. According to the SM, the "good deeds" of the Christian should not be ostentatious, but unrecognizable as good deeds and thus done in imitation of the invisibility of God.[21] They should be done knowing that "your left hand must not know what your right hand is doing."[22] Therefore, "seeing the good works" and "praising the heavenly Father" can only describe missionary goals which, if reached, presuppose conversion to God and with it a complete change of perception.[23] Those who are able to identify that "good works" are actually such and who sincerely praise the heavenly Father no longer "think" as pagans think (δοκεῖν),[24] but they know what God thinks. Such a claim can be made because, according to the Christology of the SM, Jesus revealed the principles of God's judgment as they will be applied at the last judgment.[25]

18. H. D. Betz, "Matthew VI.22f. and Ancient Greek Theories of Vision," in *Text and Interpretation: Studies in the New Testament presented to M. Black* (Cambridge: At the University Press, 1978), 43–56; see in this volume, 71–88.

19. Matt. 7:15, 20; cf. also γινώσκειν ("know") in 6:3; 7:23.

20. See BDR, section 81, 3; Bauer, *Lexicon*, s.v. "εἶδον."

21. See on this point H. D. Betz, "Eine judenchristliche Kult-Didache in Matthäus 6, 1–18," in *Jesus Christus in Historie und Theologie* (see above, n. 3), 445–57; see in this volume, 55–69.

22. Matt. 6:3: "Let not your left hand know what your right hand is doing" (μὴ γνώτω ἡ ἀριστερά σου τί ποιεῖ ἡ δεξιά σου).

23. See on "praising God" and conversion as related to "seeing" H. D. Betz, "The Cleansing of the Ten Lepers (Luke 17:11–19)," *JBL* 90 (1971): 314–28, esp. 318–19.

24. Matt. 6:7–8; see Betz, "Eine judenchristliche Kult-Didache," 451–53; in this volume, 62–64.

25. Matt. 5:3–12, 17–20; 7:21–23; see Betz, "Die Makarismen der Bergpredigt."

Furthermore, knowledge is by no means identical with hearing and knowing of the sayings of Jesus and therefore of the SM itself. Rather, the knowledge intended by the theology of the SM is to be gained by an intensive interaction between reflection and practice. The process of reflection is initiated and kept alive by the thoroughgoing rhetorical structure of the SM with its constant flow of rhetorical questions, reminders, juxtapositions, and provocative images.[26]

In addition, the relatively frequent appearance of the term "doing" (ποιεῖν) makes sure that this reflection occurs in conjunction with experience and practice. Again the word-pair "hearing and doing" comes to mind. In fact since the SM is ultimately doctrine about the understanding and implementation of the Torah, the "doing" must be the goal of the SM itself.[27] Beyond this goal, human conduct in general is described as "doing,"[28] so that the right kind of doing can be contrasted with the wrong kind of doing of the tax collectors and the pagans.[29]

Characteristically, the result of this interaction of reflection and practice is stated not in the form of objectified knowledge, but in the form of the image of "the prudent man" (ἀνὴρ φρόνιμος) in contrast to "the foolish man" (ἀνὴρ μωρός). The occurrence of this *syncrisis* motif in the concluding parable of the SM (7:24–27) is as important for the understanding of the SM as a whole as the terminology used. "Everyone who hears these sayings of mine and does them" is compared to a φρόνιμος—a practically wise, indeed shrewd individual—while the "foolish man" is "everyone who hears these sayings of mine but does not do them." The former can be called φρόνιμος ("prudent") because through sense-perception, reflection, and practice he has developed φρόνησις ("thoughtfulness"), while the latter is a fool because he stayed with sense-perception and thus lacked prudence. Such φρόνησις is valued by everyone and has no doubt been chosen intentionally. It expresses a kind of wisdom that is informed by insight into God's thought as well as by life experience

---

26. The analysis of the rhetorical and compositional structure of the SM is a different topic which will be treated in the commentary presently in preparation.
27. Matt. 5:19.
28. Evidence for this is the inclusion of the Golden Rule (Matt. 7:12).
29. Matt. 5:46, 47; cf. 5:17–20.

and self-inspection.[30] Therefore, "hearing my sayings and doing them" is here subsumed under φρόνησις. In contrast, the μωρός ("fool") stays at the superficial level of merely knowing the data of sense-perception.

What does this evidence reveal about the literary genre and function of the SM? The evidence does not provide us with the proper name of the genre. The Two Ways is a literary motif, but not a genre. The fact that the SM consists of "sayings" (λόγοι) gives us the genre of the components of the SM, but not the whole of the composition.[31] It is obvious to everyone who knows something about Hellenistic rhetoric and philosophy, however, that these various indicators which we have discussed point in a certain direction. This direction leads us outside the primitive Christian literature into Hellenistic ethical literature, where we find the presuppositions contained in the SM stated in a fuller and more systematic fashion.

II

When we evaluate the literary evidence in the SM in terms of Hellenistic rhetoric and ethical theory, we have no difficulty in locating the proper terms. The functional terms of sense-perception, reflection, and practice point to exercises like those found in the so-called diatribe literature, of which Epictetus is a good example.

According to Epictetus's philosophy, the response demanded by the SM of the hearers would have to be called ἄσκησις ("training").[32] One definition may explain this as well as many passages:

> For who is the man in training? He is the man who practices not employing his desire, and practices employing his aversion only upon

30. See G. Bertram, *TDNT* 9, s.v. "φρήν κτλ.," D 5.
31. Cf. the remark by J. M. Robinson, in J. M. Robinson & H. Koester, *Trajectories through Early Christianity* (Philadelphia: Fortress Press, 1971), 94 n. 47: "The cohesion of the collection suggests that the Sermon on the Mount (or Plain) is derived from an oral or written collection of its own, and did not first come into being in the context of Q. . . . The end seems to be the conclusion of a collection, and this not simply because of the occurrence there of the term *logoi*."
32. On this concept see B. L. Hijmans, ΆΣΚΗΣΙΣ. *Notes on Epictetus' Educational System* (Proefschrift, Utrecht, Assen: van Gorcum, 1959). See also the review by W. Theiler, *Gnomon* 32 (1960): 498–500.

7

the things that are within the sphere of his moral purpose, yes, and practices particularly in the things that are difficult to master.[33]

More specifically, Epictetus frequently defines the task of the philosopher as μελετᾶν, an almost untranslatable term combining philosophical-ethical reflection and practical experience. This activity, for which Socrates is the prototype,[34] should keep the philosopher busy from morning to night.[35] The objects of such μελετᾶν can be named variously: τὰ περὶ τῶν ἀγαθῶν καὶ κακῶν δόγματα[36] ("the philosophical doctrines regarding the good and the bad"), τὰ ἀναγκαῖα θεωρήματα[37] ("the necessary principles"), and λόγοι[38] ("philosophical sententiae"). To initiate and maintain the μελετᾶν is the purpose of Epictetus's diatribes. Epictetus also emphasizes again and again that the precondition for the proper μελετᾶν is the clarity in the philosopher's mind of "the guide-lines we must have ready at hand" in the various circumstances in life (τί πρόχειρον ἔχειν ...).[39]

Frequently the philosopher also provides sketchy lists of items to be considered as τὰ πρόχειρα.[40] In other words, the diatribes of Epictetus which were only later written down by Arrianus were originally designed to stimulate and maintain the activity of μελετᾶν in his listeners. Hence the philosophy of Epictetus cannot be identical with the diatribes but is, rather, presupposed in them. The purpose of these diatribes cannot be to inform the readers about the philosophy of Epictetus but is to make them philosophize, so that they can

33. Epictetus, *Diss.* III.12.8: τίς γάρ ἐστιν ἀσκητής; ὁ μελετῶν ὀρέξει μὲν μὴ χρῆσθαι, ἐκκλίσει δὲ πρὸς μόνα τὰ προαιρετικὰ χρῆσθαι, καὶ μελετῶν μᾶλλον ἐν τοῖς δυσκαταπονήτοις. The ed. and trans. are those of W. A. Oldfather in LCL.
34. See *Diss.*, I.25.31.
35. See esp. ibid., I.1.21–25; II.16.27; IV.1.111.
36. Ibid., II.16 (titulus); cf. IV.1.132.
37. Ibid., IV.6.16.
38. Ibid., IV.1.170.
39. Ibid., I.1.21; cf. II.1.29: "That is why I say over and over again, 'Practise these things and have them ready at hand, that is, the knowledge of what you ought to face with confidence, and what you ought to face with caution—that you ought to face with confidence that which is outside the province of the moral purpose, with caution that which is within the province of the moral purpose'" (Διὰ τοῦτο λέγω πολλάκις "ταῦτα μελετᾶτε καὶ ταῦτα πρόχειρα ἔχετε, πρὸς τίνα δεῖ τεθαρρηκέναι καὶ πρὸς τίνα εὐλαβῶς διακεῖσθαι, ὅτι πρὸς τὰ ἀπροαίρετα θαρρεῖν, εὐλαβεῖσθαι τὰ προαιρετικά"). On the concept of πρόχειρον ("at hand") see I. Hadot, *Seneca und die griechisch-römische Tradition der Seelenleitung* (Berlin: Walter De Gruyter, 1969), 58.
40. See esp. *Diss.* I.1.22; IV.1.83, 111.

develop the wisdom necessary to meet the challenges of Tyche.[41] By contrast, those who fail to engage in μελετᾶν and remain at the level of words of jargon (τὰ λεξείδια) are fools unable to cope with the events of life.[42]

For a more elaborate and systematic exposition of the philosophical theory we may turn to some of Plutarch's ethical works.[43] Plutarch has adapted Cynic-Stoic diatribe material, but to a greater degree he depends upon the Platonic-Aristotelian tradition. In spite of these differences, however, Plutarch's ethical theory has much in common with that of Epictetus. Also different is the literary form: Plutarch writes essays in which he spells out the theories which Epictetus's diatribes merely presuppose. Therefore in Plutarch's essays the "training" (ἀσκεῖν καὶ μελετᾶν) is usually found only in the exhortative sections.[44] Furthermore, Plutarch distinguishes more clearly between intellectual reflections, called ἐπιλογισμοί,[45] and practical exercises, called ἐθισμοί.[46] Both of these constitute Plutarch's concept of preventive ethical therapy.[47]

Of course, none of these philosophical terms is found in the SM or, for that matter, in the New Testament.[48] But the basic concepts about the appropriation of ethical tradition are very similar in the SM, in Epictetus, and in Plutarch. As a matter of fact, large sections of the ancient world at the time of the SM seem to have shared many of these concepts and methods differing only in philosophical school terminology and in the cultural and religious milieu. Also different, certainly, was the degree to which these methods were subjected to theoretical analysis and conceptualization.[49] But having taken all

41. See esp. ibid., II.2.21–26.
42. Ibid., II.1.30–33. Cf. also I.30.5; II.1.38; 6.14; 13.4; 16.2–3, 15; III.7.17–18; Frag. 10.
43. See H. D. Betz, ed., *Plutarch's Ethical Writings and Early Christian Literature* (Leiden: E. J. Brill,1978).
44. Ibid., 201, 214; cf. also 18, 176, 189, 268, 287.
45. Ibid., 12, 201, 286, 434.
46. Ibid., 17, 176, 284, 286, 287.
47. Ibid., 2, 7; and Index, s.v. "Psychagogy."
48. Cf., however, James 1:19-25.
49. It should be obvious that the approach taken in this paper is different from that of B. Gerhardsson, *Memory and Manuscript: Oral Tradition and Written Transmission in Rabbinic Judaism and Early Christianity* (Uppsala: Almqvist & Wiksell, 1961; 2d ed. 1964). Gerhardsson mentions the philosophical schools and their learning techniques (122ff.), but he then confines himself to the Rabbinic

these variables into account, one should not overlook the fact that the common elements enable us to understand the literary function of the SM: this document is intended to stimulate and maintain what in Hellenistic philosophical terms is called ἀσκεῖν καὶ μελετᾶν.

III

Which literary genre can be properly associated with the functional terms discussed above, and with the general structure of the SM? A literary analogue that meets these criteria is Epictetus's *Enchiridion*.[50]

The *Enchiridion* is a compilation of sayings of Epictetus, made by his student Arrianus from the philosopher's *Dissertations* (διατριβαί). In this literary sense, the *Enchiridion* is secondary compared with the *Dissertations*. In terms of the method of teaching, however, the *Enchiridion* precedes the *Dissertations*, because it contains those fundamental doctrines which serve as the basis for discussion in the *Dissertations*.[51]

Arrianus himself provides helpful information regarding the composition and purpose of the *Dissertations* in the epistolary prooemium addressed to Lucius Gellius.[52] According to this prooemium, the *Dissertations* contain the sayings (λόγοι) of Epictetus as Arrianus wrote them down in his notebooks (ὑπομνήματα). The present work, says Arrianus, was written down and published in order to fight opponents who despised not only him but also the sayings of Epictetus. These sayings, he assures us, were once powerful enough "to incite the mind of his hearers to the best things. If, now, these words of his should produce the same effect, they would have, I think, just

---

tradition, where he assumes all these learning techniques were practiced and from where they entered into early Christianity. That these assumptions cannot be substantiated has been shown by the reviewers, esp. G. Widengren, "Tradition and Literature in Early Judaism and in the Early Church," *Numen* 10 (1963): 42–83; M. Smith, "A Comparison of Early Christian and Early Rabbinic Tradition," *JBL* 82 (1963): 169–76.

50. See M. Spanneut, "Epiktet," *RAC* 5 (1962): 599–681; Th. Wirth, "Arrians Erinnerungen an Epiktet," *MH* 24 (1967): 149–89, 197–216.

51. On the background and history of these methods, see P. Rabbow, *Seelenführung. Methodik der Exerzitien in der Antike* (Munich: Kösel-Verlag, 1954), 23ff.; Hadot, *Seelenleitung,* esp. 56ff.

52. In H. Schenkl's edition, *Epictetus* (Berlin: Teubner, 1965 [rep.]), 5–6.

the success which the words of the philosophers ought to have."[53] For information about the *Enchiridion*, however, we have to turn to Simplicius's commentary upon the *Enchiridion*, in which he quotes from a letter by Arrianus. According to this statement, the *Enchiridion* was composed by selecting from Epictetus's sayings those which were most important and essential for his philosophy and which have the strongest impact upon the hearers.[54] In the *Enchiridion* itself, Arrianus calls these fundamentals "canons" or "rules" (κανόνες),[55] which the philosopher must always have at hand (πρόχειρον)[56] for his or her "training" (μελετᾶν).[57]

In terms of the literary form, the *Enchiridion* belongs to the genre of epitome, more specifically: the philosophical epitome.[58] The greatest and most famous example of the philosophical epitome in antiquity, and the specific prototype of the *Enchiridion*, was Epicurus's work *Kyriai Doxai*.[59] The concept of κανών ("canon," "rule") also comes from Epicurus,[60] as Epictetus himself acknowledges in *Diss.* II.23.21. Arrianus obviously imitates Epicurus's *tetrapharmakos*[61] (the name for the most important doctrines at the beginning of the *Kyriai Doxai*) when he also places the most important principles at the beginning of the *Enchiridion*.[62]

Epicurus, therefore, may well have been the creator of the particular type of epitome. Fortunately he also betrays why he created this type of philosophical work. Briefly stated, the purpose of the epitome

---

53. Ibid., 5, lines 16–19: ... κινῆσαι τὰς γνώμας τῶν ἀκουόντων πρὸς τὰ βέλτιστα. εἰ μὲν δὴ τοῦτό γε αὐτὸ διαπράττοιντο οἱ λόγοι οὗτοι, ἔχοι<εν> ἂν οἶμαι ὅπερ χρὴ ἔχειν τοὺς τῶν φιλοσόφων λόγους.
54. Ibid., p. III, testimonium III.
55. *Ench.* I.5. Cf. *Diss.* I.28.28, 30; II.11.13–25; II.20.21; III.3.14, 15; etc. For the importance of the term, see Hadot, *Seelenleitung*, 57, 58.
56. *Ench.* I.5; XVI; LII.2; LIII.1; and often in the *Diss.*
57. *Ench.* I.5.
58. So correctly I. Opelt, "Epitome," *RAC* 5 (1962): 944–73, esp. 951 n. 67.
59. Diog. L.X.139–54. See W. Schmid, "Epikur," *RAC* 5 (1962): 618–819, esp. 695–97, 743–46; H. Steckel, "Epikuros," *PRE.S* 11 (1968): 579–652, esp. 586–87, 598–99; furthermore N. W. DeWitt, *Epicurus and His Philosophy* (Minneapolis: University of Minnesota Press, 1954), 111ff.: "The Use of the Epitome."
60. Diog. L.X.129; also *Frag.* 31.21, line 13, ed. G. Arrighetti, *Epicuro. Opere*, 2d ed. (Turin: Einaudi, 1973), 139; *Frag.* 34.31, line 14 (ibid., 354); *Frag.* 34.32, line 7 (ibid., 356). See also H. Usener, *Epicurea* (Stuttgart: Teubner, 1966 [rep.]), 104–6.
61. So following Hadot, *Seneca*, 57, who also points to other examples of imitations of Epicurus: Seneca and the *regula vitae* of Demetrius Cynicus (56).
62. *Ench.* I.1–3.

is pedagogical, for many of his students were unable to study his *magnum opus* of the thirty-seven books Περὶ φύσεως. For these students he composed, as he himself says, the *Epistle to Herodotus:* "For those who are unable, Herodotus, to work in detail through all that I have written about nature, or to peruse the larger books which I have composed, I have already prepared at sufficient length an epitome of the whole system."[63] In other words, the *Epistle to Herodotus* is an epitome in epistolary form. What applies to this letter, however, must equally be true of the other letters: they are also *epitomai*. In addition, we know that still other *epitomai* must have existed: a μικρὰ ἐπιτομή, and a μεγάλη ἐπιτομή, the latter most likely being the source of Lucretius's *De rerum natura.*[64]

A complication seems to be created by the fact that Epicurus does not call his *Kyriai Doxai* an epitome.[65] Nevertheless, the *Kyriai Doxai* does conform to this genre. Not only have the *Kyriai Doxai* and the *Epistles* a great amount of material in common, and not only do both the *Kyriai Doxai* and the *Epistle to Herodotus* begin with the *tetrapharmakos,* but it is also true that later authors treat the *Kyriai Doxai* as an epitome.[66] As a result we can say that the *Kyriai Doxai* is one of the several *epitomai* circulating in the Epicurean school, very similar to the *Epistles* but different from them because of their epistolary form.

Which then are the characteristics of the genre of the epitome?[67] As a book title, "epitome" has been used since the 4th century B.C., the name deriving from the verb ἐπιτέμνειν ("cut short, reduce"). Latin

63. Diog. L.X.35: ... διαθρεῖν ἐπιτομὴν τῆς ὅλης πραγματείας. The translations here and in the following are by C. Bailey, *Epicurus* (Oxford: At the Clarendon Press, 1926). See also Diog. L.X.37: "I have prepared for you just such an epitome and manual of the doctrines as a whole" (ἐποίησά σοι καὶ τοιαύτην τινὰ ἐπιτομὴν καὶ στοιχείωσιν τῶν ὅλων δοξῶν).

64. The *Epistle to Pythocles* calls the *Epistle to Herodotus* the "little epitome" (μικρὰ ἐπιτομή) (Diog. L.X.85), but this designation is as doubtful as the authenticity of the letter (see Bailey, *Epicurus,* 277; Steckel, "Epikuros," 612). At least, several *epitomai* were circulating in the Epicurean school; see the *Vita Epicuri,* Diog. L.X.27; 31.

65. The *Vita Epicuri* calls the *Epistle to Herodotus* an epitome, and then mentions the *Kyriai Doxai* separately (Diog. L.X.31).

66. See also Diogenes of Oenoanda, *Frag.* 23, ed. Grilli: ἐπιτομὴ ἠθική; also the characteristic of the *Kyriai Doxai* by Cicero, *De nat. deor.* I.30.85; *De fin.* II.7.20; Lucian, *Alex.* 47.

67. See Opelt, "Epitome."

equivalents are *epitoma* and *breviarium*. As the article on "Epitome" by Ilona Opelt in *RAC* shows, many different subtypes of the genre must be distinguished, and the genre must not be confused with similar categories, such as gnomologium,[68] anthology, florilegium, catena, commentary, etc.

As a literary work, the epitome is secondary in nature. It is a condensation of a larger work, made by a redactor (who may of course be the same person as the author of the larger work) for a specific purpose. Its characteristics include brevity and precision in selection and formulation. But the epitome is not simply a collection of selected passages. Rather, the author has systematic goals and looks at the work to be epitomized as a whole. What he or she selects and composes into the new literary unit is intended to be a systematic synopsis. In composing the epitome, the author has considerable freedom to be creative, to reformulate, to transpose, to add and omit as necessary in view of the overall demands of the genre and purpose.

All of these characteristics fit the *Kyriai Doxai*, a work that includes forty philosophical *sententiae* or groupings of *sententiae* taken from the larger works of Epicurus. As a compositional unit, the *Kyriai Doxai* represents Epicurus's philosophical system as a whole. The first four sayings, the *tetrapharmakos* ("the fourfold medicine"), constitute the principles underlying everything else—a kind of summary of the summary.

Unfortunately, no consensus has been reached among scholars about the literary structure and composition of the *Kyriai Doxai*, so that H. Usener's verdict—that there is no structure at all and that for that very reason the work may even be inauthentic—is still awaiting a definitive answer.[69] For our purposes, however, it is enough to conclude that the *Kyriai Doxai* represents the literary genre of the philosophical epitome. Thanks to Epicurus himself, we are comparatively

---

68. The literary relationship between the *Kyriai Doxai* and the *Gnomologium Vaticanum Epicureum* is an intriguing problem which resembles that of the relationship between the SM and Q. See the careful recording of cross-references in the edition of P. von der Mühll, *Epicuri epistulae tres et Ratae sententiae a Laertio Diogene servatae, accedit Gnomologium Epicureum Vaticanum* (Berlin: Teubner, 1966 [rep.]); see also Arrighetti, *Epicuro*, 139ff., 505ff.; Schmid, *RAC* 5, 697–98, 771–72.

69. Usener, *Epicurea*, p. XLIV.

well informed about the literary function of his *epitomai*. Since, as we have said before, many of his students were unable to study the larger works, the whole system was epitomized "that they may keep adequately in mind at least the most general principles in each department, in order that as occasion arises they may be able to assist themselves on the most important points."[70] The epitome is not intended for outsiders or beginners, but for those "who have made considerable progress in the survey of the main principles." These students "ought to bear in mind the scheme of the whole system set forth in its essentials. For we have frequent need of the general view, but not so often of the detailed exposition."[71] The method required to obtain this knowledge is spelled out at several points. The epitome is composed in such a way that it facilitates a carefully designed learning process. The goal of this continual learning process is to keep a vision of the entire system as well as seminal formulations of doctrinal positions constantly ready in the mind of the philosopher. "For it is not possible for anyone to abbreviate the complete course through the whole system, if he cannot embrace in his own mind by means of short formulae all that might be set out with accuracy in detail."[72] The practical purpose is evident from some statements in the *Epistle to Menoeceus:* "Those things which I used unceasingly to commend to you, these do and practice, considering them to be the first principles of the good life."[73] Again, in the epilogue of that letter: "Meditate therefore on these things and things akin to them night and day by yourself, and with a companion like to yourself, and never shall you be disturbed waking or asleep, but you shall live like a god among men. For a man who lives among immortal blessings is not like to a mortal being."[74]

In order to be an Epicurean, one does not need to have the whole system worked out in detail. Rather, it is important to keep philosophizing in the Epicurean way at every stage of the student's advancement. To facilitate this educational process is the purpose of the

70. Diog. L.X.35.
71. Ibid.
72. Diog. L.X.36.
73. Diog. L.X.123: Ἃ δέ σοι συνεχῶς παρήγγελλον, ταῦτα καὶ πρᾶττε καὶ μελέτα, στοιχεῖα τοῦ καλῶς ζῆν ταῦτ᾽ εἶναι διαλαμβάνων.
74. Diog. L.X.135; also X.82, 83, 84, 85, 116.

Kyriai Doxai. Having the principal doctrines always "at hand," the philosopher is then free to develop individual topics as needed in debates or in his or her own writings. On the other hand, merely knowing the system or even the *sententiae* is not enough. The goal must be that the philosophy is to be practiced: "practicing and meditating" (πράττειν καὶ μελετᾶν) must always go hand in hand.

IV

After even this superficial survey, the similarities between the SM and Epicurus's *Kyriai Doxai*, as far as the literary genre and function are concerned, should have become apparent.[75] To be sure, the two documents are very different, although not totally unrelated, in content.[76] At any rate, the hypothesis can now be stated: the literary genre of the SM is that of an epitome presenting the theology of Jesus in a systematic fashion. The epitome is a composition carefully designed out of sayings of Jesus grouped according to thematic points of doctrine considered to be of primary importance. Correspondingly, its function is to provide the disciple of Jesus with the necessary tool for becoming a Jesus theologian. "Hearing and doing the sayings of Jesus," therefore, means enabling the disciple to theologize creatively along the lines of the theology of the master. To say it pointedly: The

75. P. Vielhauer, in his *Geschichte der urchristlichen Literatur* (Berlin: Walter De Gruyter, 1975), 316–17, has compared Epicurus's *Kyriai Doxai* and Q, and he was right in not assuming that the two documents share a common literary genre.

76. A peculiar phenomenon are the surprising parallels to the SM in Epicurus's *Kyriai Doxai*, not to mention other writings of the Epicurean school. This phenomenon seems to point to anti-Epicurean tendencies in the SM. Such tendencies are conceivable because they are found also throughout the Jewish literature of the Greco-Roman era. For the SM cf., for example, Matt. 5:3 and *K.D.* I; Matt. 5:4 and *K.D.* II; Matt. 5:5–9 and *K.D.* III; Matt. 5:10–12 and *K.D.* IV; Matt. 5:17–20 and *K.D.* XXXV–XXXVIII; Matt. 5:48; 7:24–27 and *K.D.* XX; Matt. 6:25–33 and *K.D.* X, XV, XVIII, XXI, XXVI, XXIX, XXX; Matt. 7:12 and *K.D.* XXXI, XXXII; Matt. 7:24–27 and *K.D.* V, XVI, XVII, XXV. Perhaps the "pigs" of Matt. 7:6 are veiled polemic against "Epicureans" (cf. Horace, *Ep.* I.4 and Schmid, *RAC* 5, 795, 799ff.). On anti-Epicurean tendencies in Jewish literature, see M. Hengel, *Judaism and Hellenism* (Philadelphia: Fortress Press, 1974), vol. I, 86, 87, 115, 143, 174; vol. II, 59, 92; H. A. Fischel, *Rabbinic Literature and Graeco-Roman Philosophy: A Study in Epicurea and Rhetorica in Early Midrashic Writings* (Leiden: E. J. Brill, 1973), with further literature; M. Simon, "Epikureismus und Epikureertum. Das Fortleben philosophischer Ideen," in *Hellenische Poleis*, ed. E. C. Welskopf (Berlin: Akademie-Verlag, 1974), 2017–88.

15

SM is not law to be obeyed, but theology to be intellectually appropriated and internalized, in order then to be creatively developed and implemented in concrete situations of life.

In conclusion, at least one instance should be mentioned which shows that the SM was in fact used along the lines just described. In 1 Cor. 7:10–11 Paul has to give advice to the married members of the Corinthian church. He is able to refer to a provision, contained also in the SM (Matt. 5:32), that he then develops and discusses in view of the concrete situation: "To the married I give this charge, not I but the Lord, that the wife should not separate from her husband (but if she does, let her remain single or else be reconciled to her husband)—and that the husband should not divorce his wife." Later in the same chapter, when Paul comes to speak about the so-called virgins, he has no command of Jesus at hand, but on the basis of his knowledge of the principles of faith he can go ahead and formulate his own opinion which is equally authoritative: "Now concerning the virgins, I have no command of the Lord, but I give my own opinion as one who by the Lord's mercy is competent. I think that in view of the present distress it is well for a person to remain in this condition," that is, unmarried (1 Cor. 7:25). The term νομίζω ("I think") is the evidence that Jesus' provision has accomplished its purpose. Far from being slavishly obeyed, the "saying of the Lord" has been heard, reflected upon, and understood, so that Paul is now competent to theologize and implement its intent on his own terms.

2

The Beatitudes of the Sermon on the Mount (Matt. 5:3-12): Observations on Their Literary Form and Theological Significance[1]

For Gerhard Ebeling on his 65th Birthday
6 July 1977

Not only in the Christian church and in the consciousness of humankind in general, but in contemporary New Testament scholarship as well, Jesus' so-called Sermon on the Mount (SM) remains a puzzling work. Characteristic of the older scholarship was the belief that the text of Matt. 5:3–7:27 derived directly from the historical Jesus and could thus be regarded as a source for his theology. But in recent research, this simple state of affairs is no longer taken for granted. It is certain that individual elements of the SM can be traced back to the historical Jesus; but it is equally uncertain by which methods one can obtain scientifically justifiable criteria for distinguishing between authentic sayings of Jesus and later additions. At present a redaction-historical approach is most often employed, according to which the evangelist Matthew himself compiled the SM out of Q-traditions and

---

1. Guest lecture held on 4 July 1977, at the invitation of the faculty of theology of the University of Zurich. The lecture gives a preview of a planned larger investigation of the redactor of the SM. The notes that accompany the lecture have been kept to a necessary minimum.

his own compositions. In this way the Q-portions are brought into connection, directly or indirectly, with the historical Jesus, while everything that cannot be derived from Q is explained as the creation of the evangelist.

This consensus, which we have admittedly outlined in somewhat coarse fashion, is nevertheless burdened by a number of difficulties. For reasons of time, these difficulties can only be touched upon here in passing.

1. The Q-portions of the SM agree only approximately with their Lukan parallels, so that one must assume either that Matthew had another version of Q at his disposal, or that he himself modified the wording of Q down to the minutest details. But there remains a problem in that it is not possible to explain all of these modifications on philological grounds or on the basis of the theology of Matthew.

2. The origin of the material that goes beyond Q remains a problem. It is hardly possible to designate all of this material as the creation of Matthew.[2]

3. As soon as the SM is regarded as the composition of Matthew himself, one is prevented from seeing that the text is quite artistically structured and composed in itself. Yet formal analyses indicate that the SM is a unified, integrated complex.

4. A one-sided, redaction-historical interpretation prevents one from recognizing that the SM contains a theology that is independent of Matthew and different at characteristic points.

Largely for these reasons, I developed the hypothesis that the Matthean SM is a source that has been transmitted intact and integrated by the evangelist into the composition of his Gospel.[3] But this source does not simply derive from the historical Jesus, in the sense that Jesus is the author of all the sayings in their present form and

---

2. I have attempted to demonstrate this for Matt. 6:1–18 in my essay, "A Jewish-Christian Cult *Didache* in Matthew 6:1–18," in this volume; originally published as "Eine judenchristliche Kult-Didache in Matthäus 6, 1–18" in *Jesus Christus in Historie und Theologie. Neutestamentliche Festschrift für H. Conzelmann*, ed. G. Strecker (Tübingen: J. C. B. Mohr [Paul Siebeck], 1975), 445–57.

3. Of course, the hypothesis is not completely new, but has already been put forward by others in one form or another. Cf., for example, G. Kilpatrick, *The Origins of the Gospel According to St. Matthew* (Oxford: At the Clarendon Press, 1946), 14–25.

context. Rather, the SM represents a pre-Matthean composition of a redactional nature. Thus the methods of form and redaction criticism are to be further employed; it is only that they should not be applied to the Gospel as a whole, but merely the section Matt. 5:3–7:27.

I. LOCATION

If one reflects upon the section Matt. 5:3–7:27 apart from its context, it may be compared to a precious jewel that has a long and eventful history behind it and has only lately been fitted into a suitable, but wholly different, setting—namely, the Gospel of Matthew. As is often the case with precious stones, the origin of the jewel lies in mysterious darkness. It is clear that many hands have worked at cutting and polishing it. Depending upon the light, it shines with first one then another color. All of this gives it its special radiance and charming life that never fail to have an effect upon the observer, especially when it is freed from its secondary Matthean context.

From the point of view of the history of religions, the SM belongs to early Jewish Christianity, a product of the mid-first century, when the Jewish-Christian community was still part of Judaism. The Jewish Christians who stand behind the SM and who speak through it are conscious, however, of a strained relationship to their mother faith. Like many other Jewish movements of the period, they also desire to be the "true" Judaism. They find themselves in conflict with the party of the scribes and Pharisees.[4] But they also represent a challenge to the conventional religion of the time by their relentless critique.[5] Yet non-Jews are viewed from a still-greater distance, and many passages warn against assimilation with them.[6]

But the polemical stance of the SM is also determined by the fact that it has knowledge of Gentile Christianity and sets itself off from it. Here, obviously, lies one of the critical points that served to bring the document into being in the first place.

---

4. Cf. Matt. 5:20.
5. Cf. οἱ ὑποκριταί ("the hypocrites") in Matt. 6:2, 5, 16; similarly, 7:5.
6. Cf. οἱ ἐθνικοί ("the heathen") in Matt. 5:47; 6:7 and τὰ ἔθνη ("the heathen") in 6:32.

The programmatic statements on the proper interpretation of the Torah in Matt. 5:17-20 begin with a pointed negation: "Do not think that I have come to destroy the law and the prophets" (μὴ νομίσητε ὅτι ἦλθον καταλῦσαι τὸν νόμον ἢ τοὺς προφήτας), a negation that is immediately repeated in the following clause: "I have not come to destroy but to fulfill" (οὐκ ἦλθον καταλῦσαι ἀλλὰ πληρῶσαι). To whom, then, should it have occurred to have Jesus say, "I have come to destroy the law and the prophets"? We know from other passages in the New Testament that law-free Gentile Christianity,[7] under the leadership of Paul, proclaimed this very thing, and that Paul came under attack for abrogation of the Torah.[8] Can it be a coincidence that Matt. 5:19 says that whoever relaxes one of the least of the commandments of the Torah (μίαν τῶν ἐντολῶν τούτων τῶν ἐλαχίστων) shall be called "an insignificant person" (ἐλάχιστος) in the kingdom of heaven, when (in 1 Cor. 15:9) Paul, taking up what may be his opponents' punning slur on his name (in Latin, paulus means "little" or "small"), calls himself "the least of the apostles" (ὁ ἐλάχιστος τῶν ἀποστόλων)?[9] Furthermore, against whom is the warning against the "false prophets" in Matt. 7:15-20 directed? It is aimed at those Christian prophets who do not do the works of the law. Who are the ones who cry out, "Lord, Lord," in the scene before the judgment seat of Jesus in Matt. 7:21-23, but are nevertheless cast out? They are lawless Gentile Christians, with their kyrios-Christology, who have prophesied in the name of Jesus, have cast out demons and done many mighty works, but who have not done the will of the Father who is in heaven.[10] Finally, can it be a coincidence that the wise disciple, whose life is represented in the parable of Matt. 7:24-27, builds his house "upon the rock" (τεθεμελίωτο ... ἐπὶ τὴν πέτραν)?

---

7. Thus following R. Bultmann, Die Geschichte der synoptischen Tradition, 3d ed. (Göttingen: Vandenhoeck & Ruprecht, 1957), 146-47; cf. also the Ergänzungsheft to the 4th edition (1971), 56.
8. Cf. Gal. 2:17-18; Rom. 3:31; Acts 18:13; Ps.-Clem. Hom., Ep. Petr. 2:3; Rec. I, 70,1; 71,3; 73,4, ed. Rehm.
9. Thus in agreement with J. Weiss, Das Urchristentum (Göttingen: Vandenhoeck & Ruprecht, 1917), 585. Cf. also W. D. Davies, The Setting of the Sermon on the Mount (Cambridge: At the University Press, 1966), 334-36.
10. Cf. Davies, Setting of the Sermon on the Mount, 199-200.

Can this "rock" be anything other than an allusion to Peter and his church,[11] against which Paul may be polemicizing, in concealed form, in 1 Cor. 3:11?[12]

The community of the SM is, without doubt, a Jewish-Christian minority in distress. Without lie the hostile forces of non-Jewish paganism. Gentile Christianity of a Pauline stamp, with its freedom from the law, has a bewitching charm; they are "wolves in sheep's clothing."[13] Within Judaism, the community suffers persecution from official Judaism, embodied in the stereotypes of the "scribes and Pharisees."[14] In opposition to the majority of the Jewish people, but within Judaism nevertheless, the community of the SM seeks to go its own way. The way was one that had been opened by Jesus of Nazareth, whose name is not mentioned in the SM, but who speaks throughout in the first person singular. Jesus and his proclamation are the primary causes of the present distress. He is reverenced by the community of the SM as the teacher of the proper interpretation of the Torah and the correct praxis of piety, as well as practical philosophy in general. He is awaited as the eschatological judge.[15] Yet it is strange that christological titles are not employed in the work at all.[16]

There can be no doubt that the community is prepared to take responsibility for the consequences of the teaching of Jesus, even if it means their lives.[17] But a truly disturbing problem arises for the community only when they discover that there are other Christians who have drawn very different conclusions from the teaching of Jesus. Thus the SM bears witness to a community that finds itself in the midst of a profound internal crisis. It is not only their task to maintain and defend the teachings of Jesus, but to establish, first of all, what Jesus taught and desired of others, and what he did not teach

---

11. Cf. esp. Matt. 16:18 (RSV): "You are Peter, and on this rock I will build my church" (σὺ εἶ Πέτρος, καὶ ἐπὶ ταύτῃ τῇ πέτρᾳ οἰκοδομήσω μου τὴν ἐκκλησίαν).
12. "For no other foundation can any one lay than that which is laid, which is Jesus Christ" (RSV) (θεμέλιον γὰρ ἄλλον οὐδεὶς δύναται θεῖναι παρὰ τὸν κείμενον, ὅς ἐστιν Ἰησοῦς Χριστός).
13. Matt. 7:15.
14. Matt. 5:20.
15. Matt. 7:21–23. (See on this point, however, below 151–54.)
16. With the exception of κύριος ("lord"), which is used polemically as an expression of others in 7:21–22.
17. Cf. Matt. 5:11–12.

21

and did not desire. The strange fact that such conflicting interpretations of the teaching of Jesus could arise so soon constitutes the profound dilemma of the SM in relation to the historical Jesus. As a general statement of its historical situation, one can say that the SM belongs, both theologically and in terms of history of religions, within the richly diverse Judaism of the first century.

Methodological consequences must now be drawn from the position that the community occupied within contemporary Judaism and early Christianity. Those comparative texts standing nearest literarily to the SM are, in the first instance, those which belong to the Jewish Wisdom tradition. *Pirke Abot*, with its commentary *Abot de Rabbi Natan*, and the so-called *Manual of Discipline* from Qumran are formally related, though they derive from other Jewish movements. It is of interest that the SM shares with Hellenistic Judaism an openness toward the themes and material of Hellenistic popular philosophy. Among Christian writings, the Epistle of James and the *Didache*, then portions of *The Shepherd of Hermas* and the *Pseudo-Clementines*, deserve to be mentioned. The evangelist Matthew, on the other hand, has the entire problem that gave rise to the SM behind him. The situation presupposed by his Gospel is that of the universal church which has already incorporated Jewish-Christian traditions as well as Gentile-Christian communities.[18]

It is necessary to determine the location of the SM when approaching its individual problems. In what follows I would like to select, from the wealth of issues which might be considered, a few unsolved problems related to the so-called Beatitudes. My goal in this undertaking is not to present ready answers, but to raise questions which will encourage you, my esteemed hearers, to concern yourselves with these fascinating texts from the earliest phase of Christianity.

II. ON THE FORM-CRITICAL PROBLEM
OF THE BEATITUDES

If one accepts the SM as a literary document transmitted intact and composed according to definite rules, one is immediately confronted

18. For the outlook of the evangelist himself, cf. esp. Matt. 28:18–20.

with the rather complicated problem of the Beatitudes. However familiar the macarism may be as a literary phenomenon, its history remains uninvestigated and unrelated. The following issues must be raised in particular in regard to the macarisms of the SM.

1. In Matt. 5:3–12, we have not simply a single macarism but a series of macarisms. We are familiar with such series from other literary texts of antiquity and recognize that a series of this sort constitutes a literary genre in itself. Single macarisms and series of macarisms must, therefore, be dealt with separately.

2. Connected with the phenomenon of the series of macarisms is the question of the number of the macarisms. Ten macarisms in all are brought together in Matt. 5:3–12. The number ten is hardly fortuitous, but corresponds to an ordering principle, frequently encountered in Jewish literature, which symbolizes perfection. But matters are still more complicated, for, in Matt. 5:3–12, two strata can clearly be distinguished. In Matt. 5:3–10, a series of eight macarisms, largely parallel in form, have been brought together; each consists of a distich in the third person plural, the second line of which is invariably introduced by ὅτι ("that"). In patristic exegesis, the number eight (according to other reckonings, the number seven) is discussed at great length, for it, too, must be explained in terms of number-symbolism. The number eight (or seven) symbolizes perfection as well. In Matt. 5:9–10, two further macarisms have been added secondarily. These secondary expansions bring about changes in form, though it is not clear for what reason. In any case, the symbolism remains constant, since both the number eight (seven) and the number ten express perfection. As a *theologumenon,* perfection plays an important role in the SM.[19]

3. The phenomenon of the series of macarisms raises the problem of how individual macarisms are related to one another. Again there are wide-ranging discussions among the church fathers on this point. They noticed that the first in the series of macarisms speaks of the basic virtue of humility, while the last deals with the vision of God and deification. Thus some patristic expositors interpreted the design as a stepladder for the ascent of the soul from the elementary virtue of

19. Cf. Matt. 5:48.

humility to mystical union with God. Though one may be properly skeptical toward such speculative ideas, it remains necessary to find an explanation more appropriate to the text for why the Beatitudes are arranged in their present order.

4. In itself the series of macarisms is by no means uniform, but is made up of four distinct types, each of two lines, with the exception of v. 12, which is a tristich.

a. The first and no doubt the "leading" macarism is found in v. 3. It has its counterpart in v. 10. The first line contains the macarism as such, "Blessed are the poor in spirit," formulated in the third person plural. The designation of those addressed is unusual, a matter of which we shall still have to speak. The second line constitutes a ὅτι-clause, in which the grounds for the macarism are stated. However, the ὅτι-clause belongs to the macarism in only a qualified sense. The phrase "to them belongs the kingdom of heaven" was originally a verdict that had its place in the last judgment and is anticipated here.

b. The second type is found in vv. 4–9. Again the first line contains the macarism, cast in the third person plural, together with the designation of those who are addressed, while the second line is a ὅτι-clause giving the basis for the blessing. But in this instance the ὅτι-clause consists of an eschatological promise, formulated in the future passive. These promises arise through an eschatological interpretation of the *ius talionis*. The series comprised by vv. 4–9 contains macarisms that correspond to individual scenes in which the fate of the righteous in paradise is described. Thus one can see in this section a greatly abbreviated apocalyptic vision of the world to come.

c. The third type is found only once, in v. 11. The macarism is now formulated in the second person plural and is not connected with a designation of those addressed. The second line takes the form of a ὅτι-clause; it presents three situations of persecution that the addressees must be prepared to undergo.

d. The fourth type is a tristich, represented by v. 12. Again formulated in the second person plural, it begins with a double summons to "rejoice and be glad" (RSV), then passes over into a ὅτι-clause in the second line, which provides the necessary justification. This line consists of a Jewish dogmatic judgment: "Great is your reward in heaven." This verdict is then furnished with its justification in the third line: "for so they persecuted the prophets who were before you." In other words, a historical verdict is rendered by which the present persecution of the community is equated with the persecution of the prophets, that, in accordance with Jewish thought, results in eschatological reward. One must read the argument in reverse, so to speak. The historical verdict rendered in v. 12c leads to the dogmatic judgment in v. 12b, and both together constitute the basis for the macarism in v. 12a.

5. One must assume that the introduction of the SM by this series of macarisms is intentional. But what purpose is behind it? What is the function of this series of macarisms in the present literary composition? What is the relationship between the introductory series of macarisms and the rest of the SM?

6. As one turns to individual macarisms, the question arises of how the type of macarism found in the SM is to be evaluated in respect to the ancient literary genre to which it belongs. As soon as one seeks a solution to this problem, it becomes clear with what a complicated literary creation we are dealing. Viewed in broad outlines, we may roughly distinguish in ancient literature between the religious macarism (for example, Ps. 1:1), the secular macarism (in which one is praised on account of wealth, strength, beauty, etc.), the "macarism of the wise man" (so called by B. Gladigow, in which one is praised for wisdom and virtue), and the satirical macarism (for example, *Eth. En.* 103, 5–6: "Blessed are the sinners; they saw all their days. And now they have died in prosperity and wealth ...").[20] Now which of these categories corresponds to the type of macarism found in the SM, assuming that one may regard them as a unity? The answer to this question shall further concern us in what follows; the other problems touched upon must be left to one side for now.

---

20. Cited according to the edition of M. A. Knibb, *The Ethiopic Book of Enoch* (New York and Oxford: Oxford University Press, 1978), vol. II, 240.

III. THE FORM AND SIGNIFICANCE
OF THE FIRST MACARISM

The first macarism in Matt. 5:3 (RSV) is composed, as we have said, of two lines, and runs as follows:

Blessed are the poor in spirit,
for theirs is the kingdom of heaven.
μακάριοι οἱ πτωχοὶ τῷ πνεύματι,
ὅτι αὐτῶν ἐστιν ἡ βασιλεία τῶν οὐρανῶν.

Since this macarism is found in an ostensibly religious text, one should not hesitate to reckon it to be the type of the religious macarism. But things are not so simple. To clarify the matter, we shall first turn our attention to the second line.

1. As has already been mentioned, the clause "for theirs is the kingdom of heaven" is an anticipatory eschatological verdict actually belonging to the account of the last judgment. One can still discern its original function in the so-called Parable of the Great Judgment in Matt. 25:31–46, where the eschatological judge, the Son of man, says to those about to enter into paradise (v. 34): "Come, you blessed of my Father, inherit the kingdom prepared for you from the foundations of the world." The curse upon those who must depart into hell is correspondingly formulated in Matt. 25:41 (RSV): "Depart from me, you cursed, into the eternal fire prepared for the devil and his angels."

Thus in Matt. 5:3, we have before us an eschatological judgment passed proleptically upon the members of a given religious community. In connection with the macarism, this kind of eschatological pronouncement has a long history in Greek as well as in Jewish religion. If one wishes to gain a proper understanding of Matt. 5:3, one must become familiar with this history, at least in broad outline.

Surely the earliest instance of such a macarism is found in the *Homeric Hymn to Demeter* (480–83):

Happy is he among men upon earth who has seen these mysteries;
but he who is uninitiate has no part in them;
never has lot of like good things once he is dead,
down in the darkness and gloom.[21]

21. The translation is that of H. G. Evelyn-White, *Hesiod, The Homeric Hymns*

ὄλβιος ὃς τάδ' ὄπωπεν ἐπιχθονίων ἀνθρώπων·
ὃς δ' ἀτελὴς ἱερῶν, ὅς τ' ἄμμορος, οὔ ποθ' ὁμοίων
αἶσαν ἔχει φθίμενός περ ὑπὸ ζόφῳ εὐρώεντι.[22]

The macarism is formulated in the third person and is addressed to those who have been initiated into the Eleusinian mysteries. In the course of the initiation, they have "seen these things"—a mysterious way of referring to the rites, and one which is only understandable to the initiate. We still do not know what sort of vision was involved; but it is certain that in some manner the destiny of the soul in the afterlife, which awaited the initiate, was revealed. Pindar, who also quotes the macarism,[23] says that the initiate "knows the end of life," and that "he also knows the beginning given by god" (οἶδε μὲν βίου τελευτάν, οἶδεν δὲ διόσδοτον ἀρχάν). Therefore, that which the initiate has seen has imparted a certain knowledge. What kind of knowledge was it? As we have already stated, nothing can be said with certainty; but if the Pseudo-Platonic *Axiochus* (371D) discloses that a "privileged seat" (προεδρία) at the banquet in the Elysian Fields was part of it, then we can in general conclude that the content of this "knowledge" would have been the destiny of the soul of the initiate in the afterlife. This immediately gives rise to the further question of whether this knowledge actually consisted of the teaching of Orphic mythology on the bliss and punishment of the soul in the afterlife.[24] Though nothing definitive can be said on the basis of present research, it is good, nevertheless, to call attention at this point to some remarkable textual finds. Macarisms like that in the *Hymn to Demeter* are found on the so-called Orphic gold plates, which have long been known but which have only recently received serious attention. As G. Zuntz correctly observed in his commentary,[25] the gold plates contain numerous citations among which are also macarisms. The following example is typical:

---

and *Homerica,* LCL (Cambridge: Harvard University Press, 1959), 323.
22. Cited according to the edition of N. J. Richardson, *The Homeric Hymn to Demeter* (Oxford: Oxford University Press, 1974), 134. See also the commentary to these lines, 313–15.
23. Frag. 121, ed. Bowra.
24. See on this point F. Graf, *Eleusis und die orphische Dichtung Athens,* RVV 33 (Berlin: Walter De Gruyter, 1974), 79–80.
25. *Persephone* (Oxford: Oxford University Press, 1971), 322–23.

Blessed and happy are you; you will be a god rather than man. ὄλβιε καὶ μακαριστέ, θεὸς δ' ἔσηι ἀντὶ βροτοῖο.[26] The purpose of the gold plate was as follows.[27] One buried such a gold plate with the initiate in the grave, putting it in his or her hand or laying it in the ear. The plate obviously contained the all-important formulas needed to reach the Elysian Fields, the passwords and magical charms which the initiate had learned in the mystery rites, but which could easily be forgotten. Without them, it was impossible to find one's way past the gods of the underworld. Thus the macarism is one of the most important things the initiate comes to "know" through initiation and must be regarded as an indispensable element of one's eschatological salvation.

In relation to Matt. 5:3, it is important to emphasize that in every instance—in the Homeric *Hymn to Demeter*, in Pindar, on the gold plates, etc.—macarisms are quoted which are taken over from the initiation itself, and are only secondarily adduced as an aid to the memory. Without being too bold, one can say the same thing of the macarisms in the SM. Their present setting and function are secondary; they serve as a reminder, heightened by arrangement in a series, with all its complexity. We can be certain that the religious macarism originally belonged in the context of liturgical initiation from the evidence of other well-known texts.[28]

In the field of Jewish literature, the type of the religious macarism is encountered chiefly in apocalyptic writings. How it is employed is made particularly clear in *Slavonic Enoch*. Here we are told how the seer makes an extended journey through the underworld, and afterward returns to earth. In a lengthy farewell address, he imparts his "knowledge" to "his sons" and, of course, to the reader. His knowledge, we are expressly told, embraces both the world to come and the consequences for life in this world; that is to say, it consists of rather extensive paraenetic discourses. Enoch begins his address in charac-

---

26. Cited according to the edition of Zuntz, *Persephone*, 301.
27. Thus according to Zuntz, *Persephone*, 335. For these important references I am indebted to W. Burkert's essay, "Orphism and Bacchic Mysteries: New Evidence and Old Problems of Interpretation," The Center for Hermeneutical Studies in Hellenistic and Modern Culture, Colloquy 28 (Berkeley, Calif., 1977).
28. For example, Apuleius, *Met.* XI, 16, 22–23, ed. Griffiths, or on syncretistic Jewish soil, *Jos. and As.* 16:7–8, ed. Philonenko.

teristic terms: "And now, my children, I know all things, for this is from the Lord's lips, and this my eyes have seen from beginning to end."²⁹ Then he recounts once more all he has seen and heard, frequently introduced by the familiar phrase, "I saw." What is interesting is that the prophet proceeds, on the basis of his knowledge of the other world, to compose a series of macarisms that have a remarkable similarity to Matthew 5.³⁰ A similar situation is found in another apocalyptic text, *4 Ezra* 8:46–54. God has granted an audience through his angel to the seer Salathiel-Ezra, in which the angel answers the questions of the seer. The angel admonishes him in conclusion: "But think rather on your own lot, and seek after the splendour which your brothers shall inherit." Afterward, the angels dismiss him with the promise:

For for you
  is opened Paradise,
    planted the Tree of life;
  the future age prepared,
    plenteousness made ready;
  a City builded,
    a Rest appointed;
  Good works established,
    wisdom preconstituted;
The (evil) root is sealed up from you,
  infirmity from your path extinguished;
And death is hidden,
  Hades fled away;
Corruption forgotten,
  sorrows passed away;
and in the end, the treasures of immortality are made manifest.³¹

These examples, which might easily be multiplied, are enough to demonstrate that here, too, an initiation of a seer, and through him of the reader, in the secrets of the other world has taken place. Out of his "knowledge" macarisms are born. The seer has seen that the right-

29. Cited according to the translation of N. Forbes and R. H. Charles, *APOT*, vol. 2, 455.
30. *Slav. En.* 42:6ff.; 52:1ff.
31. Cited according to the translation of G. H. Box in Charles, *APOT*, vol. 2, 597–98.

eous are those on earth who are humble and who humble themselves; it is these who shall inherit paradise. For this reason, he can promise his faithful, those who have followed him upon this path, the salvation of the world to come at present. The words with which the angel comforts the seer apply to them:

> Thou, however, hast many times ranged thyself with the ungodly.
> This must not be!
> But even on this account thou shalt be honorable before the Most High;
> because thou hast humbled thyself, as it becomes thee,
> and hast not assigned thyself a place among the righteous;
> and so thou shalt receive the greater glory.[32]

The second line of the macarism in Matt. 5:3 is, therefore, to be regarded as an eschatological verdict reached on the basis of knowledge about the fate of humankind in the afterlife. There is thus a remarkable parallel within the phenomenology of religion between the ancient Greek mysteries of Demeter and other mysteries, and Jewish apocalyptic. Both religions impart to their adherents, in initiations of the most various kinds, the secrets of the world beyond and their own lot at present. It is for this reason that the verdict awaited at the last judgment, both in the mysteries and in Jewish apocalyptic, can already be rendered in the earthly present.

2. As already indicated, the characteristic feature of the first line of the macarism in Matt. 5:3 is the designation of those addressed. But before raising the question of who is addressed as "poor in spirit," it is necessary to deal with the matter of literary form. This manner of speaking about those addressed points to a further peculiarity in the form of this macarism.

Put briefly, there is evidence at this point of the influence of another type of macarism, which B. Gladigow termed the "macarism of the wise man." As Gladigow has shown,[33] this type of macarism arose out of critical reflection on the conventional macarism, in which a person is praised on account of wealth, health, fame, etc. This critical reflection puts the system of values expressed in the conventional, secular macarism fundamentally in question. Its basis is human

---

32. *4 Ezra* 8:48–49, cited according to the translation of G. H. Box in Charles, *APOT,* vol. 2, 597.
33. "Der Makarismus des Weisen," *Hermes* 95 (1967): 404–33.

experience, which has repeatedly shown that material possessions and the values associated with them are an uncertain affair. Philosophical skepticism had long concluded that no mortal could be called "happy." On the contrary, mortals are constantly exposed to danger, catastrophes, and the accidents of nature throughout their lives. Only the dead, who are freed from the ups and downs of life, can be called happy. Or, one might also say, only those may be called happy who have never seen the light of day. Such themes are commonplace in Greek as well as in Jewish Wisdom literature.

One might refer, for example, to the famous encounter between the Greek wise man Solon and the Persian king Croesus in *Herodotus* 1, 30–32. After the king had shown his guest all his treasures and had complimented him on his experience of the world and his wisdom, he asked the question whether Solon had ever met a man more blessed than his fellows. To Croesus's surprise, Solon named first a certain Tellos of Athens, then the brothers Cleobis and Biton of Argos. Solon went on to explain why he had named these three persons: they combined great virtue with those things for which men are customarily praised. For this reason they were honored by their fellow citizens with a public burial, and in the case of Cleobis and Biton, by the erection of statues. It is the end of life that is decisive. A man is accounted "blessed" ($\ddot{o}\lambda\beta\iota o s$) when he has lived his life well and ended it well. But before a man is dead, he can only be called "lucky" ($\epsilon\dot{v}\tau\nu\chi\dot{\eta}s$). Then Solon holds a long discourse before the king on the conditions of human life in general. Heaven is envious and loves to lay traps for humanity. Human life is short, seventy years at most. And these years are spent under the dominion of chance. All things, even riches, can be transformed into their opposites from one day to the next. For this reason one must wait to the end of life to see if a person is to be called "blessed."

The theme is dealt with from the opposite point of view in a dialogue between Socrates and the sophist Antiphon in Xenophon, *Mem.* 1, 5, 6ff. Antiphon has observed that Socrates' practice of philosophy has not led, as one would expect, to an increase in his personal fortune. On the contrary, Socrates lives in such wretched poverty that no one, not even a slave, could endure his standard of living. His fare is miserable, and his threadbare cloak is changed

31

neither summer nor winter. He has no shoes. And that modest sum of money which makes independence possible, he is also without. Thus he designates Socrates a "professor of misery" (κακοδαιμονίας διδάσκαλος). The attack then furnishes Socrates with the opportunity to present the doctrine of *encrateia*. He asserts that he is by no means poor, but on the contrary has no need of wealth and luxury. His manner of life keeps his body healthy and in good condition. He can even hope that he will become a better man because he has better friends than those who live in luxury. Socrates concludes by contrasting the two concepts of *eudaimonia:* Antiphon assumes, along with the great mass of fools, that luxury and extravagance bring happiness. Socrates, on the other hand, sees happiness as the absence of desires, for this state is divine. To have need of nothing comes nearest the divine, and is most in keeping with human nature and the cosmos.

It is generally known that this idea gained prominence in Cynic philosophy. At work here was the principle of the overturning of all values: wealth is no longer praised, but voluntary poverty. Riches do not live up to their promise, whereas poverty is by no means a condition of misery, but the precondition for freedom, virtue, wisdom, *eudaimonia.* Under the influence of Antisthenes, the concepts "wealth" and "poverty" were further spiritualized, so that they became traits of the soul.

In the course of reflection the macarism was thus transformed and brought in line with the philosophical trend of the day. The following macarism, for example, is attributed to Empedocles: "Blessed, he who has earned wealth from divine thoughts, wretched, he who cherishes a dark delusion concerning the gods" (ὄλβιος, ὃς θείων πραπίδων ἐκτήσατο πλοῦτον, δειλός δ', ὧι σκοτόεσσα θεῶν πέρι δόξα μέμηλεν).[34]

True wealth is now viewed as the possession of divine thoughts, and the "knowledge" of which Pindar and the Homeric *Hymn to Demeter* speak is interpreted as philosophical knowledge. On this basis, the history of the "macarism of the wise man" can now begin. Obviously, content and terminology conform to the views of the various philo-

34. H. Diels and W. Kranz, *Die Fragmente der Vorsokratiker*, 6th ed. (Berlin: Weidmann, 1951–52), 31 B 132 (I, 365).

sophical or religious schools. But the macarism of the wise man remains an "anti-macarism"; that is to say, it is consciously formulated in opposition to the conventional macarism and stands its values on its head.

Naturally, this "macarism of the wise man" is encountered frequently in Cynic and Stoic traditions. But it is also found in popular philosophy, collections of *gnomai*, and anecdotes on the lives of philosophers. In this literature as well, the macarism can take on a religious coloring as, for example, in one of the sentences of Sextus: "Blessed is the man whose soul is not held up as he journeys to God" (μακάριος ἀνήρ, οὗ τῆς ψυχῆς οὐδεὶς ἐπιλήψεται εἰς θεὸν πορευομένης).[35]

In this secondary religious context the "macarism of the wise man" is also found in great numbers in Old Testament–Jewish Wisdom literature, in apocalyptic, and in early Christian literature. In most of the macarisms of this type it is not difficult to show how conventional values are stood on their head. When one finds in Sir. 25:8, for example, "Happy is the man who lives with an intelligent wife" (μακάριος ὁ συνοικῶν γυναικὶ συνετῇ), it is clear that the macarism is aimed at the conventional belief that he is happy who has a rich and beautiful wife. In apocalyptic, one sees how talk of individual insecurity takes on cosmic dimensions. Cosmic catastrophes such as the apocalyptist describes serve to justify the overthrow of values. For this reason apocalyptic macarisms are frequently anti-macarisms praising those who do not measure up to conventional values. In the context of Jewish theology, it is not the "righteous" who are blessed—those who adhere to the conventional standards of piety—but those who actually fulfill the law.

IV. SUMMARY

We may sum up: the macarism in Matt. 5:3 is a mixed form of a rather complicated sort. The first line, "Blessed are the poor in spirit" (RSV) is an anti-macarism opposed to the conventional macarism "Blessed are the rich." The first line reflects the critical unmasking of a naive,

---

35. Sent. 40, text and translation according to the edition of H. Chadwick, *The Sentences of Sextus* (Cambridge: At the University Press, 1959), 16.

but religiously sanctioned, materialism. By contrast, it is not the economically poor who are called "blessed," but the "poor in spirit." This disputed term, as we now know, is a Semitism and derives from the Jewish "piety of the poor."[36] But what does the expression mean? It has two principal aspects: first, it represents a correction of the notion that those who are economically poor are to be called blessed, an idea that is again termed naive. Rather, humanity in general is recognized to be miserable. On this the SM is in complete agreement with Jewish *Anawim*-piety on the one hand and certain elements of Greek philosophy on the other. It is a matter of consciously accepting human existence. In the categories of Jewish theology such an attitude belongs to the virtues of self-abasement and humility, marks of the true righteousness.

If human beings are ·such miserable creatures, wherein is their salvation? The answer, the second principal aspect, is provided by the next line: "for theirs is the kingdom of heaven" (RSV). The teacher who formulated the macarism "knows" the kind of righteousness that is rewarded in the hereafter. Thus he is able to promise the kingdom of heaven to those who measure up to the required righteousness here and now.

The combination of these lines results in a sophisticated literary product whose elements have a long history both in Judaism and in Greek culture, a history that has been absorbed by the macarism. The macarism in Matt. 5:3 presupposes the conventional macarism and its critique by the "macarism of the wise man." But by the combination of both it goes far beyond the elements of which it was built and constitutes a new form of the religious macarism. Matt. 5:3 is therefore neither cultically defined like the macarism of the *Hymn to Demeter* nor simply secular. In comparison with the *Hymn to Demeter*, Matt. 5:3 introduces an ethical-paraenetic dimension. Conditions of an ethical sort, which one missed in the ancient mysteries, are laid down for admission into paradise. Compared finally with the apocalyptic macarism, Matt. 5:3 has wiped out the entire apocalyptic framework.

These variations can only be understood as the result of critical

---

36. Cf. the material in H.-Th. Wrege, *Die Überlieferungsgeschichte der Bergpredigt*, WUNT 9 (Tübingen: J. C. B. Mohr [Paul Siebeck], 1968), 6ff.

discussion. In analyzing this debate, one should not hastily have recourse to the historical Jesus, but should consider the impact of the Christology of the SM as well. According to this Christology, Jesus himself was the authoritative interpreter of the Torah, the one who "knew" what would and would not be accounted righteous in the last judgment.

Thus we may conclude that in the course of its transformation the macarism in Matt. 5:3 has been elevated to the status of a fundamental theological definition. Formally the macarism is equipped to take on this role. It contains everything one must know to pass through this life into paradise. In this respect the macarism is closely related to the Orphic gold plates of which we spoke at the beginning.

In my view, the first macarism is unfolded and variously developed in the following macarisms (Matt. 5:4–12). Together they constitute the self-consciousness of the community which expresses itself in the sayings "You are the salt of the earth" (5:13, RSV) and "You are the light of the world" (5:14–16, RSV). The rest of the SM is nothing else than the concretization and elucidation of the first macarism. It is on the basis of this statement that the interpretation of the Torah is carried out (5:17–48 and 7:12). In 6:1–18 the life of practical piety is constituted anew, while in 6:19–7:12 the conquest of everyday anxieties is undertaken. This outline illustrates how clearly the material has been organized and challenges us to a detailed literary analysis which cannot, of course, be carried out here.

It is a further task to integrate properly the SM and its theology in the history of early Christianity. The traditional antithesis of "law" and "gospel" does not do justice to the situation represented here. The SM derives from a Jewish-Christian group in which law and gospel are strongly intertwined. It was Pauline theology that first destroyed this synthesis which the SM, despite all its tensions, is concerned to maintain intact.

Had Paul, the former Pharisee, been familiar with the SM, it seems certain that he would have regarded its understanding of the Torah and its concept of righteousness as little more than an abridgment of the law.[37] Even as a Christian, Paul allowed only that Pharisaic

---

37. Cf. Gal. 6:13: "For not even the circumcised themselves keep the law" (οὐδὲ γὰρ οἱ περιτεμνόμενοι αὐτοὶ νόμον φυλάσσουσιν).

Judaism was authentic Judaism.[38] The solution of the SM must have appeared an idle compromise. It could only have provided confirmation for his thesis of "Christ as the end of the law."[39] But for a non-Pharisaic Jewish-Christian inspired by the Jewish *Anawim*-piety and the teachings of Jesus of Nazareth, the SM could point the way to a "better righteousness"[40] within Judaism.

---

38. Cf. Gal. 5:3: "I testify again to every man who has become circumcised, that he is obliged to do the whole Law" (μαρτύρομαι δὲ πάλιν παντὶ ἀνθρώπῳ περιτεμνομένῳ ὅτι ὀφειλέτης ἐστὶν ὅλον τὸν νόμον ποιῆσαι).
39. Cf. Gal. 3:23–25; Rom. 10:4.
40. Matt. 5:20.

3

The Hermeneutical Principles
of the
Sermon on the Mount
(Matt. 5:17-20)[1]

In his description of Jesus' teaching on the law in his *Dogmatik des christlichen Glaubens,* Gerhard Ebeling rightly urges us to consider that "What Jesus discloses of his own authority must demonstrate its legitimacy first of all in relation to that absolute embodiment of authority, the Mosaic law, and in confrontation with it."[2] With regard to the teaching of Jesus, the evidence indicates that early Christianity was historically united on the fact that Jesus taught the fulfillment of the Torah in the love-commandment.[3] But opinions on how this teaching was to be conceived in particular were sharply divided in the various groups that made up early Christianity. This was the case above all with the question of how the love-commandment could lead to the fulfillment of the Torah, and which theological consequences were to be drawn from this teaching. The pointed debates that were held on these subjects may still be discerned in the New Testament, if only in fragmentary form. Although now embedded in the context of

1. The English version of this paper was presented by invitation to the Annual Meeting of the New Testament Society of South Africa held in Pretoria, 27 July 1982.
2. Vol. II (Tübingen: J. C. B. Mohr [Paul Siebeck], 1979), 428.
3. The distribution of the evidence in the sources presents a clear picture: Matt. 5:43–48; Luke 6:27–36; Gal. 5:14; Rom. 13:8–10; James 2:8; Mark 22:31 par.; Matt. 19:19. See D. Lührmann, "Liebet eure Feinde (Lk 6,27–36/Mt 5,39–48)," *ZThK* 69 (1972): 412–38 and *Essays on the Love Command,* trans. by R. H. Fuller and I. Fuller (Philadelphia: Fortress Press, 1978).

secondary discussions, certain formulations with the character of slogans point to the basic positions adopted in these debates. Thus what Paul refers to as "the law of Christ" in Gal. 6:2 (RSV) contains without doubt an entire program for the understanding of the Torah as summarized in the love-commandment, cited earlier in Gal. 5:14.[4] Paul himself would hardly have introduced such a concept as "the law of Christ" into the discussion, but since it was already in use, obviously as the watchword of his opponents, he now makes every effort to incorporate it into his argument. His own understanding is more nearly embodied in the formula "Christ the end of the law" (Rom. 10:4), which he was repeatedly obliged to defend against the charge of antinomianism.[5] By contrast the Epistle of James speaks provocatively of "the royal law" (2:8) and "the law of liberty" (1:25; 2:12; RSV). Paul, on the other hand, finds it possible to bring together concepts such as "freedom" and "law" only in the form of an involved and complicated definition: "The law of the spirit of life in Christ Jesus has set you free from the law of sin and death" (Rom. 8:2). What Paul manages to hold together here with great difficulty, the Gospel of John opposes in dualistic fashion: "The law was given through Moses; grace and truth came through Jesus Christ" (1:17, RSV).

Regarded in this theological and historical context, it becomes clear that the teaching of Jesus in the Sermon on the Mount was not handed on merely as a traditional complex of pious reminiscence, or on account of a need that was later felt for the guidance of moral principles. Compared with the work of the evangelists, and also with that of Paul, the portrayal of the teaching of Jesus in the SM must be regarded as a wholly independent theological achievement. It manifests its independence not only in its resolute attempt to demonstrate that the teaching of Jesus was orthodox in terms of contemporary Jewish theology,[6] but also in its effort to clothe this demonstration in

4. Compare H. D. Betz, *Galatians* (Philadelphia: Fortress Press, 1979), 274–76, 298–301.

5. Compare Gal. 3:19–25, and on this passage see Betz, *Galatians*, 161–80. The fact that Paul's attitude toward the Torah remains controversial yet today is due neither to malicious intentions nor to want of intelligence, but rather to differently based theological presuppositions.

6. For important observations on this point, I am indebted to H. J. Schoeps, "Jesus und das jüdische Gesetz," in his *Studien zur unbekannten Religions- und Geistesgeschichte* (Göttingen: Musterschmidt, 1963), 41–61.

the form of an epitome, and thus to make of it a kind of systematic theology.[7] But what, above all, distinguishes the SM from virtually every other New Testament text is that it formulates the hermeneutical principles which guided Jesus in his interpretation of the Torah—by bringing together in Matt. 5:17–20 four guiding principles, to which is added the so-called Golden Rule and its interpretation in 7:12.[8]

The four guiding principles have been carefully thought out, formulated, and set in relation to one another.[9] In each individual saying the following items of major importance for hermeneutics are defined, both with respect to subject matter and in relation to each other: the text, the teacher, the teaching, and the recipients of the teaching. In the process the recipients of the teaching become, in turn, teachers themselves.

1. There was never a doubt in the early Christian tradition[10] about

7. See the more detailed exposition in my article, "The Sermon on the Mount: Its Literary Genre and Function," *JR* 59 (1979): 285–97. [See in this volume 1–16.]

8. The juxtaposition of the guiding principles is the work of the pre-Matthean redactor of the SM, in my opinion, not a part of the final redaction of the Gospel of Matthew. The concise observations of R. Bultmann, *The History of the Synoptic Tradition*, 2d ed. (New York: Harper & Row, 1968), 138, were already leading in this direction. Since D. Lührmann, *Die Redaktion der Logienquelle* (Neukirchen: Neukirchener Verlag, 1969), has convincingly demonstrated that the presynoptic source material in Q already gave evidence of redactional handling (on Matt. 5:17–20, see esp. 106, 116–21), investigation must be carried further in this direction. Compare my review in *ThLZ* 96 (1971): 428–29, and also my article "Die Makarismen der Bergpredigt (Matthäus 5,3–12). Beobachtungen zur literarischen Form und theologischen Bedeutung," *ZThK* 75 (1978). [See in this volume, 17–36.] Most recent investigations, on the other hand, impute the composition of Matt. 5:17–20 to the final redaction of the evangelist. In my opinion, this treatment is methodologically misleading. The latest attempts of this sort are the works of U. Luz, "Die Erfüllung des Gesetzes bei Matthäus," *ZThK* 75 (1978): 398–435; I. Broer, *Freiheit vom Gesetz und Radikalisierung des Gesetzes. Ein Beitrag zur Theologie des Evangelisten Matthäus*, SBS 98 (Stuttgart: Katholisches Bibelwerk, 1980); and C. Heubült, "Mt 5,17–20. Ein Beitrag zur Theologie des Evangelisten Matthäus," *ZNW* 71 (1980): 143–49.

9. M. Dibelius (*The Sermon on the Mount* [New York: Charles Scribner's Sons, 1940], 23) correctly emphasized this: "A few sentences prominently placed at the beginning of the entire section express the whole doctrine of a new Christian law in a few words: your righteousness shall exceed the righteousness of the Scribes and Pharisees. It may be questioned whether this small section Matthew 5:17–20 does not reflect the attitude of some Jewish-Christian communities rather than that of our Lord himself. But at any rate the closing phrase quoted above expresses very well the meaning of the commandments as given. The new righteousness, that is indeed the subject of this section of the Sermon on the Mount."

10. See the fundamental works by A. von Harnack, "Geschichte eines program-

the programmatic character of the first principle enunciated in Matt. 5:17, though the interpretation of the saying remains in dispute to this day.[11] Its literary form alone can only be comprehended as the result of a long and complicated debate. The opening words, μὴ νομίσητε, in the sense of "do not think it right . . ." or "do not share the opinion . . . ," are both polemically and apologetically intended, and are only meaningful on the supposition that there are those who are inclined to think as they should not.[12]

But now what is rejected in the name of Jesus is not a certain belief which is designated as false, but a saying of Jesus which is first cited in full as follows (RSV): "I have come to abolish the law and the prophets" (ἦλθον καταλῦσαι τὸν νόμον ἢ τοὺς προφήτας).

In the following sentence this false saying of Jesus is simply corrected, in that a disputed concept—καταλύειν[13] —is replaced by another, clearly the right one—πληροῦν.[14] Thus in its correct form the saying must run as follows: "I have come to fulfill the law and the prophets" (ἦλθον πληρῶσαι τὸν νόμον ἢ τοὺς προφήτας).

The phenomenon of a false Jesus-saying is indeed unusual, but is not without parallel in the literature.[15] But the question is: has the SM picked up a saying of Jesus which was actually in circulation, and which must then have been regarded as authentic by the bearers of the tradition?[16] Or are we dealing with an imitation, on the pattern of

---

matischen Worts Jesu (Matth. 5,17) in der ältesten Kirche," *SPAW.PH* (1912): 184–207; idem, "'Ich bin gekommen.' Die ausdrücklichen Selbstzeugnisse Jesu über den Zweck seiner Sendung und seines Kommens," *ZThK* 22 (1912): 1–30; cf. also Bultmann, *History*, 145ff., 150ff.; S. Légasse, "Mt 5,17 et la prétendue tradition paracanonique," in *Begegnung mit dem Wort. FS H. Zimmermann*, BBB 53 (Bonn: Hanstein), 11–21.

11. The extensive literature on this saying cannot be discussed here. See Broer, *Freiheit*, 11–12, although I certainly consider Broer's methods unsuccessful.

12. For the background significance of νομίζω, cf. Matt. 10:34; Acts 8:20, 17:29; 1 Cor 7:36; 1 Tim 6:5, as well as H. Kleinknecht, *TDNT* 4, 1023–25, 1028–29; W. Fahr, ΘΕΟΥΣ ΝΟΜΙΖΕΙΝ. *Zum Problem der Anfänge des Atheismus bei den Griechen*, Spudasmata 26 (Hildesheim: Olms, 1969), whose treatment of the New Testament passages is unfortunately inadequate.

13. To this legal concept, compare Gal. 2:18 and Betz, *Galatians*, 121 n. 70, as well as Eph. 2:14–15.

14. This legal concept appears in the same context in Gal. 5:14; cf. also Rom. 8:4; 13:8. See Betz, *Galatians*, 275.

15. Besides Matt. 10:34, cf. also 7:21, and H. D. Betz, "Eine Episode im Jüngsten Gericht (Mt 7:21-23)," *ZThK* 78 (1981): 1–30. [See in this volume, 125–27.]

16. Cf. the collection of parallel passages in von Harnack, "Geschichte eines

the ἦλθον-sayings, and hence a spurious composition, produced only in order to be repudiated?[17] Could it be that we are dealing with a deliberate caricature, a bowdlerization of a saying of Jesus actually in circulation? The latter is no doubt the most probable, for in the extracanonical Jesus-tradition a number of similar sayings are found with which Matt. 5:17 bears comparison. That such bowdlerizations actually occurred is shown by a tale which Karl Georg Kuhn[18] rightly characterized as a satire in *b Shab.* 116a. In this story the following citation from the Gospels is put into the mouth of "a corrupt philosopher" (that is to say, a Christian theologian): "I have not come to take away from the Torah of Moses, but I have come in order to add to it."[19]

The date of this Rabbinic satire cannot be determined,[20] but it refers either to the pre-Matthean SM, or to the Gospel of Matthew (Matt. 5:17, 19), or to still other Jewish-Christian traditions which it thus intends to disclaim. It should also be pointed out that satirical formulations occur elsewhere in the SM.[21]

The "authentic" Jesus-saying, which remains to be formulated in 5:17b, is not satirical, but is no less contrived or artificial on that account. Strictly speaking this saying exists only as a theological concept in the mind of the reader. The text is intentionally written so that the reader cannot simply read-off the correct saying as he can the false one, but he must construct the saying himself out of the building materials that the text provides.

From a hermeneutical point of view Matt. 5:17 is of fundamental significance for an understanding of the SM in two respects. First of all, the character of the text of the SM is established in a formal way. In keeping with the genre of the epitome,[22] the SM as a whole con-

programmatischen Worts."

17. Cf. E. Arens, *The HΛΘON-Sayings in the Synoptic Tradition* (Göttingen: Vandenhoeck & Ruprecht, 1976), 91–116.

18. K. G. Kuhn, "Giljonim und sifre minim," in *Judentum, Urchristentum, Kirche. FS J. Jeremias,* BZNW 26 (Berlin: Walter De Gruyter, 1960), 24–61, esp. 50–58. Cf. also S. Pines, *The Jewish Christians of the Early Centuries According to a New Source* (Jerusalem: The Israel Academy of Sciences and Humanities, 1966), 5.

19. Quoted according to the German translation of Billerbeck, vol. 1, 241.

20. On the dating, see J. Jeremias, *New Testament Theology,* vol. I (London: SCM Press, 1971), 83 n. 7.

21. Cf. Matt. 5:13, 15, 46–47; 6:2, 5, 7, 16; 7:3–5, 21–23, 26–27.

22. See my "The Sermon on the Mount" (see above, n. 7).

sists of sayings of Jesus, that is, of words that were actually spoken. They are drawn from the broader Jesus-tradition, and are formulated in such a way that they should be "heard and obeyed." Thus in relation to Jesus' own proclamation, the SM is a secondary literary creation, a critical compilation of sayings of Jesus that have been recognized as decisive for instruction in proper theological thought and practice. Therefore one has to distinguish between three kinds of "texts": (1) the text of the proclamation of the historical Jesus that is represented here, (2) the text of the SM that is simply to be read, delivered, and recited, (3) and the text that is still to be constructed in thought and life. The last-mentioned text is the actual text with which the SM is concerned. By contrast, the written text of the SM performs only an auxiliary function, yet one which is necessary because of the disputed meaning of Jesus' message.

This definition of the text stands behind the singular construction of Matt. 5:17. The statement in v. 17a, which is given a wholly negative value, is formulated in such a way that its meaning can simply be read-off the surface of the text. Thus it constitutes a non-text, which compels the reader to compose the intended text from personal knowledge and experience, based on the building materials given. The real text of the SM is not written down, as it were, but first comes into being and continues to exist as a living word in the mind of the reader.

Furthermore, the theological content of 5:17 is of fundamental importance. As a definition the verse seeks to comprehend Jesus' interpretation of the Torah in its historical reality. The existence of both sayings of Jesus not only reflects the options that were available, but presupposes that the message of Jesus was a matter of dispute and that it had led to mutually opposed conclusions on the significance of Jesus' coming in general. The SM now takes up a definite position in the debate over the theological significance of Jesus' interpretation of the Torah.

In the first place it is established that the distinct character of this interpretation is the source and foundation of Jesus' community. The significance of his coming (that is, the aim and result of his historical existence) was his interpretation of the Torah—and nothing more. If the SM has nothing to say on important doctrinal matters such as the crucifixion, resurrection, and institution of the sacraments, it is not due to ignorance, but, rather, has the same motive as the polemic against prophecy, exorcism, and wonderworking in Matt. 7:21-23— namely, to differentiate the path chosen by the author of the SM from the directions pursued by other early Christian groups.

Furthermore, the SM makes clear that the purpose of Jesus' interpretation was by no means the abolition of the Torah, but its fulfillment. Behind its use of the technical terms "abolish" (καταλύειν) and "fulfill" (πληροῦν) lies the debate within Judaism over whether Jesus was rightly or wrongly judged to be a heretic. To be accused of having propagated the abolition of the law and the prophets was an extremely serious matter within Judaism at all periods, for it amounted to nothing less than being branded a heretic and an apostate.[23] In the Hellenistic world in general, Jesus would have been regarded as an anarchist and a rebel.[24] The SM seeks to refute the charge of heresy by insisting that Jesus' interpretation of the Torah was and is "orthodox" in the Jewish sense: his teaching, like that of any other orthodox teacher, was not in itself Torah but merely its interpretation, the sole purpose of which was to fulfill the will of God.[25]

2. The second hermeneutical principle (v. 18) seeks to define in what sense the followers of Jesus' teaching are to regard the Torah as authoritative Scripture.[26] From a formal point of view v. 18 again constitutes a saying of Jesus, introduced by a formula well known from Jesus' preaching—"truly I say to you" (ἀμὴν λέγω ὑμῖν). But the use of this introductory formula alone does not enable us to form a judgment on the historical value of v. 18, since the formula is also

23. A characteristic description of the apostate is found in Abot 3.15, according to the edition and translation of R. Trevers Herford, *Pirke Aboth. The Ethics of the Talmud: Sayings of the Fathers* (New York: Schocken Books, 1962), 80: "R. Eleazar the Modiite said: He who profanes holy things and despises the festivals, and shames his associates in public and makes void the covenant of Abraham our father, and gives interpretations of Torah which are not according to Halachah, even though he possess Torah and good deeds he has no portion in the world to come." The words $w^e h\check{a}m^e g\check{a}llae\ pan\hat{\imath}m\ b\check{a}tt\hat{o}r\bar{a}$ indicate an arrogant attitude with regard to the Torah, which according to the SM was definitely not true of Jesus.
24. See W. Nestle, "Asebieprozesse," *RAC* I (1950): 735-40.
25. Cf. Matt. 7:21; 6:10.
26. The connection with γάρ ("for") signifies that v. 18 is the basis as well as the development of v. 17. See G. Bornkamm, *Gesammelte Aufsätze* (Munich: Chr. Kaiser, 1971), vol. IV, 76.

employed frequently in sayings that are clearly secondary in nature.[27] We may only be certain that a saying introduced in this manner claims to derive its authority from Jesus. Yet because the saying's content has its origin in Jewish tradition, Jesus' authority here is only that he declared the decision in this saying to be binding on his followers.

The definition itself consists of a composition of three distinct parts. Without doubt the principal statement is located in the middle of the verse (18b), bracketed by two temporal qualifications (vv. 18a and c):

v. 18a   till heaven and earth pass away
v. 18b   not even one iota or one dot will pass away from the law
v. 18c   until it all comes to pass.
v. 18a   ἕως ἂν παρέλθῃ ὁ οὐρανὸς καὶ ἡ γῆ,
v. 18b   ἰῶτα ἓν ἢ μία κεραία οὐ μὴ παρέλθῃ ἀπὸ τοῦ νόμου,
v. 18c   ἕως ἂν πάντα γένηται.

The principal assertion in v. 18b defines the Torah as a written text in the following respect. The fact that the Torah is referred to by means of ἰῶτα ("iota") and κεραία ("dot," lit. "hook") implies that the text under consideration is written in Hebrew script: only for such a text would "iota" and "dot" serve as distinguishing characteristics.[28] Furthermore, the conclusion in question must be drawn *a minori ad maius:* what is true of the smallest letter must, *ipso facto,* be true of all the rest. Inferences such as these make it clear that, in keeping with Jewish theology, the Hebrew text of the Torah was the scriptural authority for the members of Jesus' movement, and that this text was considered binding down to its smallest letter.[29] Such a declaration is astonishing because the SM is itself written in Greek, and was part of a Greek linguistic milieu. The same may be said of the scriptural citations, particularly of those found in the antitheses in 5:21-48.

27. See H. D. Betz, "Eine judenchristliche Kult-Didache in Matthäus 6:1-18," in *Jesus Christus in Historie und Theologie. FS. H. Conzelmann* (Tübingen: J. C. B. Mohr [Paul Siebeck], 1975), 455. [In this volume, 67.]

28. ἰῶτα here refers to the Hebrew letter *yodh,* while κεραία is proverbial in Greek as well (cf. Philo, *In Flacc.* 131). For comparative material, see Billerbeck, vol. 1, 244, 247-49; Bauer, *Lexicon;* G. Schwarz, "ἰῶτα ἓν ἢ μία κεραία (Matthäus 5,18)" *ZNW* 66 (1975): 268-69.

29. Compare Paul's very different view in Gal. 5:14, the summary in 5:3 of the view he had held before he became a Christian, and the position of the Letter of James (James 2:10-11).

There is no indication that the SM as a whole was translated from Hebrew, and one's attention is otherwise seldom drawn to Semitic figures of speech.[30] Consequently the decision to restrict the definition of scriptural authority to the Hebrew text of the Torah must have had special motives, and can be explained as an attempt at polemical delimitation.

This definition of scriptural authority, however, gives rise to a problem that demands an explanation. As the term παρέρχεσθαι ("pass away") indicates, the Torah, in its character as Scripture, participates in the createdness of the world, and thus is subject to transience.[31] But how can this transience be compatible with the absolute authority of Scripture?

The answer provided by the SM is that the authority of Scripture is temporally limited. Thus the SM gives rise to a seeming paradox: the scriptural authority of the Torah will not pass away so long as the conditions of this transitory world persist.

It is the task of the two frame-sentences in vv. 18a and c to specify the time at which the conditions of the transitory world will be annulled. This temporal limit is derived from apocalyptic expectation, as is evident from two didactic formulas. The first of these formulas employs the well-known apocalyptic *topos:* "until heaven and earth pass away" (v. 18a).[32] The second formula is conceived as a parallel to v. 18a and is also of apocalyptic origin: "until all is accomplished" (v. 18c, RSV).[33] Accordingly, these definitions aim at a solution that differs radically from that of other Jewish sects for whom the written Torah was eternally valid,[34] and from that of Paul for whom the end of the (Jewish) Torah coincided with the coming of

---

30. Words like ἀμήν ("truly") in 5:18, 26; 6:2, 5, 13, 16; γέεννα ("Gehenna") in 5:22, 29, 30; μαμωνᾶς ("Mammon") in 6:24; ῥακά ("fool") in 5:22 had long since entered into colloquial speech.

31. So correctly also Bornkamm, *Gesammelte Aufsätze,* 77–78. In the use of παρέρχομαι ("pass away") in 5:18a and b, the cosmological-apocalyptic meaning (cf. Mark 13:30 par.; 2 Cor. 5:17; 2 Peter 3:10) and the juristic meaning (cf. Mark 13:31 par.; Luke 15:29) are played off against one another.

32. See for instance Mark 13:31 par.; Luke 16:17; 1 Cor. 7:31; Rev. 21:1. For further citations, see Billerbeck, vol. 3, 840ff.

33. See also Mark 13:30 par.; Rev. 1:1, 19; 4:1, etc.

34. See the material in Billerbeck, vol. 1, 245–47. As he often does, he here interprets Rabbinic theology into Matt. 5:18.

Jesus.[35] But while the Pauline solution must have been considered heretical by non-Christian Judaism, the same cannot be said of the SM. It merely asserts that the written Torah was given under historical conditions, and that these conditions will come to an end with history itself.[36] Until then, the community of the SM remains within the bounds of Judaism.

3. The third hermeneutical principle seeks to define the binding force of Jesus' interpretation of the Torah (v. 19). After the obligation to observe the written text of the Torah has been confirmed in v. 18, and after the fulfillment of God's will has been ordained as the goal of Jesus' interpretation of the Torah in v. 17, there follows logically the question of the binding force of Jesus' interpretation of the Torah.[37] On the basis of the first two hermeneutical principles alone one might be tempted to conclude that Jesus' interpretation was not binding, so long as the text of Scripture was left undisturbed and the will of God was fulfilled. Any such interpretation of the Torah, including that of Jesus, would represent little more than the opinion of one Jewish school among many, and in the last analysis would be only second-rate.

The position adopted by the SM in this matter takes the form of a "sentence of holy law,"[38] formulated in antithetical *parallelismus membrorum:*[39]

v. 19a Whoever then abolishes one of the least of these commandments and teaches the people in this way
v. 19b shall be called least in the kingdom of heaven;
v. 19c but whoever does them and teaches them
v. 19d this one shall be called great in the kingdom of heaven.
v. 19a ὃς ἐὰν οὖν λύσῃ μίαν τῶν ἐντολῶν τούτων τῶν ἐλαχίστων καὶ διδάξῃ οὕτως τοὺς ἀνθρώπους,

---

35. Cf. Gal. 3:19-25 and Betz, *Galatians,* 161-80.
36. Philo advocates a similar view in *De vita Mosis 2: 14-15,* when he writes of the Mosaic law: "and we may hope that they will remain for all future ages as though immortal, so long as the sun and moon and the whole heaven and universe exist" (πρὸς τὸν ἔπειτα πάντα διαμενεῖν ἐλπὶς αὐτὰ αἰῶνα ὥσπερ ἀθάνατα, ἕως ἂν ἥλιος καὶ σελήνη καὶ ὁ σύμπας οὐρανός τε καὶ κόσμος ᾖ).
37. The connection is established by οὖν ("therefore").
38. See E. Käsemann, "Sentences of Holy Law," in his *New Testament Questions of Today* (Philadelphia: Fortress Press, 1969), 78.
39. See Jeremias, *New Testament Theology,* vol. I, 14ff.

v. 19b   ἐλάχιστος κληθήσεται ἐν τῇ βασιλείᾳ τῶν οὐρανῶν·
v. 19c   ὃς δ᾽ ἂν ποιήσῃ καὶ διδάξῃ,
v. 19d   οὗτος μέγας κληθήσεται ἐν τῇ βασιλείᾳ τῶν οὐρανῶν.

The protases of both conditional sentences (vv. 19a and c) contrast two conceivable legal situations with one another, while the accompanying apodoses (vv. 19b and d) draw the consequences which result in accordance with the eschatological *ius talionis*. The legal situations described in the conditional portions of both sentences have as their theme certain modes of conduct and teaching in respect to specific commandments (ἐντολαί), while the accompanying apodoses state the eschatological rank which corresponds respectively to the mode of conduct and teaching. A number of difficult problems are connected with this formal description of the "sentence of holy law."

First of all, the question arises for whom v. 19 was actually formulated. The answer can hardly be in doubt in light of the activities described in vv. 19a and c. The terms "abolish" (λύειν) and "do" (ποιεῖν) designate the kind of conduct that was on the one hand prohibited, and on the other hand required of the community of the SM, in relation to the teaching of Jesus. The proper response was to hear (ἀκούειν) and to act (ποιεῖν) in accordance with the teaching, whereas merely hearing and doing nothing leads to ruin—both in this world and in the world to come.[40] While this rule applies to all, that which is stated in v. 19 must be taken to refer specifically to teachers who are at work in the community.[41] It is said that when their teaching occurs in the proper manner, it takes place as "doing and teaching" (ποιεῖν καὶ διδάσκειν). That is to say, the content of the teaching is first lived out as an example by the teacher. In this way the student always has before his or her eyes not only the words of Jesus,

---

40. I have worked out the details of this in "The Sermon on the Mount" (see above, n. 7).
41. Cf. also *Did.* 4:13; *Barn.* 19:11. In the background there seems to be an ancient legal principle which had already been stated in Deut. 4:2; Prov. 30:6; Eccl. 3:14. Also noteworthy are Gal. 1:8–9 (cf. Betz, *Galatians*, 50ff.) and Rev. 22:18–19. Cf. W. C. van Unnik, "De la regle Μήτε προσθεῖναι μήτε ἀφελεῖν dans l'histoire du canon," *VigChr* 3 (1949): 1–36; W. Herrmann, "Zu Kohelet 3,14," *WZ[L].GS* 3 (1953/54): 293–95; C. Schäublein, "Μήτε προσθεῖναι μήτ᾽ ἀφελεῖν . . . ," *MH* 31 (1974): 144–49. On the tradition-historical problem, see esp. H. Schürmann, "'Wer daher eines dieser geringsten Gebote auflöst . . . ' Wo fand Matthäus das Logion Mt 5,19?" in his *Traditionsgeschichtliche Untersuchungen zu den Evangelien* (Düsseldorf: Patmos-Verlag, 1968), 126–36.

but the teacher who lives them out as well. In fact, this procedure corresponds, so far as we know, to contemporary Jewish methods of teaching.⁴² By way of contrast the teacher who seeks to discredit the teaching of Jesus sets up his false teaching in opposition to the true, and then teaches this false doctrine to people.⁴³

But a further question arises: what is to be understood by "the least of these commandments" (ἐντολῶν τούτων τῶν ἐλαχίστων)? What portion of the teaching is meant by this expression? Are these "commandments" (ἐντολαί) to be identified with the statements of the Torah (νόμος), or with the commands of Jesus? It is evident from 5:17 and 18, as well as 7:12, that the term νόμος is used in the SM to designate the written Torah, which cannot itself serve as the content of the teaching. Thus the term ἐντολαί must refer to the commands of Jesus, which then form the teaching material of the SM.⁴⁴

But to what does "these" (τούτων) refer?⁴⁵ What is probably meant is the teaching of Jesus as presented from 5:21 on. How much is to be included in the commands of Jesus? It is hard to provide a conclusive answer to this question, since the term ἐντολή ("commandment") does not occur elsewhere in the SM. Are the "commandments" to be identified with the so-called antitheses of 5:21-48,⁴⁶ in which the formula "but I say to you" (ἐγὼ δὲ λέγω ὑμῖν) repeatedly introduces

---

42. Cf. Billerbeck, vol. 1, 527–29; H. D. Betz, *Nachfolge und Nachahmung Jesu Christi im Neuen Testament* (Tübingen: J. C. B. Mohr [Paul Siebeck], 1967), 11–12.

43. Linguistically, λύειν ("abolish") and ποιεῖν ("do") denote mutually opposed viewpoints held by early Christian teachers with regard to Jesus' exposition of the Law. These concepts are not to be confused with καταλύειν ("abolish") and πληροῦν ("fulfill") in v. 17. So correctly W. Grundmann, *Das Evangelium nach Matthäus*, 2d ed. (Berlin: Evangelische Verlagsanstalt, 1971); differently, Luz, "Die Erfüllung des Gesetzes bei Matthäus," 409 n. 55.

44. The linguistic usage of νόμος ("law") and ἐντολή ("commandment") that is under discussion here seems peculiar because in the SM, νόμος refers to the Torah collectively, while ἐντολή, which appears only once (in 5:19), refers to Jesus' own interpretation of an individual command. This is a reasonable conclusion in view of the consistent use of ἐντολή ("commandment") in other ancient Jesus traditions as, for example, Mark 1:28, 31 par.; 1 Cor. 14:37; *1 Clem.* 13:3; *2 Clem.* 4:5; *Did.* 1:5; 2:1; 4:13; 13:5, 7.

45. Cf. the discussion of the proposed possibilities in Grundmann, *Das Evangelium nach Matthäus*, 149 n. 41; H.-Th. Wrege, *Die Überlieferungsgeschichte der Bergpredigt* (Tübingen: J. C. B. Mohr [Paul Siebeck], 1968), 41 n. 3.

46. Cf. F. Dibelius, "Zwei Worte Jesu," *ZNW* 11 (1910): 188–92; C. E. Carlston, "The Things That Defile (Mark VII.14) and the Law in Matthew and Mark," *NTS* 15 (1968/69): 75–96, esp. 76–77.

Jesus' interpretation of the Torah? Or are all of the commands of Jesus contained in the SM his "commandments" (ἐντολαί), and therefore identical with the "words" (λόγοι) of 7:24–27? Or is the frame more narrowly drawn, so that only the main part of the SM (5:21–7:12) is to be regarded as the "commandments" (ἐντολαί) of Jesus? The so-called Golden Rule and its application in 7:12 does indeed constitute the conclusion of the body of the SM, and reflects back on it. The problem is made still more difficult by the fact that the commands of Jesus are classified as "least" (ἐλάχισται), though it is nowhere said what is meant by this expression. Surely the author makes reference here to the division of the commandments into commands of greater and lesser importance, or easier and more difficult. Such a division has its parallels, above all, in Pharisaic and Rabbinic theology.[47] Does such a classification presuppose that the community of the SM would have made such a distinction between more and less important commands of Jesus?[48] If this is the case, does it mean that only the lesser commandments are contained in the SM, while the more important commands are to be sought elsewhere? Since there is no basis otherwise for this supposition, the other possibility alone remains: that the commandments of Jesus as a whole were classified as "of little importance." But such an evaluation can only be meant ironically: that is to say, it constitutes, indirectly, a polemic against the emphasis on the "heavy" or "difficult" commands in Pharisaic theology.

What mattered according to Pharisaic theology was the fulfillment of the commands of the Torah which, because of their difficulty, were judged to be more "important." It is clear from the presynoptic tradition that Jesus and the primitive Christian community polemicized with special vehemence against this Pharisaic teaching.[49] What was maintained above all in this polemic was that the degree of external difficulty involved in the fulfillment of a command (that is, the quan-

47. On Rabbinic teaching, cf. the texts in Billerbeck, vol. 1, 249, 900–905, and E. E. Urbach, *The Sages* (Jerusalem: Magnes Press, 1975), vol. I, 324ff.
48. Cf. Dibelius, "Zwei Worte Jesu," 188–90; Grundmann, *Das Evangelium nach Matthäus*, 149–50.
49. Cf. esp. the debates about pure and impure in Mark 7:1–23 par., about the great commandment in Mark 12:28–34 par., and the anti-Pharisaic polemics in Matt. 23:1–39.

titative cost) cannot simply be equated with the fulfillment of God's will demanded by the Torah.[50] Thus it appears that, in contrast to Pharisaic theology, the commands of Jesus were ironically and polemically judged to be "of little importance" and "easy to fulfill."[51]

When the matter is viewed from the Pharisaic standpoint, one can, in fact, only come to the conclusion that the commands of Jesus in the SM are "light" or "easy." On the other hand, it is precisely the matter of the criteria for determining what is easier and what is more difficult to fulfill that is the theme of the antitheses of the SM. We cannot pursue the problem further here, but we may say at least that what is demonstrated there is that the commands of Jesus only appear to be easy to fulfill at first glance; on closer analysis the fulfillment turns out to be very difficult indeed. To be sure, the degree of difficulty in this instance is not measured by the external, quantitative cost, but by the inner, qualitative resistance in people, which must be overcome in the course of fulfillment.

Therefore it is probable that v. 19 seeks to establish the binding force of Jesus' interpretation of the Torah for teachers in the community of the SM. Corresponding to this is an eschatological classification of teachers. And here the rule of the eschatological *ius talionis* is again in operation. The place which the early Christian teacher will occupy in the coming kingdom of God is determined by the degree of his or her loyalty to the teaching of Jesus.[52]

A remarkable contradiction results from this evaluation, for contrary to what one would expect, a place in the kingdom of God is not denied even to the disloyal teacher who seeks to discredit Jesus' teaching.[53] For if such a teacher receives no more than the disparaging title "least" (ἐλάχιστος) in the coming kingdom, nevertheless it

---

50. As the admonitions of the rabbis show, the problem was chiefly an inner-Jewish one. Cf. esp. *Abot* 2,1 according to the translation of Herford, *Pirke Aboth,* 38–39: "Rabbi said: . . . And be careful in the case of a light precept as in that of a weighty one, for thou knowest not how the rewards of the precepts are given. . . ." Note also the comment by Billerbeck, vol. 1, 902, who rightly remarks, "A great deal of room was given here to one's subjective judgment."

51. Cf. Matt. 11:30; Acts 15:10, 19–20, 28–29; 1 John 5:3; *Did.* 6:3.

52. To this question, cf. also the disciples' discussion of rank in Mark 9:35 par., 10:35–45 par. On Rabbinic teaching, see Billerbeck, vol. 1, 249–50, 774, 920–21.

53. Similarly also Käsemann, *New Testament Questions of Today,* 85–87; differently E. Schweizer, *Das Evangelium nach Matthäus* (Göttingen: Vandenhoeck

corresponds exactly to the disdain which he or she has shown for the teaching of Jesus as "trifling" and unimportant for instruction. Ever since Johannes Weiss,[54] scholars have repeatedly called attention to the fact that the use of the title "least" (ἐλάχιστος) here may represent a wordplay on the name of the apostle Paul. We may recall that Paul was not reluctant to apply the name to himself in 1 Cor. 15:9.[55] If, as we also believe, this passage also alludes to the name of Paul, it is all the more remarkable that he is not absolutely denied entrance into the kingdom of God, but that only the better places remain barred to him. We may believe, moreover, that Paul would have been thoroughly pleased with such a verdict.[56] This implies that a form of Christian teaching guided by theological principles other than those of the SM is recognized as legitimate in a relative sense, even if it remains excluded for the teachers of the community of the SM.[57] For this community the orthodox teacher is one who is committed to Jesus' interpretation of the Torah, and for whom the SM itself constitutes the teaching material. Thus one may assume that in the honorific title "great" (μέγας), which is awarded this teacher in the kingdom of God, the teacher or the authors of the SM express their own conception of their vocation.

4. The fourth and final hermeneutical principle (v. 20) defines the goal of the teaching of Jesus as understood by the SM. The teaching of Jesus does not merely ensue on its own account; its goal, as one would expect, is eschatologically determined, and follows logically from the three preceding definitions.[58]

& Ruprecht, 1973), 62, on Matt. 5:19; Luz, "Die Erfüllung des Gesetzes bei Matthäus," 410.

54. Cf. J. Weiss, *Earliest Christianity* (New York: Harper & Brothers, 1959), vol. II, 753; R. Bultmann, *Theology of the New Testament* (New York: Charles Scribner's Sons, 1951), vol. I, 54; differently Luz, "Die Erfüllung des Gesetzes bei Matthäus," 411. The pun is found already in 1 Sam. 9:21 (LXX), involving the name Saul. I am indebted here to Professor Jon Levenson.

55. The Deutero-Pauline author of Ephesians considered this self-assessment worthy of imitation (3:8); the author of the pastoral epistles reinterpreted it (1 Tim. 1:15–16).

56. The teacher not committed to the teachings of Jesus must not simply be ranked among the false prophets (7:15–20) or the lawless (7:21–23), however.

57. But the relationship corresponds to that of the two versions of the Gospel upon which the early church agreed at the Jerusalem Conference (Gal. 2:7–8). See Betz, *Galatians*, 95–99.

58. The connection is again established by γάρ ("for"). Cf. v. 18.

From a formal point of view v. 20 is couched in a form that imitates the sayings on the entrance into the kingdom of God:[59]

v. 20a   For I tell you:
v. 20b   "Unless your righteousness surpasses that of the scribes and Pharisees,
v.20c   you will never enter into the kingdom of heaven."
v. 20a   λέγω γὰρ ὑμῖν ὅτι
v. 20b   ἐὰν μὴ περισσεύσῃ ὑμῶν ἡ δικαιοσύνη πλεῖον τῶν γραμματέων καὶ Φαρισαίων,
v. 20c   οὐ μὴ εἰσέλθητε εἰς τὴν βασιλείαν τῶν οὐρανῶν.

Only the last part of the sentence (v. 20c), however, follows the pattern of the sayings on the entrance into the kingdom of God. The first part exhibits a much more complicated structure. The introductory formula, "for I tell you that" (λέγω γὰρ ὑμῖν ὅτι) (v. 20a), lacks the "truly" (ἀμήν) found in v. 18, and appears to be formulated with the antitheses—in which it is often repeated—in mind.[60] The introductory formula is followed by a "sentence of holy law" of the casuistic sort, in which the basic condition for admission to the kingdom of God is established (v. 20b).[61] The condition for admission is only indirectly defined with respect to its content. What is at stake, to be sure, is the divine demand for "righteousness" (δικαιοσύνη) with which the reader, in harmony with the representatives of all other movements in Jewish and Christian theology, must comply.[62] Nor can there be any doubt that what the expression "your righteousness" (ὑμῶν ἡ δικαιοσύνη) has in mind is not a righteousness that comes from God on the basis of the redemptive act of Jesus Christ, but a righteousness that must be produced by the disciples of Jesus.[63] But what is most decisive still remains to be said; for what divided the

59. This type of saying is also used in Matt. 7:21 (cf. also 7:13). See Betz, "Eine Episode im Jüngsten Gericht," 1–2. [See in this volume, 125–26.]
60. Matt. 5:22, 28, 32, 34, 39, 44; cf. also 6:25, 29.
61. Cf. Matt. 5:19, 32; 6:14; 7:12. On this form of legal saying, see Bultmann, *History*, 130ff.; H. W. Gilmer, *The If-You Form in Israelite Law*, SBLDS 15 (Chico, Calif.: Scholars Press, 1975).
62. The concept of righteousness (δικαιοσύνη), understood entirely in the Jewish sense, underlies the whole SM (Matt. 5:6, 10, 20, 45; 6:1, 33; cf. 7:13–14, 21–23); it is also closely bound up with the idea of reward (5:12, 46; 6:1, 2, 5, 16).
63. Failure to attain righteousness (δικαιοσύνη) is equivalent to lawlessness (ἀνομία), 7:21–23.

various schools of contemporary Judaism above all was the question of *how* the demand of God could be fulfilled. What distinguishes the definition of the SM is that the way to righteousness can only be spoken of in comparison and contrast. It is enough to state that it must differ from the righteousness of the scribes and the Pharisees, both quantitatively and qualitatively, and that it must surpass their righteousness.[64]

But the question remains: why does the SM see its antitype precisely in the teaching of the scribes and the Pharisees? The expression "the scribes and the Pharisees" already presupposes a certain amount of stereotyping which reflects the debate that had been carried on since the time of Jesus, and even since John the Baptist.[65] From the historical point of view, Jesus obviously developed his conception of the Torah in discussion with the scribes and the Pharisees. The SM looks back at this debate, but also takes part in it retrospectively, as is clear from the antitheses.

Hence the "righteousness" (δικαιοσύνη) demanded by God cannot simply be produced by the external observance of regulations, as practiced by the scribes and the Pharisees. What was most at fault about the scribes and Pharisees was that their praxis was not capable of producing that "qualitative surplus" which is alone acceptable to God. The righteousness demonstrated by the SM, on the other hand, requires a renunciation of merely external observance and a turning toward the inner disclosure of the human heart before God.

This is the principal reason the commands of Jesus in the SM cannot simply be regarded as legal provisions, subject to outward fulfillment. Rather they are to be regarded as a set of instructions whose purpose is to educate the disciples of Jesus so that they may be able to recognize for themselves the demands of God that apply to them, and thus do justice in their thought and conduct to the will of God. This alone, according to the SM, will be recognized as "righteousness" (δικαιοσύνη) by the divine judge in the last judgment.

---

64. On the piling up of comparatives in περισσεύειν πλεῖον ("have abundance in excess of"), see BDF, par. 246. Cf. also Matt. 5:47.
65. In the SM, the word-pair occurs only in 5:20, but elsewhere in the synoptic tradition it is widely distributed. Cf. H. F. Weiss, *TDNT* 9, 38–39; Wrege, *Die Überlieferungsgeschichte*, 42.

4

A Jewish-Christian
Cultic Didache in Matt. 6:1-18:
Reflections and Questions
on the
Problem of the Historical Jesus

The central problem of current historical-critical research on Jesus remains the unsolved matter of the sources. Recent investigations of the complex of traditions embodied in the Gospels indicate that this material has already been subjected to redactional influences.[1] Thus the field occupied by the process of tradition at the presynoptic level is measurably extended. Here, too, the key word is "complexity": the layers of tradition are manifold, as are the literary forms and theological concepts that have exerted an influence upon the conglomerate and left their stamp upon it. To the degree that the area of presynoptic tradition has been enlarged, the categories and concepts hitherto employed in scholarship have become obsolete: as form and redaction criticism tend to blend, so anonymous traditions can also bear an individual stamp, etc. But while the field of presynoptic tradition has widened, the material which one once thought possible to trace back to the historical Jesus has narrowed. One can now say that only radical skepticism remains toward the use of previous criteria such as "authentic" and "inauthentic" in the study of the Jesus-tradition. The

1. See esp. the work of D. Lührmann, *Die Redaktion der Logienquelle* (Neukirchen-Vluyn: Neukirchener Verlag, 1969), and my review in *ThLZ* 96 (1971): 428-29.

question is, naturally, whether the criteria employed up to now must not be subjected to critical examination.

This state of affairs surely stands in striking contrast to the bulk of literature on Jesus that has appeared in the last few years.[2] It appears that research in this area, despite all efforts, is once again in its inception. "Thus at the end of the 'new' debate carried on between Bultmann and his students, the question of the historical Jesus arises again, a question which, at least in principle, one long thought to have left behind: the question of the relationship of the Gospels and the traditions they embody to the earthly Jesus."[3]

In what follows, the long-neglected pericope Matt. 6:1–18 will be analyzed briefly.[4] Then on the basis of this analysis the source-critical question will be discussed in relation to the problem of the historical Jesus.

I

The pericope Matt. 6:1–18 represents an identifiable, self-contained whole which Matthew took over from the tradition, probably together with the Sermon on the Mount. It is another matter how this pericope is related to Q.[5] In any event, it is by no means necessary to attribute to the redactor Matthew everything not to be found in Q.[6] Moreover, it is entirely probable that the complex of sayings in Matt. 6:1–18 had already passed through a long process of tradition, of which the material still bears some trace. Inclusion of the pericope in the

2. Cf. the overview in H. Conzelmann, "Ergebnisse wissenschaftlich-theologischer Forschung? Neue Taschenbücher über Jesus," *Evangelischer Erzieher* 23 (1971): 254–62; E. Grässer, "Motive und Methoden der neueren Jesus-Literatur," *VF* 18/2 (1973): 3–45.

3. J. Roloff, *Das Kerygma und der irdische Jesus* (Göttingen: Vandenhoeck & Ruprecht, 1970), 34.

4. For reasons of space, the analysis must understandably be limited to what is absolutely necessary. For the most recent discussion of the pericope, cf. H.-Th. Wrege, *Die Überlieferungsgeschichte der Bergpredigt* (Tübingen: J. C. B. Mohr [Paul Siebeck], 1968), 94–107; see also the review of this work by D. Lührmann, *ThLZ* 95 (1970): 199; W. Grundmann, *Das Evangelium nach Matthäus*, 2d ed. (Berlin: Evangelische Verlagsanstalt, 1971), 190–208; J. Jeremias, *New Testament Theology*, vol. I, Eng. trans. J. Bowden (London: SCM Press, 1971), passim.

5. Cf. Lührmann, *Redaktion*, 118–19.

6. Cf. W. L. Knox, *The Sources of the Synoptic Gospels* (Cambridge: At the University Press, 1957), vol. II, 7ff., 25–26.

A JEWISH-CHRISTIAN CULTIC *DIDACHE*

Matthean SM only represents, therefore, the final stage in the process.[7]

From a form-critical point of view, Matt. 6:1-18 constitutes a cultic *didache*.[8] As the following analysis makes clear, the form in itself is carefully organized and composed.

6:1	A. General paraenesis embracing the entire pericope[9]
6:1a	I. Comprehensive cultic-ethical exhortation and warning
	II. General description of the conduct to be rejected
6:1b	III. Statement of the consequences of not following the preceding paraenesis
	1. Account of the case of not observing, that is, of rejecting, the conduct described in A, II
	2. Statement of consequence in view of the expectation of eschatological reward and, at the same time, the theological justification for the imperative in A, I
6:2-6, 16-18	B. Specific cultic paraenesis in reference to three cultic acts:
6:2-4	I. Almsgiving
6:2a	1. Statement of the cultic act
6:2b-e	2. Prohibition of the improper performance of the cultic act

7. An independent tradition is found in *P. Oxy.* 654, no. 6 in J. Fitzmyer, *Essays on the Semitic Background of the New Testament* (London: Geoffrey Chapman, 1971), 384–87; but I do not share Fitzmyer's view on the origin of the logion. Cf. also the Coptic *Gospel of Thomas*, logion 6; *Did.* 8; *Didascalia Apostolorum*, ed. R. H. Connolly (Oxford: At the Clarendon Press, 1929), 143–44.

8. The question of the form-critical designation is raised by R. Bultmann, *History of the Synoptic Tradition*, 2d ed. (New York: Harper & Row, 1968), 133. He rightly rejects the term "didactic poem" and lays stress upon the "composition" with its "Church catechism in character" (133 n. 1). Elsewhere he speaks of "rules of piety" (146). We have chosen the term "*didache*" after the title of the early Christian writing of the same name.

9. Bultmann, *History*, 133, 150, also raises the question of the origin of the "introduction" (6:1). But it is not necessary to ascribe it to the evangelist Matthew. Cf. also G. Strecker, *Der Weg der Gerechtigkeit*, 3d ed. (Göttingen: Vandenhoeck & Ruprecht, 1971), 152; Wrege, *Überlieferungsgeschichte*, 97.

6:2b	a. Imperative (negative)
6:2b–c	b. Caricature of the conduct to be rejected
6:2d	c. Statement of the (improper) objective
6:2e	d. Description of the consequences of improper conduct in the form of an Amen-saying
6:3–4	3. Instruction in the proper performance of the cultic act
6:3a	a. Statement of the cultic act
6:3b	b. Description of the proper performance of the act by means of a proverbial saying
6:4a	c. Statement of the (proper) goal of the instruction
6:4b	d. Theological justification for the instructions and promise of eschatological reward
6:5–6	II. Prayer
6:5a	1. Statement of the cultic act
6:5b–e	2. Prohibition of the improper performance of the cultic act
6:5b	a. Imperative (negative)
6:5c	b. Caricature of the conduct to be rejected
6:5d	c. Statement of the (improper) objective
6:5e	d. Description of the consequence of improper conduct in the form of an Amen-saying
6:6	3. Instruction in the proper performance of the cultic act
6:6a	a. Statement of the cultic act
6:6b	b. Description of the proper performance of the act by means of a popular concept
6:6c	c. Statement of the (proper) goal of the instruction (abbreviated)
	d. Theological justification for the instructions and promise of eschatological reward
6:16–18	III. Fasting
6:16a	1. Statement of the cultic act
6:16b–e	2. Prohibition of the improper performance of the cultic act
6:16b	a. Imperative (negative)

6:16b–c	b. Caricature of the conduct to be rejected
6:16d	c. Statement of the (improper) objective
6:16e	d. Description of the consequences of improper conduct in the form of an Amen-saying
6:17–18	3. Instruction in the proper performance of the cultic act
6:17a	a. Statement of the cultic act
6:17b	b. Description of the proper performance of the act
6:18a	c. Statement of the (proper) goal of the instruction
6:18b	d. Theological justification for the instructions and promise of eschatological reward

The analysis at first glance reveals a rather complicated text. Formal division indicates that there are two principal sections (A, B) which are closely related to one another.

Section B contains three cultic paraeneses, all of which exhibit the same structure. In each case they begin with a statement of the cultic act (I, 1; II, 1; III, 1). This is followed by a prohibition of the improper performance of the act. These prohibitions are again divided and organized in the same manner (I, 2; II, 2; III, 2): the imperative (a) is followed by a caricature of the behavior to be rejected (b), and its objective (c), together with an Amen-saying (d) in which the consequences of proper conduct are described. The Amen-sayings agree with one another word for word. The three sets of instructions for the proper observance of the cult (I, 3; II, 3; III, 3) are also placed at the same point in their respective paraeneses. In each instruction, the cultic act is again given (a), the proper performance is described (b), and the goal is stated (c). The composition is brought to a close by a statement of the theological justification of the paraenesis and the eschatological "promise"[10] based upon it (d). These concluding portions of the paraenesis also correspond to one another word for word.

Furthermore, the regular change from the second person plural in

10. Bultmann, *History*, 133.

59

the first description of the action (II, 1; III, 1; otherwise in I, 1) to the second person singular in the second account (I, 3a; II, 3a; III, 3a) is striking.

The composition of section A is similar to that of section B, but contains some characteristic differences. At the beginning stands a general cultic-ethical exhortation and admonition to righteousness (δικαιοσύνη) (A, I). This introductory exhortation establishes the fact that the reward promised in section B is a reward that is acceptable to the Father in heaven (A, III, 2) and is bestowed in return for righteousness (δικαιοσύνη) to be wrought by human beings. The imperative "pay attention" (προσέχετε) acknowledges the demand for righteousness (δικαιοσύνη) and presupposes that its attainment is dependent upon a certain kind of conduct, and is thus imperiled. The cultic *didache* as a whole is nothing other than a set of instructions for observing the ethical exhortation in the realm of the cult.

The introductory sentence passes over immediately into a characterization of the general behavior to be rejected (A, II); this characterization recurs in section B, applied in each case to the cultic act under consideration (B, I, 2; II,2; III, 2).

The sentence that concludes section A is formulated in an entirely negative manner and specifies the consequences which will result from not following the paraenesis (A, III). First the case of one who does not follow the paraenesis is briefly mentioned; that is, one assumes that the conduct rejected in A, II has actually taken place. The consequences follow from belief in an eschatological reward. Thus the indicative statement in A, III, 2 takes the form of a conclusion drawn from a previously held doctrine. This conclusion, formulated negatively here, recurs positively in section B in a twofold manner: once in the form of a warning in the Amen-sayings (B, I, 2d; II, 2d; III, 2d), and again as a theological justification in B, I, 3d; II, 3d; III, 3d. Consequently, what we have before us in A, III, 2 is the theological foundation which bears the weight of the entire paraenetic edifice.

The content corresponds to the formal structure. As the general paraenesis states at the beginning, the text sets itself the goal of making righteousness (δικαιοσύνη) possible by the proper observation of three chosen cultic acts. Compliance with the three sets of cultic instructions (B, I; II; III), therefore, satisfies the demand for righteousness expressed in A, I.

The three sets of positive instructions (B, I, 3; II, 3; III, 3) make use of literary forms that go beyond the purely cultic. This suggests that the cultic acts in themselves are merely occasions that make the general conduct demanded in the introduction (A, I) more concrete. The view expressed here presupposes the tendency to make critical distinctions in respect to the cult. Nevertheless, cultic acts are not thereby rendered superfluous, but are filled with a significance that demands theological justification.

To comprehend the inner logic that gives rise to the cultic *didache* one must reflect upon the following theological presuppositions. Of fundamental importance is the concept of the hidden God who dwells "in heaven" (6:1), who is "in secret" (6:6, 18), and who "sees in secret" (6:4, RSV). The concept of reward is also presupposed. The righteousness (δικαιοσύνη) demanded of humans is recognized as the condition of redemption. But reward for good deeds can be bestowed only once. Thus the devout person who is in need of reward to bring about redemption in the last judgment (6:1b: "before your Father in heaven") must avoid the anticipation of reward in this life (6:1a: "before the people") under all circumstances. The concept of the imitation of God (*imitatio Dei*) serves to make this possible, in accordance with which the proper performance of the cultic act must take place "in secret."[11]

This doctrinal basis gives rise then to a marked criticism of the cult as its reverse side. Simply put, the eschatological reward is anticipated, and thus wasted, if righteousness (δικαιοσύνη) is performed before the eyes of others, so that it may be observed by them and receive their approval (6:1). How this happens concretely in the cultic actions mentioned here is described in the corresponding caricatures (6:2, 5, 16).

11. G. Vermès, *Jesus the Jew* (London: William Collins Sons, 1973), 78, believes that 6:1-4 alludes to the "Chamber of Secrets" in the temple of which the Mishnah in *Shekalim* 5, 6 speaks (Eng. trans. H. Danby): "Into the Chamber of Secrets the devout used to put their gifts in secret and the poor of good family received support therefrom in secret." But this fails to explain the two other cultic acts, apart from the fact that Matthew 6 and the Mishnah mean something entirely different by the term "secret."

From the point of view of the history of religions, the cultic *didache* in Matt. 6:1-18 is completely in keeping with the religious thought and practice of Judaism. At no point does it betray "Christian" influence. This is the case with respect to the concept of the hidden God who "sees in secret," the notion of the heavenly Father, the concept of reward, and the idea of the imitation of God. The criticism of the cult as well (6:2, 5, 16) is an inner-Jewish phenomenon, and is by no means necessarily Christian on account of its critical stance. It may be that the *didache* exhibits an anti-Pharisaic tendency,[12] but it is hardly possible to determine the precise location of its theology within contemporary Judaism.

II

It is generally recognized that 6:7-15 constitutes a secondary insertion.[13] But it remains a matter of question whether the evangelist Matthew was responsible for the insertion or whether it was already part of the material which he incorporated into his Gospel. We may be certain that Matthew did not compose the section himself. If it is likely that Matt. 5:3-7:27 already existed as a pre-Matthean composition, then it may be assumed that 6:7-15 was already a part of this material. Regarded as a separate entity, 6:7-15 is also a cultic *didache* confined, of course, to the subject of prayer.[14] Its affinity to B, II is obvious, and this no doubt was the reason for its insertion at this point in 6:1-18.

Yet 6:7-15 is in itself a rather complicated unit composed of three parts: the didactic section proper (6:7-9a), a prayer (the Lord's Prayer in 6:9b-13), and a "sentence of holy law" (6:14-15). It results, in detail, in the following structure:

---

12. Thus W. Bousset and H. Gressmann, *Die Religion des Judentums im späthellenistischen Zeitalter,* 4th ed. (Tübingen: J. C. B. Mohr [Paul Siebeck], 1966), 181; more recently J. Neusner, *From Politics to Piety* (Englewood Cliffs, N.J.: Prentice Hall, 1973) 67ff.

13. Bultmann, *History,* 133, assumes the secondary character and the special position of Matt. 6:7-13. See also the *Ergänzungsheft* to the 4th Germ. edition, ed. G. Theissen and P. Vielhauer (Göttingen: Vandenhoeck & Ruprecht, 1971), 54.

14. Cf. Jeremias, *Theology,* 194: "a short teaching passage on prayer composed of sayings of Jesus."

6:7-15   C. A paraenesis on prayer
6:7-13   I. Prayer
6:7a   1. Statement of the cultic act
              2. Prohibition of its improper performance
                 a. Imperative (negative)
                 b. Caricature of the conduct to be rejected and
                    comparison with non-Jewish practice of
                    prayer
6:7b   c. Description of the theory of prayer under-
                    lying the non-Jewish practices
6:8a   d. Warning against assimilation to the non-
                    Jewish practice
6:8b-13   3. Instruction in the proper performance of the
                 cultic act
6:8b   a. Theological justification for the instruction
6:9a   b. Statement of the cultic act
6:9b-13   c. Citation of the Lord's Prayer as the authori-
                    tative example of prayer
6:14-15   II. Forgiveness of sins
              (a "sentence of holy law" formulated in antithetical
              parallelismus membrorum)[15]

In comparison with sections A and B, section C exhibits structures
which, while formally similar, contain certain significant differences.
Like A and B, section C begins with a mention of the cultic act (C, I,
1), then follows with a prohibition of improper performance in the
form of a caricature (C, I, 2ab). What is new in contrast to A and B is
the account of the theory of prayer which underlies the rejected
practice (C, I, 2c) and the warning against assimilation (C, I, 2d). As
in sections A and B, there follows a set of instructions for the proper
practice of prayer (C, I, 3), but in this case the theological justification
is given first (a), followed by the designation of the cultic act (b).
Another new element is the citation of the Lord's Prayer as a primary

15. Cf. Jeremias, *Theology*, 16, 19, 25, 192, 194.

example of prayer (c).[16] Likewise without analogy in A and B is the "sentence of holy law" in C, II.[17]

Several aspects may be mentioned here as well from the point of view of the history of religions. This section too remains entirely within the orbit of Jewish thought, but instead of inner-Jewish polemic, section C contains polemic against "the Gentiles" (that is, the non-Jews), whose theory and practice of prayer are ridiculed. Along with the warning against assimilation to "the Gentiles," this polemic points to the Diaspora as the context in which the composition arose.

The theological concepts in section C are also different from those found in sections A and B. Prayer is justified by the doctrine of divine omniscience (C, I, 3a), not by the idea of the hiddenness of God. This represents an implicit rejection of the "Gentile" view that God must be informed about humanity's needs through prayer. In this conception, the ideas of reward and the imitation of God have no role to play, though both notions are presupposed by the "sentence of holy law" in C, II. One should also observe that the Lord's Prayer (I, 3c) stands in certain tension theologically to its justification (I, 3a).

16. Bultmann, *History*, 141, raises the question "whether the Lord's Prayer in Matt. 6:7–13 is put in place of some previous antithesis, which had to be removed to make place for it, or whether it is more likely that Matt. 6:7f. is a formulation (by Matthew?) analogous to the other sections fashioned specially to bring the Lord's Prayer into this particular context. I think this latter is more likely, for in that case the complex would have consisted originally of one saying each about almsgiving, prayer, and fasting; the duplication of instructions about prayer must be secondary. In any case we may suppose that the need for catechetical formulations, constructed like each other, and easy to remember, has led to the assimilation of alien material into such forms." Bultmann's redaction-critical account fails to explain the particulars of 6:7–13, of course; moreover, the literary phenomenon of analogous constructions which he has no doubt rightly identified leaves room for other possibilities.

17. Bultmann, *History*, 147, holds that 6:14–15 is a later Christian construction used by Matthew "as a commentary on one of the petitions of the Lord's Prayer" (148). Bultmann, 133, sees that the "promise" is lacking in 6:7–13, but he does not observe that this lack calls into question the one-sided redaction-critical explanation he has provided. On 6:14–15 as a "sentence of holy law," see E. Käsemann, "Sentences of Holy Law in the New Testament," in his *New Testament Questions of Today* (Philadelphia: Fortress Press, 1969), 77; K. Berger, "Zu den sogenannten Sätzen heiligen Rechts," *NTS* 17 (1970/71): 10–40, esp. 3, 17, 19.

III

What, then, is the relationship of the pericope Matt. 6:1–18 to the historical Jesus? On the basis of the preceding analysis and from the application of the former criteria[18] one must conclude that the pericope cannot be used to reconstruct the message of Jesus.[19] But at the same time the problem is thus by no means settled, but has only just begun.

Theologically the passage remains rooted in "Judaism." But this does not exclude the possibility that the work is also "Christian," for it could well be the product of Jewish Christianity. This can even be the case if no specifically Christian views are to be found in the text. It is highly questionable methodologically simply to equate Christian with Gentile Christian, and then to set this in opposition to what is Jewish. To the extent that Jewish Christianity remains within Judaism, one must search for other *indicia*.

It is possible, and even probable, that not only sections A and B but section C as well, including the Lord's Prayer, had their origin in Jewish Christianity. Since Jesus was a Jew, he can in principle have been the author of all sections of the pericope.[20] But that does not mean that Jesus had to have been simply in conformity with "Judaism," for this would be overlooking the fact that a variety of viewpoints were found *within* Judaism. Both the Lord's Prayer and sections A, B, and C give expression to original forms of Jewish theology. Even where the criticism of Judaism is undertaken, it represents an inner-Jewish critique. The theological conceptions

---

18. On the problem of the criteria for distinguishing between "authentic" and "inauthentic," see N. Perrin, *Rediscovering the Teaching of Jesus* (New York: Harper & Row, 1967), 15ff.; Jeremias, *Theology*, chap. 1; critically, D. G. A. Calvert, "An Examination of the Criteria for Distinguishing the Authentic Words of Jesus," *NTS* 18 (1972): 209–18; J. G. Gager, "The Gospels and Jesus: Some Doubts about Method," *JR* 54 (1974): 244–72.

19. Most scholars attribute the pericope to the historical Jesus. Bultmann constitutes an exception, *History*, 149: in "6:2–18 the exalted Jesus is thought of as speaking." But this assumption touches on only one of the possibilities.

20. The fact that the Jewish concept of reward is found in Matt. 6:1–18 speaks neither for nor against the deriving of this passage from Jesus. Differently, E. Haenchen, *Der Weg Jesu* (Berlin: Walter De Gruyter, 1968), 117; cf. Jeremias, *Theology*, 215–16 (with additional literature).

found in the various subsections cannot be easily harmonized, but betray a certain independence. All of this means that the "criterium of dissimilarity"[21] is of no further assistance in dealing with our pericope.

We can hardly form a reliable estimate of the antiquity of the traditions contained in the passage 6:1–18. It is often assumed that the Lord's Prayer goes back to the earliest stage of the tradition and thus can be attributed to the historical Jesus with the greatest accuracy.[22] But caution is in place even here. It is difficult to date liturgical material such as the Lord's Prayer.[23] In view of the wealth of parallels in Jewish prayer literature, one can only assume that the petitions contained in the prayer are older than Jesus, and that only the specific combination in the Lord's Prayer points to him.[24] It is even a question whether, in view of the variableness of the tradition, one can go back to an "original form"—such as that of Jesus. It is a well-known fact that prayers are seldom fixed word for word before they are committed to writing in various liturgies. One may even recall that the Lord's Prayer has not been entirely fixed to this day, but is still in use in various forms. Also, the context of Matt. 6:7–15 in which the Lord's Prayer is found is most likely a product of Diaspora Judaism. The Lukan parallel (11:1–4) is of an entirely different sort and contains an unusual reference to John the Baptist. If all of these questions apply to section C, then the same must be said with respect to the relative antiquity of sections A and B.

The "criterion of multiple attestation" likewise provides no useful

21. Cf. on this point Perrin, *Rediscovering the Teaching of Jesus*, 39–40; and Gager, "Gospels and Jesus," 256–59.

22. Thus, for example, Jeremias, *Theology*, 193–203; Perrin, *Rediscovering the Teaching of Jesus*, 41, 47.

23. Perrin, *Rediscovering the Teaching of Jesus*, 108, 151–52, thinks of the possibility to specify the table-fellowship with Jesus as the *Sitz im Leben* of the Lord's Prayer.

24. Jeremias's account is typically ambiguous: on the one hand he calls the Lord's Prayer "a new prayer" (*Theology*, 193), while on the other hand he admits that the petitions were "not newly constructed by Jesus," but derive "from the Jewish liturgy" (198). The contradiction is resolved "dogmatically": "The Jewish community and the disciples of Jesus pray ... in the same words. Yet there is a great difference between them. In the Kaddish, a community is praying which is still completely in the courts of waiting. The Lord's Prayer is prayed by men who know that God's gracious work, the great turning-point, has already begun" (199).

result in relation to our text. Only the Lord's Prayer is attested more than once,[25] but this evidence does not apply to the entire context. If one were to make use of the criteria established by J. Jeremias, the Amen-sayings would furnish decisive proof of the authenticity of this passage.[26] But in this instance the Amen-sayings are an inseparable part of the composition and cannot have existed apart from it. Even if the introduction of certain sayings with the word "amen" does go back to Jesus, the sayings in our text can only be regarded as imitations like those found elsewhere in the Gospel traditions. They offer no proof of the authenticity of this passage.

Can Matt. 6:1–18 be integrated, then, into the framework of the proclamation of Jesus as reconstructed from other texts? Since this passage is not attested elsewhere in the synoptic tradition, the question must be answered negatively (apart from the Lord's Prayer, perhaps). It is true that the Lord's Prayer contains a concept of decisive importance in the proclamation of Jesus—the kingdom (βασιλεία). But the prayer "Your kingdom come" is found elsewhere in Jewish literature.[27] Moreover, the notion of the kingdom of God is found nowhere else in our pericope.

Thus our verdict in general must be that the passage 6:1–18 (with the possible exception of the Lord's Prayer)[28] cannot be attributed to Jesus. If this verdict is allowed to stand, further questions immediately arise. How is it possible that not only Matthew but the entire tradition at every stage preceding him assumed Jesus to be the author? These Jewish-Christian tradents must at least have stood in close

25. Cf. Wrege, *Überlieferungsgeschichte,* 97–109; S. Schulz, *Q. Die Spruchquelle der Evangelisten* (Zurich: Theologischer Verlag, 1972), 84–93.

26. Cf. on this point Jeremias, *Theology,* 35–36; K. Berger, *Die Amen-Worte Jesu* (Berlin: Walter De Gruyter, 1970), 30, 33, 77, 81, 92; and his article, "Zur Geschichte der Einleitungsformel 'Amen, ich sage euch'," *ZNW* 63 (1972): 45–75, esp. 71–72.

27. For the texts, see Billerbeck, vol. 1, 418–19.

28. Schulz, *Q,* 87, sees "in the Lord's Prayer the 'prayer formula' of the earliest Jewish-Christian Q-community in Palestine," that arose "in imitation of late Jewish prayers and prayer-formulae" (93). But the question is whether one can identify "the Q-community" so readily with Jewish Christianity. Does not the heterogeneous tradition of the Lord's Prayer in Q and in Matt. 6:1–18 point to a more varied tradition within Jewish Christianity? Does it not indicate that Jewish Christianity was no uniform entity in itself? Such an instance of multiple attestation of the Lord's Prayer in the presynoptic tradition actually increases the likelihood that it derived from Jesus.

connection with Jesus chronologically and theologically.[29] They must have believed that their theological views were consistent with those of Jesus. But the question is, what weight should be granted to such an assertion?

A further question is related to this. It is implied that the author of section C sees his teaching on prayer (in 7:7-9a) exemplified in the Lord's Prayer and wishes to base his teaching upon it. The theology found in sections A and B is likewise implicitly attributed to Jesus. Thus even if the passages under consideration are the work of Jewish Christians, they nevertheless claim that it was Jesus who gave impetus to this form of Jewish thought. This implicit claim cannot merely be rejected out of hand, but we must ask whether some evidence of the "impact of Jesus" upon the text can be detected. No doubt the text is the product of a discontent that has led to a new attitude toward the cult. One might even say that what lies before us in Matt. 6:1-18 is a kind of "program of reform."[30] In evaluating this matter, one must bear in mind which cultic acts are mentioned and which are left out of the account. Moreover, the order in which they occur is important.

First of all, the concentration of this passage on what we would call "personal piety" is striking. The official cult is nowhere mentioned and is therefore rejected as inessential. The individual occupies the center of attention. In respect to personal religious conduct, radical asceticism is recommended: true religion as such cannot be observed by human beings. The sequence of cultic actions discussed reflects their priority. Thus almsgiving—what we would call social work— takes first place. The greatest attention is devoted to prayer. Fasting is divested of its negative traits by scathing religious critique and is interpreted anew.[31]

---

29. Thus already Bousset and Gressmann, *Religion,* 178 n. 4, who call attention to the relationship between the Lord's Prayer and the instructions of several Jewish teachers who were thought to stand near Christianity; Eliezer ben Hyrcanus must be mentioned here in particular, on whom see the study by J. Neusner, *Eliezer ben Hyrcanus,* Part I, II (Leiden: E. J. Brill, 1973).

30. G. Schille, *Das vorsynoptische Judenschristentum* (Stuttgart: Calwer Verlag, 1970), 43-46, and B. Gerhardsson, "Geistiger Opferdienst nach Matth 6,1-6," in *Neues Testament und Geschichte,* O. Cullmann zum 70. Geburtstag (Zurich: Theologischer Verlag, 1972), 69-77.

31. Cf. Roloff, *Kerygma,* 230-31, who, on the one hand, attributes 6:16-18 to

On the whole, one can say that a form of Jewish Christianity comes to expression here that shows no interest in the temple cult and is probably anti-Pharisaic in tendency. Was this form of Jewish Christianity akin to what is now being called "charismatic Judaism," of which virtually every trace has disappeared?[32] Was impetus given to this cultic *didache* by Jesus himself? Or did it arise within a kind of Judaism that stood near to Jesus, but with which his name came to be connected only at a later date? These questions show that the problem of the historical Jesus and the sources from which his teaching is to be reconstructed necessarily involve a question derived from the history of religions: the question of the type of Judaism to which Jesus and his earliest followers belonged. Even if, for want of sources, we can discover nothing more about this form of Judaism and Jewish Christianity, we must leave open the possibility, and even probability, of an image of Jesus which is completely different from that of the synoptic tradition and its Gentile-Christian redactors.

Jewish Christianity, and then contradicts himself by speaking of a "demarcation from Judaism" in connection with these verses.

32. This term is employed by Vermès, *Jesus the Jew*, 69ff. But one should not content oneself with this concept which is still much too unclear; rather one should attempt to trace out the contours which can be recognized.

5

Matt. 6:22–23 and
Ancient Greek Theories
of Vision

The debate between Judaism and Hellenism not only predates Christianity, but has also influenced the early Christian literature at its oldest level of tradition. The Q-logion about the eye as the lamp of the body (Matt. 6:22–23//Luke 11:34–36),[1] puzzling as this saying doubtless is, shows evidence of the intellectual struggle between Judaism and Hellenism.

A. Jülicher[2] correctly observed that the passage looks harmless but is in fact one of the most difficult to interpret in the entire gospel tradition. And J. Amstutz[3] perceptively remarked that the more work is done on the logion, the more obscure it becomes. Even as early as 1912 P. Fiebig[4] had proposed a moratorium on further attempts to explain the riddle of Matt. 6:22–23 and par. New Testament scholarship surely ignored the moratorium, but no one has yet succeeded in satisfactorily explaining the mysterious word of Jesus. Although no exhaustive survey of the recent studies can be provided here, the general situation may best be exemplified by the study of E. Sjöberg.[5] He goes to great lengths to recover the presumed Aramaic original of the logion, but in the end he himself seems to feel the inconclusive nature of the evidence. In an addition after the proofreading he gives

1. Cf. also the Coptic *Gospel of Thomas*, logion 24.
2. *Die Gleichnisreden Jesu*, 3d ed. (Tübingen: J. C. B. Mohr [Paul Siebeck], 1910), vol. II, 98.
3. J. Amstutz, ΑΠΛΟΤΗΣ. *Eine begriffsgeschichtliche Studie zum jüdisch-christlichen Griechisch* (Bonn: Hanstein, 1968), 96.
4. *Die Gleichnisreden Jesu* (Tübingen: J. C. B. Mohr [Paul Siebeck], 1912), 151.
5. "Das Licht in dir. Zur Deutung von Matth. 6, 22f Par.," *Studia Theologica* 5

credit to J. Munck for having called his attention to Plato's *Timaeus* 45B–46A. It is indeed in this direction that one must look for a solution to the problem.[6] In the following pages a beginning of such an interpretation is attempted. Limited space requires that the paper be confined to the essential points of discussion and pieces of evidence. For the same reason, the discussion will be limited to Matt. 6:22–23, because Luke 11:34–36 and the Coptic Gospel of Thomas, logion 24, represent quite different doctrines.

I. ON THE FORM AND COMPOSITION

v. 22a   The lamp of the body is the eye.

v. 22b   If then your eye is healthy/good, your whole body is full of light.

v. 23a   If, however, your eye is sick/evil, your whole body is dark.

v. 23b   If, therefore, the light which is in you is darkness— what darkness!

v. 22a   Ὁ λύχνος τοῦ σώματός ἐστιν ὁ ὀφθαλμός.

v. 22b   ἐὰν οὖν ᾖ ὁ ὀφθαλμός σου ἁπλοῦς, ὅλον τὸ σῶμά σου φωτεινὸν ἔσται·

v. 23a   ἐὰν δὲ ὁ ὀφθαλμός σου πονηρὸς ᾖ, ὅλον τὸ σῶμά σου σκοτεινὸν ἔσται.

v. 23b   εἰ οὖν τὸ φῶς τὸ ἐν σοὶ σκότος ἐστίν, τὸ σκότος πόσον.

The logion has four lines, but its composition, structure, and form have not been analyzed convincingly. R. Bultmann[7] in his *Geschichte*

(1951): 89–105.

6. This suggestion can be found in part of the older literature, but it did not make its way into the commentaries. J. J. Wettstein, *Novum Testamentum Graecum* (Amsterdam: Officina Dommeriana, 1751), vol. I, 330–31, quotes some pertinent passages from the Greek literature and concludes: *Comparat Christus animum corpori, & judicium oculis, similitudine etiam apud Philosophos usitata,* "Christ compares the mind and the body, and the judgment and the eyes, through a similitude used also by the philosophers." The matter was clearly stated by J. Lindblom, "Det solliknande ögat," *Svensk Teologisk Kvartalskrift* 3 (1927): 230–47; and by G. Rudberg, *Hellas och Nya Testamentet* (Stockholm: Diakonistyrelsen bokförlag, 1929), 150–51.

7. 4th ed. (Göttingen: Vandenhoeck & Ruprecht, 1971), 77, 91, 95; Eng. trans:

der synoptischen Tradition presents a very cautious and tentative discussion. He treats Matt. 6:22–23 as a logion and puts it into the subsection called "Material Formulations" ("sachlich formulierte Grundsätze"). He saw that the logion is composed of several elements. Verse 22a could be the original unit, which was then to be interpreted by vv. 22b–23a. But because of what Bultmann perceived as a poverty in content in Matt. 6:22a, the double-logion in vv. 22b–23a may well have been the starter, and v. 22a as well as 23b later additions. Luke 11:34–36 he took to be a later, expanded version. Although Bultmann's suggestions have been taken over by many scholars they are nothing but possibilities—none of them is even a probability.

1. The introductory sentence v. 22a looks proverbial.[8] For that reason it may have been thought suitable as an introduction. It certainly later became a proverb together with many other sayings of the Sermon on the Mount. The logion itself, however, takes v. 22a more seriously, so that in the present composition it is regarded as a *definition* of the human eye and a description of its functioning. The following commentary shows that it is "cited" only to be critically evaluated.

2. Verses 22b–23a are antithetical *parallelismus membrorum*, connected with v. 22a by way of *chiasmus*. While v. 22a names the lamp (ὁ λύχνος) first and the eye (ὁ ὀφθαλμός) second, the eye is discussed first in vv. 22b–23a, and the lamp second in v. 23b. The introductory words ἐὰν οὖν (v. 22b), ἐὰν δέ (v. 23a), and εἰ οὖν (v. 23b) suggest that the statements function as a commentary, proceeding from the objective phenomena stated in the third person singular (v. 22a) to the paraenetic second person singular in vv. 22b–23b. The commentary itself has two parts, the interpretation of the eye as the organ of vision (vv. 22b–23a), and the interpretation of the image of the lamp (v. 23b). The first part can be subdivided again into the description of the proper and of the defective functioning of the eye.

The History of the Synoptic Tradition, 2d ed. (New York: Harper & Row, 1968), 74, 87, 91.

8. Cf. *Deutsches Sprichwörter-Lexicon,* ed. K. F. W. Wander (Leipzig: Brockhaus, 1867), vol. I, col. 172, n. 87: "Die augen sind des leibs latern." For a comprehensive treatment of the eye and its symbolism, see W. Deonna, *Le symbolisme de l'oeil* (Bern: A. Francke, 1965).

3. The second part of the commentary (v. 23b) interprets how the image of the lamp should be correctly understood. The light burning in the lamp is now identified as "the light in you" (τὸ φῶς τὸ ἐν σοί). This identification as well as the form of the oxymoron[9] is evidence that we have definitely moved from a physiological to a moral level of thought. The oxymoron introduces the paradoxical possibility that "the light within you" may well be "darkness," and it concludes with an exclamation of surprise, "What a darkness!" (τὸ σκότος πόσον). Of course, this exclamation is a rhetorical device, making inescapably clear that no time is to be wasted on trivialities and absurdities, but that matters of ultimate human concern are at stake.

4. It should be noted that this compositional structure has a parallel in one of the main sources for Greek theories of cognition, Theophrastus's *De sensibus*.[10] Theophrastus begins his essay by reporting on the theories of cognition proposed by earlier philosophers. He then criticizes these theories by pointing out their inner consequences and resulting faults, which cause greater dilemmas than those they were intended to explain. The whole procedure of report, critique, and dilemma is, of course, informed and shaped not only by the sources but also by Theophrastus's own theory. Compared with Theophrastus's work, Matt. 6:22–23 is obviously extremely short. It looks like a condensation into a *mashal* of what in an elaborated form would be a treatise. At any rate, the formal structure of Matt. 6:22–23 seems to be as follows:

v. 22a   I. Definition of the human eye

vv. 22b–23b II. Physiological and paraenetical commentary

vv. 22b–23a   1. Interpretation of the eye as the organ of vision

v. 22b   a. The condition for proper vision

            (1) The condition of the eye is sound

            (2) The expected positive result

v. 23a   b. The condition for defective vision

            (1) The condition of the eye is not sound

---

9. So Jülicher, *Gleichnisreden*, vol. II, 99.

10. Theophrastus, *De sensibus*, ed. G. M. Stratton, *Theophrastus and the Greek Physiological Psychology Before Aristotle* (New York and London: George Unwin, 1917). See also the parallel composition in Epictetus, *Diss.* III.3.20–22.

(2) The expected negative result
v. 23b   2. Interpretation of the image of the lamp
        a. Assumption of a paradoxical possibility
        b. An exclamation of (seeming) surprise

II. THE THEME

In terms of the thematic content of Matt. 6:22–23, we enter into the territory of the ancient theories of sense perception, especially vision. This territory is very diversified and includes such fields of research as theory of elementary cognition, theory of light and color, physiology of the eye, therapy of the eye. None of these fields can of course be adequately treated here, but only the main points of contact can be mentioned.[11]

1. The style of definition with regard to the human eye is found as early as Pythagoras who, according to anonymous Pythagoreans, called the eyes "gates of the sun."[12] This image reminds us of mythological notions, as when sun and moon are considered to be the eyes of a cosmic deity, or the human eyes to correspond to sun and moon. The interpretation of Pythagoras's saying is not clear.[13] Are the eyes "gates of the sun" in the sense that the sunlight enters through them into the body? Or is the sun the image for the inner "light of the soul," which again can be identical with the mind ($\nu o\hat{v}s$)? Or are several meanings combined as in another saying of the philosopher, "not to speak without light" ($\mu\grave{\eta}\ \lambda\acute{\epsilon}\gamma\epsilon\iota\nu\ \check{a}\nu\epsilon\upsilon\ \phi\omega\tau\acute{o}s$)?[14] At any rate, Pythago-

---

11. On this subject matter, see esp. the following studies: J. I. Beare, *Greek Theories of Elementary Cognition from Alcmaeon to Aristotle* (Oxford: At the Clarendon Press, 1906); A. E. Haas, "Antike Lichttheorien," *Archiv für Geschichte der Philosophie* 20 (1907): 345–86; H. Lackenbacher, "Beiträge zur antiken Optik," *Wiener Studien* 35 (1913): 34–61; R. Bultmann, "Zur Geschichte der Lichtsymbolik im Altertum," *Philologus* 97 (1948): 1–36, reprinted in his *Exegetica* (Tübingen: J. C. B. Mohr [Paul Siebeck], 1967), 323–55; W. Luther, "Wahrheit, Licht und Erkenntnis in der griechischen Philosophie bis Demokrit," *ABG* 10 (1966): 2–240. Especially important is W. Beierwaltes, *Lux intelligibilis. Untersuchung zur Lichtmetaphysik der Griechen* (Ph.D. Diss., Munich, 1957); D. Bremer, "Licht als universales Darstellungsmedium; Materialien und Bibliographie," *ABG* 18 (1974): 185–206, where a good bibliography is included (197–206).
12. Diels-Kranz, 58 B 1 a (vol. I, p. 450, line 13).
13. See on this problem Beierwaltes, *Lux intelligibilis,* 31–33.
14. Jamblichus, *Vita Pyth.* 84, p. 48, 22, ed. Deubner.

rean tradition also contained the dualism of light (φῶς) and darkness (σκότος), which according to some sources goes back to a Chaldean named Zaratas.[15] Furthermore, the Pythagoreans seem to have introduced the separation of body (σῶμα) and soul (ψυχή),[16] a dualism also presupposed in Matt. 6:22–23. There the concept of σῶμα comes close to that of body-tomb (σῶμα/σῆμα), but ψυχή is not mentioned. Instead, Matt. 6:23 has "the light in you" (τὸ φῶς τὸ ἐν σοί), a concept which even in Jewish thought is not unknown and is often identified with that of the soul.[17]

Two sayings of Heraclitus are important for the study of Matt. 6:22–23. Perhaps the preference for the eye rather than the ear is proverbial in origin: ὀφθαλμοὶ γὰρ τῶν ὤτων ἀκριβέστεροι μάρτυρες,[18] "The eyes are more accurate witnesses than the ears."

Another saying, critical of the eye and ear as organs of sense perception, is intentionally obscure: κακοὶ μάρτυρες ἀνθρώποισιν ὀφθαλμοὶ καὶ ὦτα βαρβάρους ψυχὰς ἐχόντων,[19] "Bad witnesses are eyes and ears to men, if they have barbarian souls." The phrase "barbarian souls" is difficult to understand. According to Diels-Kranz these are souls who, like barbarians, cannot properly understand the information given by the senses. Heraclitus would then be saying that he does not doubt the value of sense perception per se,[20] but he contends that those who do not use the organs with "consideration" (φρόνησις) cannot interpret what they have perceived.[21] The failure lies in the fact that they do not possess reason (the λόγος).[22] On the whole, however, G. S. Kirk is correct in his exposition of Heraclitus: "His criticism of men is based upon the fact that the truth is there to

---

15. Hippolytus, *Refut.* I.2.12.
16. Cf. Diels-Kranz, 58 B 1 a (I, 450, 5). See also W. Burkert, *Weisheit und Wissenschaft* (Nürnberg: Carl, 1962), 98ff.; Eng. trans.: *Lore and Science in Ancient Pythagoreanism*, Eng. trans. E. L. Minar, Jr. (Cambridge: Harvard University Press, 1972), 120ff.
17. Cf. Billerbeck, vol. 1, 432ff.
18. Diels-Kranz, 22 B 101 a (I, 173, 15–16). See M. Marcovich, *Heraclitus* (Merida, Venezuela: The Los Andes University Press, 1967), 23–24; Deonna, *Le symbolisme de l'oeil*, 1ff.
19. Diels-Kranz, 22 B 107 (I, 175, 1–2). See Marcovich, *Heraclitus*, 45–48.
20. Diels-Kranz, 22 B 55 (I, 162, 11–12).
21. Ibid., 22 B 17 (I, 155, 6–8).
22. Ibid., 22 B 72 (I, 167, 9–11).

be observed, is common to all, but they cannot see it: apprehension of the Logos is no mystical process but the result of using eyes, ears, and common sense."[23] There can be no doubt that although Matt. 6:22–23 does not mention the ear, it gives preference to the eye. This is similar to the idea that the eye alone is not capable of recognizing the truth, but that another factor must enter into the process of vision.

2. The dualism of light and darkness is preeminent in the cosmology and epistemology of Parmenides.[24] In his thought light and darkness are metaphors for "truth" versus "untruth," "knowledge" versus "ignorance," and "being" versus "non-being." These principles also determine the process of vision.[25] Darkness is to the highest degree the nature of the corpse, which has no capacity for cognition.[26] If, however, the human mind is illuminated by light, cognition of being can take place. Consequently, the organ of cognition is no longer the eye (which is devalued)[27] but thought.[28] Also in Matt. 6:22–23 the eye and the capacity to see are distinguished, and in the final analysis the capacity to see depends on another factor not named in Matt. 6:23, which qualified both "the light within you" and the eye.

3. The comparison of the eye to a lamp we find first in Empedocles' poem Περὶ φύσεως.[29] Empedocles compared the process of vision to a man who wishes to go out in a winter night and who because of the darkness outside equips himself with stormlamps. When Aphrodite[30] created the human eye it was a kind of lamp she constructed: the eternal fire was wrapped in fine membranes and thin veils behind the pupil. Within the eye, water flowed around the fire, but the eye lets the light pass from the inside out because it is so much finer.[31] Empedocles, therefore, assumed a fire-light within the eye behind the

---

23. G. S. Kirk, *Heraclitus: The Cosmic Fragments* (Cambridge: At the University Press, 1954), 376.
24. See Beierwaltes, *Lux intelligibilis,* 34–36.
25. Cf. Diels-Kranz, 28 B 9 (I, 240ff.).
26. Ibid., 28 A 46 (I, 226, 10ff.).
27. Cf. the expression ἄσκοπον ὄμμα ("inconsiderate eye") in ibid., 28 B 7 (I, 234, 34).
28. Ibid., 28 B 4 (I, 232, 7); 28 B 7 (I, 235, 1).
29. Ibid., 31 B 84 (I, 342, 4–9).
30. Cf. ibid., 31 B 85, 86, 95 (I, 343; 345).
31. Ibid., 31 B 84 (I, 342, 10–14).

pupil. Like a lantern this light shines through the eye and thus facilitates the process of vision.[32]

At this point we note a clear difference between Empedocles and Matt. 6:22–23: both use the term "the lamp" (ὁ λύχνος), but in Matt. 6:22–23 the light is not in the eye, but somewhere else in the body. This difference is no doubt intended and not simply accidental.

4. The philosophers of the following periods continued to build their own theories of cognition and sense perception, but the foundations laid by the pre-Socratics remained decisive presuppositions. Theophrastus, who has transmitted to us important doxographical material in his *De sensibus*, has also attempted to sort things out historically. Basically, he finds, there are two conceptions of the process of cognition.[33] Parmenides, Empedocles, and Plato share the principle of "similarity" (τῷ ὁμοίῳ), while Anaxagoras and Heraclitus start from the principle of "contrast" (τῷ ἐναντίῳ). The first group assumes that the agent of cognition is located within beings and that cognition, especially vision, occurs by way of an "effluence" (ἀπόρροια) from within the body toward the objects outside, where they meet with entities akin to them in nature. The other group proceeds from the theory that opposites attract one another. This principle also underlies Democritus's theory of "air-imprints,"[34] by which he tried to explain why, if one looks into the eye, one perceives in the pupil a reduced "appearance" (ἔμφασις) of the world outside, including perhaps the observer. Employing Empedocles' notion of "effluence," Democritus thinks that the "appearances" occur in this way: the objects seen send out atoms which produce "air-imprints" (ἀποτύπωσις) when they hit the air. The medium of the air then transports these "air-imprints" into the eye, a process facilitated by the sun. The fire-atoms of the sunlight compress the air, so that the "imprints" can be received, and the light guides the "air-imprints" through channels into the eye. After they have passed to the pupil, the "appearances"

---

32. The fiery nature of the eye was observed earlier by the physician Alcmaeon, ibid., 24 A 5 (I, 212, 5). See also Beare, *Greek Theories*, 16ff.
33. *De sens.* §1–2, ed. Stratton, 6.
34. On Democritus's theory, I follow W. Burkert, "Air-Imprints or Eidola: Democritus' Aetiology of Vision," *Illinois Classical Studies* 2 (1977): 97–109, where further literature is also listed.

occur and are then transmitted to the rest of the body, including the soul which, according to Democritus, is part of the body and a material entity.

The conditions for vision are established if the physiology of the eye meets the needs of the passage of the "appearances." The external membranes must be thin and dense, the inner parts spongy and free from fat and meaty tissue, the veins must serve to pass the "appearances" on into the body, etc.[35] Complicated as Democritus's ideas about vision and disturbance of vision certainly are, the conditions for vision or disturbance of vision are always physiological in nature. The same is true for Epicurus and his famous theory of "images" (εἴδωλα).[36] These "images" are constantly produced and emitted by the objects seen. Separating from them they float into the eye. Since this theory was also promoted later by Epicurean philosophers, among them especially Lucretius,[37] we may assume that it was rather widely known in the New Testament era.

Looking again at Matt. 6:22–23, one will have to conclude that the passage, by intention or accident, implicitly rejects the atomistic and Epicurean theories of vision, while approving of the Empedoclean and Platonic traditions at least to the extent that vision occurs through light passing from the inside out.

5. The theory of cognition and, as part of it, of vision, is the topic of discussion especially in Plato's *Republic,* books VI and VII, and *Timaeus.* Notably, Plato uses the form of parable to explain the matter: the Parable of the Sun (*Rep.* VI.507B–509C), the Parable of the Parallel Lines (*Rep.* VI.510B–511B), and the Parable of the Cave (*Rep.* VII.514A–518B).[38]

In connection with the Parable of the Sun, Plato first calls to mind the difference between the phenomena and the ideas: "And the class of things [namely, phenomena] we can say can be seen but not

---

35. Cf. Diels-Kranz, 68 A 135 (II, 114, 28–115, 3; 116, 3–4).
36. See C. Bailey, *The Greek Atomists and Epicurus* (Oxford: At the Clarendon Press, 1928), 406ff.; Burkert, "Air-Imprints," 103ff.
37. *De rer. nat.* IV.311–52, ed. H. Diels. Cf. also Epicurus's saying: "But even when he has lost his eye-sight, he [the sage] takes part in life" (ἀλλὰ καὶ πηρωθέντα τὰς ὄψεις μεθέξειν αὐτὸν τοῦ βίου). Citation according to G. Arrighetti, *Epicuro, Opere,* 2d ed. (Turin: Einaudi, 1973), 27: Frag. [1] 119, 8–9.
38. See Beierwaltes, *Lux intelligibilis,* 37ff.

thought, while the ideas can be thought but not seen."[39] Next, "vision" (ἡ ὄψις) is the topic of consideration. Vision, according to Plato, is to be regarded as a higher sense compared with the others because it needs a third element, light, without which it cannot function: "Though vision may be in the eyes and its possessor may try to use it, and though colour be present, yet without the presence of a third thing specifically and naturally adapted to this purpose, you are aware that vision will see nothing and the colours will remain invisible."[40] The origin and cause of this light is the god Helios, and therefore the eye can rightly be named "the most sunlike of all the instruments of sense."[41] But vision is identical neither with the eye nor with the sun; Helios is the "cause" (αἴτιος)[42] of vision, and the eye receives "the power which it possesses as an influx, as it were, dispensed from the sun."[43] Then (*Rep.* 508C) the discussion turns from the visible world to the world of thought. Here Plato discusses first the phenomena of the disturbance of vision.

We see normally as long as we direct our eyes toward objects illuminated by the light of day; but "when the eyes are no longer turned upon objects upon whose colours the light of day falls but that of the dim luminaries of night, their edge is blunted and they appear almost blind, as if pure vision did not dwell in them."[44] These observations are then applied to the ways in which the soul perceives the truth: "When it is firmly fixed on the domain where truth and reality shine resplendent it apprehends and knows them and appears to possess reason; but when it inclines to that region which is mingled with darkness, the world of becoming and passing away, it opines only and its edge is blunted, and it shifts its opinions hither and thither, and again seems as if it lacked reason."[45] This is the result as far as insight into the truth is concerned:

39. *Rep.* VI.507B; text and Eng. trans. are according to P. Shorey, ed., *Plato. The Republic,* vol. II, LCL (Cambridge: Harvard University Press; London: William Heinemann, 1935).
40. *Rep.* VI.507D/E.
41. Ibid., 508B.
42. Ibid.
43. Ibid.
44. Ibid., 508C.
45. Ibid., 508D.

This reality, then, that gives their truth to the objects of knowledge and the power of knowing to the knower, you must say is the idea of good, and you must conceive it as being the cause of knowledge, and of truth in so far as known. Yet fair as they both are, knowledge and truth, in supposing it to be something fairer still than these you will think rightly of it. But as for knowledge and truth, even as in our illustration it is right to deem light and vision sunlike, but never to think that they are the sun, so here it is right to consider these two their counterparts, as being like the good or boniform, but to think that either of them is the good is not right. Still higher honour belongs to the possession and habit of the good.[46]

The problem of the disturbance of vision is given special consideration in the Parable of the Cave. Plato distinguishes between two kinds of disturbances of the eye: the one when a person comes out of the light into darkness, and the other when a person changes from darkness to light.[47] What this means for philosophy is explained by the parable. The cave dwellers who have never seen anything else but the shadows on the wall can only take those shadows for reality itself. If, however, one of the cave dwellers were "freed from his fetters and compelled to stand up suddenly and turn his head around and walk and to lift up his eyes to the light,"[48] he would only feel pain in his eyes because of the dazzle and glitter of the light and see nothing. Even "if someone told him that what he had seen before was all a cheat and an illusion, but that now, being nearer to reality and turned toward more real things, he saw more truly,"[49] he would turn back to the cave and to those objects of vision that he is able to discern. Plato's solution to the problem is gradual adjustment to the light, so that at its end cognition of reality can truly occur.

The second kind of disturbance of vision happens when the same man, now accustomed to live in the light, returns to the darkness of the cave. Of course, his vision of things has now completely changed, and "if he recalled to mind his first habitation and what passed for wisdom there, and his fellow-bondsmen, do you not think that he

---

46. Ibid., 508E–509A.
47. Ibid., VII.518A.
48. Ibid., 515C.
49. Ibid., 515D.

would count himself happy in the change and pity them?"[50] Such a man would no doubt lose all interest in returning to the cave. But if one imagines he would indeed return he would have the problem of disturbed sight again. At this point Plato describes the situation of the philosopher, obviously with the destiny of Socrates in mind:

> Now if he should be required to contend with these perpetual prisoners in "evaluating" these shadows while his vision was still dim and before his eyes were accustomed to the dark—and this time required for habituation would not be very short—would he not provoke laughter, and would it not be said of him that he had returned from his journey aloft with his eyes ruined and that it was not worthwhile even to attempt the ascent? And if it were possible to lay hands on and to kill the man who tried to release them and lead them up, would they not kill him?[51]

As Plato points out in the following interpretation of the parable, he intended to speak about "the soul's ascension to the intelligible region."[52] The goal is to see the idea of good and to accept it as "the cause for all things of all that is right and beautiful, giving birth in the visible world to light, and the author of light and itself in the intelligible world being the authentic source of truth and reason, and that anyone who is to act wisely in private or public must have caught sight of this."[53]

Based upon this assessment Plato outlines the task of the philosopher:

> Whenever he saw a soul perturbed and unable to discern something, he would not laugh unthinkingly, but would observe whether coming from a brighter life its vision was obscured by the unfamiliar darkness, or whether the passage from the deeper dark of ignorance into a more luminous world and the greater brightness had dazzled its vision. And so he would deem the one happy in its experience and way of life and pity the other, and if it pleased him to laugh at it, his laughter would be less laughable than that at the expense of the soul that had come down from the light above.[54]

This situation is for Plato also the starting point of *paideia*. Educa-

50. Ibid., 516E–517A.
51. Ibid.
52. Ibid., 517B.
53. Ibid., 517C.
54. Ibid., 518A.

tion, he emphasizes, cannot "put true knowledge into a soul that does not possess it, as if they were inserting vision into blind eyes."[55] Rather, education corresponds to the turning around of the liberated man in the cave; it is the "art of changing around" the soul: "not an art of producing vision in it, but on the assumption that it possesses vision but does not rightly direct it and does not look where it should, an art of bringing this about."[56] The capacity of vision itself is never lost, and so "the excellence of thought, it seems, is certainly of a more divine quality, a thing that never loses its potency."[57] It is only the application of the faculty that must be converted, from the useless and harmful to a useful and beneficient. Plato at this point inserts an interesting illustration: "Have you never observed in those who are popularly spoken of as bad, but smart men, how keen is the vision of the little soul, how quick it is to discern the things that interest it, a proof that it is not a poor vision which it has, but one forcibly enlisted in the service of evil, so that the sharper its sight the more mischief it accomplishes?"[58]

In addition to the *Republic,* the *Timaeus* treats the eye and the processes of vision *in extenso.*[59] A detailed comparison between the two works cannot be presented in this paper, but a few points may be brought out. In the *Timaeus* Plato makes use of Empedocles' idea of the fire in the eye as he calls the eyes "fire-bearing eyes" (φωσφόρα ὄμματα). Vision involves three kinds of light: (1) the daylight dispersed by the sun in the air; (2) the light contained in the eyeball and flowing out of it toward the objects seen; and (3) the light that is part of the colors of the objects. Vision takes place through a cooperation of all these lights, a process later called συναύγεια ("meeting of rays").[60]

Accordingly, whenever there is daylight round about, the visual current issues forth, like to like, and coalesces with it and is formed into a single

55. Ibid., 518C.
56. Ibid., 518D.
57. Ibid., 518E.
58. Ibid., 519A.
59. *Tim.* 45Aff. See F. M. Cornford, *Plato's Cosmology* (London: Paul, Trench, Trubner, 1937), 151ff.
60. See on this concept Beare, *Greek Theories,* 45.

homogeneous body in a direct line with the eyes, in whatever quarter the stream issuing from within strikes upon any object it encounters outside. So the whole, because of its homogeneity, is similarly affected and passes on the motions of anything it comes in contact with or that comes into contact with it, throughout the whole body, to the soul, and thus causes the sensation of vision.[61]

Disturbance of vision happens, for example, at night, because then the eternal fire is cut off, so that the internal fire, when it issues, meets with something that is unlike it, and therefore vision is prohibited.[62]

6. This survey has covered at least superficially the major theoretical presuppositions of Greek philosophy, insofar as they are needed for the interpretation of Matt. 6:22–23. It is, of course, understood that even after Plato these basic conceptions were constantly reproduced, criticized, and modified in many different ways. Jewish thinking, which had for a long time paid an extraordinary amount of attention to the eye,[63] entered only hesitatingly into this debate. Philo, however, takes over the whole Platonic tradition, most likely in a middle-Platonic version: it is not the eyes that see, but the mind (νοῦς) that sees through them.[64] In a long section on the faculty of vision in De Abrahamo 150–66 Philo follows the doctrines of the Timaeus, but he strongly emphasizes that the faculty of vision is under the influence of the emotions (πάθη), a Stoic concept.[65]

III. THE CONCEPT OF VISION
IN MATT. 6:22–23

After our survey of Greek theories of vision, it should now become evident that Matt. 6:22–23 contains quite different ideas on the

61. *Tim.* 45 C–D, Eng. trans. Cornford, 153.
62. *Tim.* 54D.
63. See the large collection of references in A. Rosenzweig, *Das Auge in Bibel und Talmud* (Berlin: Mayer and Müller, 1892); also W. Michaelis, "ὀφθαλμός," *TDNT* 5, 375ff.
64. *De Post. Caini* 126. Cf. Epicharmus, Diels-Kranz, 23 B 12 (I, 200, 16); Cicero, *Tusc.* I.20.46. On Philo, see M. Freudenthal, *Die Erkenntnislehre Philos von Alexandria* (Berlin: Calvary, 1891); H. Schmidt, *Die Anthropologie Philons von Alexandreia* (Würzburg: Triltsch, 1933), 75–79; F.-N. Klein, *Die Lichtterminologie bei Philon von Alexandrien und in den hermetischen Schriften* (Leiden: E. J. Brill, 1962).
65. On the doctrine of *pathos* in Philo, see Schmidt, *Die Anthropologie*, 86ff.

subject. The introductory thesis (v. 22a), which may have been taken over from the proverbial or Wisdom tradition, is granted only qualified approval. The commentary (vv. 22b–23b) treats it rather critically, and this critique seems justified because the image of the "lamp of the body" leaves unexplained what relationship we are to assume exists between the "lamp" and the "body." Is τοῦ σώματος a *genitivus objectivus* or *subjectivus?*

In effect the commentary vv. 22b–23b rejects the concept that the eye itself sees. The eye, we are informed, not only facilitates vision, but may also prohibit it. The philosophers who, as we learned in the previous section, also investigated the phenomena and causes of defective vision focused almost entirely upon the physiological conditions of the eye. At this point, Matt. 6:22–23 presents its own corrective point of view, suggesting that merely physiological considerations cannot decide whether or not the eye is capable of seeing.

To make this point clear, a quite peculiar pair of contrasting terms is introduced: ἁπλοῦς and πονηρός. The wide-ranging discussions that have developed around this word-pair cannot to any adequate degree be evaluated here.[66] The terms leave it unclear whether they are to be taken in the physiological ("healthy" versus "sick") or ethical sense ("simple, sincere, generous," versus "evil, wicked"). Perhaps this ambiguity is intended. Naturally, the hearer will think first of the physiological facts, but will then be moved to the ethical level of meaning. As a term describing the physiology of the eye, ἁπλοῦς is certainly unusual, while as ethical terms both ἁπλοῦς and πονηρός are quite common.[67] At any rate, the introduction of ethical terms opens up the completely new possibility that the ethical disposition of a person determines whether or not the eyes function properly. It appears that the merely physiological explanations are polemically

66. On this difficult concept, see the investigations by C. Edlund, *Das Auge der Einfalt. Eine Untersuchung zu Matth. 6,22–23 und Luk. 11,34–35* (Copenhagen: Ejnar Munksgaard, 1952); R. Vischer, *Das einfache Leben. Wort- und motivgeschichtliche Untersuchungen zu einem Wertbegriff der antiken Literatur* (Göttingen: Vandenhoeck & Ruprecht, 1965); J. Amstutz, ΑΠΛΟΤΗΣ. See also H. Bacht, "Einfalt," *RAC* 4 (1959): 821–40.

67. Cf. esp. Test. XII Iss. III.4 (β–γ, S¹), ed. Charles: πορευόμενος ἐν ἁπλότητι ὀφθαλμῶν ("Walking as I did in singleness of eye"). IV.6: μὴ ἐπιδεχόμενος ὀφθαλμοὺς πονηροὺς ἀπὸ τῆς πλάνης τοῦ κόσμου ("Shunning eyes (made) evil through the error of the world").

replaced by ethical considerations. From a Jewish ethical point of view, the entire approach of Greek philosophical tradition is called into question. Although the terms ἁπλοῦς and πονηρός are derived from Greek ethical language, the concern that they express is typically Jewish.

If the eye itself does not contain the light, where is it located? Verse 23b introduces another familiar concept—the "light within," the *lumen internum*.[68] But this concept, too, is immediately subjected to radical criticism. Contrary to what we would expect, the *lumen internum* is not connected with the "soul," and we look in vain for concepts like the "eye of the soul," the "intelligible light," or the mind (νοῦς). Instead we are told the "light within you" may even become "darkness." This suggestion is flatly directed against the Greek philosophical tradition, according to which the *lumen internum* is divine in nature and can never be turned into its opposite, "darkness." In other words, this suggestion must be another correction of the Platonic-Stoic anthropology, and it follows from the first correction. If the eye is affected by human sinfulness the same must be true for the "inner light," because nothing human is exempt from sin. In conclusion: If even the *lumen internum* is subject to sin and, on that account, can turn into its opposite, it can no longer be regarded as the *ultima ratio* upon which humanity can rely in its battle against the "desires" caused by the senses. The eye is not the real cause of sin, but the *lumen internum* itself when it has turned into darkness. This result, then, finds its dramatic expression in the exclamative "What a darkness!" (τὸ σκότος πόσον).

What does this result mean for the introductory definition v. 22a? Is it accepted or rejected? At the end, after having heard the critical commentary vv. 22b–23b, we are able to reaffirm the definition. Indeed, if the *lumen internum* shines, the eye is the lamp of the body. It can then illuminate the body, qualify the eye as ἁπλοῦς, and thus make it function properly.

Where, however, does the paraenetical edge of the logion lie? It appears that having heard and understood the logion the thoughtful

---

68. See Beierwaltes, *Lux intelligibilis*, 42 n. 3; H. Conzelmann, "φῶς," *TDNT* 9, esp. 334–35.

and conscientious person will be worried: What if my inner light is darkness? How can it be made bright again? The logion is designed to provoke this concern, but it does not answer it. It leaves the concerned hearer alone and restless, and this open-ended situation seems to be the paraenetical goal of the passage.

6

Cosmogony and Ethics in the Sermon on the Mount[1]

The question of the soteriological basis of the Sermon on the Mount preserved in Matthew (5:3–7:27) proves, on closer examination, to be far more complicated than it first appears. Investigation discloses not only that the SM combines a series of soteriological motifs, but that this combination results in a concept found nowhere else in the New Testament. In the study that follows, the hypothesis employed in previous essays—that the evangelist took over the SM from a pre-Matthean source, which had already undergone revision by a redactor, and embodied it in the final form of his Gospel—is made the object of discussion.[2] Consequently, we must investigate the soteriological concept of this pre-Matthean source, a concept characteristically different from that of the Gospel author. Thus it will be necessary, first of all, (I) to discuss the problem itself, so as then, (II) by means of an analysis of the decisive text, Matt. 6:25–34, to discover the fundamental principles of the soteriology of the SM. Finally, (III) these principles will be discussed with respect to the SM as a whole.

I. THE PROBLEM

For a more precise understanding of the present problem it is impor-

1. This essay is an expanded version of a paper first presented at the Symposium on Cosmology and the Ethical Order, held at the University of Chicago, 15–17 October 1982. The paper was also discussed with a group of New Testament colleagues from the "cluster" of theological schools in Chicago on 5 January 1983. To all who offered criticism and encouragement I am greatly indebted.
2. The essays are included in this volume.

tant, first of all, to obtain clarity as to its particular aspects and presuppositions.

1. As we have sought to show in a series of essays, the SM as found in Matthew's Gospel is a presynoptic source that has been preserved in its entirety. In our view, this source does not derive from Jesus of Nazareth directly, but from Jewish-Christian groups residing in Jerusalem sometime around the middle of the first century A.D.[3] The author (there may have been several)[4] drew his material from the tradition of Jesus' sayings and, by careful selection, formulation, arrangement, and composition, created a kind of compendium of the teaching of Jesus. The epitome comes most readily to mind as the literary genre of the SM. In its function as an epitome, the SM served to instruct the members of the above-mentioned Jewish-Christian community.[5]

2. Chronologically, and in respect to its cultural and religious milieu, the community of the SM stood nearer to the historical Jesus than most other early Christian groups. If, indeed, a synopsis of the theology of Jesus was composed by this community in debate with non-Christian Judaism on the one hand,[6] and with nascent Gentile Christianity on the other,[7] then the SM would represent, in its way, a contribution to the subject "Was lehrte Jesus wirklich?"[8] But one should not conclude from this possibility that every part of the SM can simply be traced back to the historical Jesus. As was demonstrated in my inaugural address at the University of Chicago, the genre epitome is open in principle to the transformation, revision, and even emenda-

---

3. See esp. 125 n. 1.

4. When reference is made in what follows to "the author," it is no indication that a decision has been made as to whether there were one or several authors of the SM. The SM pretends, of course, to have Jesus as its author, a claim justified only in the wider sense of the notion of authorship. The text of the SM does not betray whether there were one or several authors.

5. See the essay, "The Sermon on the Mount (Matt. 5:3–7:27): Its Literary Genre and Function," above, 1–16.

6. See esp. Matt. 5:17–20 and the essay, "The Hermeneutical Principles of the Sermon on the Mount (Matt. 5:17–20)," above, 37–57.

7. See esp. Matt. 5:19 (and on this, see above, 46–51); 7:21–23; and the essay, "An Episode in the Last Judgment (Matt. 7:21–23)," below, 125–57.

8. So the title of the well-known book by Norman Perrin in Germ. trans., *Was lehrte Jesus wirklich? Rekonstruktion und Deutung* (Göttingen: Vandenhoeck & Ruprecht, 1972); originally entitled *Rediscovering the Teaching of Jesus* (London: SCM Press, 1967).

tion of individual parts.[9] Undoubtedly, many sayings in the SM go back in one form or another to the historical Jesus. But there are also sayings, and even entire compositions, for which there are no synoptic parallels, and whose derivation from Jesus cannot, therefore, be established.[10] Moreover, many sayings in the SM clearly give the impression that they were written in retrospect on Jesus and his ministry,[11] and thus were composed by the redactor himself. It is implied, of course, in sayings such as these—which derive from the redactor—that they are based upon the teaching of Jesus; that is, they are meant to give expression to Jesus' teaching. Thus while the composition of the SM as a whole does not derive from the historical Jesus, it represents the redactor's intention to summarize that which was typical and of decisive importance for the master.

3. All the teachings presented in the SM may be interpreted in the context of Palestinian Judaism around the middle of the first century A.D. Within this pluralistic Jewish society, the Jesus movement was only one group among many. In the SM, Jesus is regarded as the authoritative teacher and interpreter of the Jewish Torah. There is no reason to attribute to Jesus a higher status than that of Moses,[12] or to speak of him as a "new Moses"[13] —not even in the so-called antitheses in Matt. 5:21-48. For the Jewish Christianity which comes to expression in the SM, Jesus' interpretation of the Torah is "orthodox" in the Jewish sense.[14] This principle is not contradicted by the fact that Jesus' interpretation of the Torah is presented in opposition to

9. See above, 1-16.

10. See esp. Matt. 6:1-18 and the essay, "A Jewish-Christian Cultic *Didache* in Matt. 6:1-18: Reflections and Questions on the Problem of the Historical Jesus," above, 55-69.

11. Esp. Matt. 5:17 and 7:21-23. See on these passages this volume 37-43, 125-57.

12. There is no evidence that the SM views Jesus as being superior to Moses. The SM is concerned with demonstrating how Jesus' teaching confirmed the Torah (on this point see esp. my essay, "Hermeneutical Principles," in this volume, 37-53). In response to criticism of its view (5:17), the SM takes the position that Jesus was opposed to the literal interpretation of the Torah, but not to the Torah itself. For a different view, see the review of present scholarship on the subject in W. Schrage, *Ethik des Neuen Testaments,* NTD Ergänzungsreihe 4 (Göttingen: Vandenhoeck & Ruprecht, 1982), 54-69, esp. 67.

13. On this notion, see W. D. Davies, *The Setting of the Sermon on the Mount* (Cambridge: At the University Press, 1966), 25-108.

14. See above, 37-53.

Pharisaism.[15] The Jesus movement, like Jesus himself[16] and John the Baptist[17] earlier, primarily came into conflict with Pharisaic Judaism, for the very reason that it stood *nearer* to Pharisaism than to other Jewish groups.[18] The controversy was, therefore, inner-Jewish, not anti-Jewish. The same may be said of the rejection of conventional Judaism in the SM; it, too, is an inner-Jewish phenomenon. Thus, according to the SM, Jesus' authority depends upon that of the Torah, though naturally in accordance with his particular interpretation.

4. The primitive Christian kerygma of the death and resurrection of Jesus plays no role in the SM.[19] If this kerygma was known to the community of the SM, as one may surmise on the basis of Matt. 7:21–23, it had in any case been rejected.[20] Moreover, the community of the SM refused to indulge messianic expectations with regard to Jesus or the kingdom of God. But that Jesus was awaited as eschatological defender and intercessor for his followers fits well in the context of contemporary Judaism. Thus the SM lacks not only a Christology, but the soteriology based upon it as well. The soteriology of the SM is none other than that of the Jewish Torah.

5. The SM is an expressly polemical text and reflects conflicts in a number of directions. Alongside the inner-Jewish controversy with

---

15. The scribes and Pharisees are mentioned only in Matt. 5:20, but since this statement introduces the main part of the SM, it extends over the whole of the text. Conventional Judaism is attacked under the epithet "hypocrites" (6:2, 5, 16; 7:5), but the term is not used exclusively of the Pharisees (see esp. 7:5).

16. That Jesus' theology was anti-Pharisaic is clear from primitive sayings such as Mark 8:15//Matt. 16:6//Luke 12:1; Matt. 23:2, etc. For further references, see H. Braun, *Spätjüdisch-häretischer und frühchristlicher Radikalismus*, 2d ed., BHT 24, vol. 2 (Tübingen: J. C. B. Mohr [Paul Siebeck], 1969), 12; K. Weiss, *TDNT* 9 (1973; Eng. trans., 1974), s.v. "Φαρισαῖος," section B, I, 1; J. Neusner, *From Politics to Piety: The Emergence of Pharisaic Judaism* (Englewood Cliffs, N.J.: Prentice-Hall, 1973), 70–71; G. Vermès, *Jesus the Jew: A Historian's Reading of the Gospels*, 2d ed. (Philadelphia: Fortress Press, 1981), 34–36; E. Schürer, *The History of the Jewish People in the Age of Jesus Christ*, rev. ed. (Edinburgh: T. & T. Clark, 1979), vol. 2, §26.

17. See esp. Luke 7:29–30; Matt. 3:7; cf. Matt. 21:31–32.

18. See on this point Neusner, *From Politics to Piety*, 71–72; Weiss, *TDNT* 9, 37–39.

19. Even mention of Jesus' crucifixion is lacking in passages where one would expect it: Matt. 5:10–12; 7:21–23. Cf. Matt. 10:38//Luke 14:27; Matt. 23:34–35// Luke 11:49–51; 1 Thess. 2:14–16.

20. See on this point my essay, "An Episode in the Last Judgment," in this volume, 125–57.

Pharisaism and conventional Judaism, there is an inner-Christian polemic against Gentile Christianity. Of great importance, finally, is the deep-seated debate with the Greco-Roman world. This aspect of the SM's polemic is difficult to grasp, because it is presented to a large extent in veiled form. Here belong the subtle debates with the concepts of Greek philosophy in a wider sense,[21] as well as the attitude that the SM takes toward the political situation. The characteristically veiled nature of the political attitude indicates that the community regards itself as a threatened minority.[22] Of course the Romans represent a threat, but there is also a threat from the Jewish authorities. Thus references to the political environment invariably assume a negative form. Assimilation to pagan culture is sharply rejected throughout.[23] Otherwise, its views are clothed in images and metaphors clear only to the initiated.[24] And beyond this, silence reigns— doubtless a strategy of self-defense in view of their absolute powerlessness politically, a strategy also adopted later by the rabbis. Despite such conditions, it is noteworthy that the SM betrays no sign of defeatism, despair, or apocalyptic panic.[25] On the contrary: however unimportant the community of the SM may have been in the political affairs of the day, it lived in unbroken confidence that it would endure and prevail against the storms of history and the hardships of human life.[26] Seen in this way, the SM can almost be called a "manual for survival."

These presuppositions give rise to the problem of the soteriology of the SM: after the kerygma of the death and resurrection of Jesus has been eliminated as the basis for soteriology, of what does the soteriology of the SM consist? Which possibilities come into consideration?

21. This has been demonstrated in my essay, "Matt. 6:22–23 and Ancient Greek Theories of Vision," in this volume, 71–87.
22. See esp. Matt. 5:11–12, 13–16, 38–42, 43–48; 7:12, 13–14, 15–20, 21–23, 24–25.
23. Matt. 5:46–47; 6:7, 32.
24. The prime example of this strategy is the puzzle in Matt. 7:6.
25. The SM shows no trace of apocalypticism, but supports traditional Jewish eschatology. The end of the world will occur sometime in the future (Matt. 5:18, see on this passage above, 43–46). There will be a last judgment (5:21–22; 6:14–15; 7:2, 21–23), a heaven (5:3–12, 16, 18, 19, 20, 34, 45, 48; 6:1, 9, 10, 14, 20, 26, 32; 7:11, 21), and a hell (5:22, 29, 30; 7:19, 21–23).
26. See Matt. 5:3–12, esp. v. 5; 5:13–16; 7:24–25.

Whatever soteriological concepts are to be discussed, they must be at home in contemporary Judaism, and must be grounded in Jesus' teaching as evidenced by other texts.

As a person, Jesus has a saving function in the SM only in an indirect sense. His authority as a teacher of the Torah does not lie in his person,[27] but in the Torah he teaches.[28] This teaching is not limited to himself alone, but is perpetuated by the teachers of the community of the SM,[29] though it would not have existed without the historical Jesus of Nazareth. The question of how one came to be indebted to Jesus for the proper interpretation of the Torah is not raised in the SM.

Furthermore, Jesus' role as intercessor for his own followers in the Day of Judgment (7:21–23) in no way negates the soteriological function of the Torah; he merely testifies before God as to whether or not his followers were faithful in observing the Torah he taught. Again, the soteriology does not depend upon the Torah in general, but on the Torah taught by Jesus, for which reason he, as advocate, is only responsible for his own followers.[30] Other Jewish teachers, one must conclude, were accountable for their own students.

One of the main concepts in the SM is the concept of "kingdom of heaven" ($\dot{\eta}$ $\beta a\sigma\iota\lambda\epsilon\acute{\iota}a$ $\tau\hat{\omega}\nu$ $o\dot{\nu}\rho a\nu\hat{\omega}\nu$). How is this concept related to the Torah? One must first say that the notion of the kingdom of God is otherworldly and eschatological in orientation in the SM (Matt. 5:19, 20; 6:10, 33; 7:21). But this otherworldly kingdom is simultaneously at work in the present; certain persons may already participate in it at present as an eschatological promise (5:3, 10). Does this mean that

---

27. This is not contradicted by the expression "on account of me" ($\dot{\epsilon}\nu\epsilon\kappa\epsilon\nu$ $\dot{\epsilon}\mu o\hat{\nu}$) in Matt. 5:11, a reference to slander as the cause of the harassment of the congregation. The situation is different, however, in Q, which has a Christology. Cf. esp. Mark 8:35//Matt. 16:25; Luke 9:24; Mark 10:29//Matt. 19:29; Matt. 10:18, 39; Mark 13:9//Matt. 24:18/Luke 21:12. Cf. Luke 6:22; 18:29.

28. Throughout the SM Jesus speaks in the first person singular. Therefore, the phrase "but I say to you" ($\dot{\epsilon}\gamma\grave{\omega}$ $\delta\grave{\epsilon}$ $\lambda\acute{\epsilon}\gamma\omega$ $\dot{\upsilon}\mu\hat{\iota}\nu$) refers not only to the antitheses Matt. 5:21–48, but to the SM as a whole, which is called "these my sayings" ($\mu o\upsilon$ $\tau o\grave{\upsilon}s$ $\lambda\acute{o}\gamma o\upsilon s$ $\tau o\acute{\upsilon}\tau o\upsilon s$) in 7:24, 26. See also 7:21–23.

29. See Matt. 5:19 and the interpretation given above, 46–51.

30. The reason for the rejection of Gentile Christians in 7:21–23 is their "lawlessness" ($\dot{a}\nu o\mu\acute{\iota}a$). Their failure to obey the Torah is a failure to produce the required righteousness ($\delta\iota\kappa a\iota o\sigma\acute{\upsilon}\nu\eta$). See on this point below, 125–57.

the kingdom of God comes into conflict with the Torah in respect to soteriology?

It is clear that in the sense of the SM, these concepts correspond to one another. In the Torah as taught by Jesus the kingdom of God is described as an important concept. One who studies and practices this Torah can count upon eschatological reward (5:12, 46; 6:1, 2, 5, 16). With the help of the Torah taught by Jesus, the righteousness demanded by God in the last judgment can actually be produced (5:6, 10, 20, 48; 6:1, 33). The task of Jesus' disciples in this life is "to seek after the kingdom [of God] and his righteousness" (6:33), guided by the Torah that Jesus taught.

Thus there is no doubt that the concept of the kingdom of God has priority. The Torah taught by Jesus is nothing less than the way revealed by God which corresponds to his kingdom and which leads one into it (7:13–14). The Torah has a soteriological function, therefore, only in a derived sense. The soteriology of the SM is identical with the activity of God, that is to say, with his kingdom.

Yet the manner in which the kingdom of God is described in the SM is unparalleled in the New Testament. To be sure, the SM agrees with the other New Testament texts that the kingdom of God is not to be understood in an exclusively eschatological and otherworldly sense. But on the matter of how the kingdom of God is at work in the present, the SM goes its own way. It is striking that reference is made neither to apocalyptic traditions nor to the miracles of Jesus. Rather, the SM has recourse to a theology of creation. What it falls back upon is not, of course, the creation account of Genesis, but the doctrine of the *creatio continua*. In the exposition of this doctrine ancient mythological fragments of what can only be called a cosmogony in the strict sense are drawn upon. This characteristic doctrine is found in the central text, Matt. 6:25–34, which will be analyzed more closely in what follows.

II. INTERPRETATION OF MATT. 6:25–34

The character of the pericope in Matt. 6:25–34 is already manifest in the language, for which reason the exegetical analysis will be preceded by a translation and an analysis of the literary composition.

Translation[31]

v. 25 Therefore I say to you:
Do not be anxious about your soul/life[32]
what you shall eat [or what you shall drink],[33]
nor about your body/person,[34] what you shall put on.
Is not the soul/life more than nourishment,
and the body/person more than clothing?

v. 26 Look at the birds of the sky:[35] they neither sow
nor harvest nor gather into barns,
but your heavenly Father feeds them.
Are not you of greater value than they?

v. 27 Then, which of you by worrying

31. The translation is based on Nestle-Aland, 26th ed. (4th rev. printing, 1981). In addition, A. Huck's *Synopsis of the First Three Gospels, with the Addition of the Johannine Parallels,* 13th ed. rev. by H. Greeven (Tübingen: J. C. B. Mohr [Paul Siebeck], 1981), has been consulted.

32. The translation of ψυχή (found nowhere else in the SM) is extremely difficult. Should it be rendered "soul" or "life"? Should one look for the influence of Greek philosophical anthropology? Modern scholarship is frequently marked by a strange prejudice against Greek ideas—which can hardly be overlooked at this point. Bauer's *Lexicon* (901) formulates the problem aptly: "it is often impossible to draw hard and fast lines between the meanings of this many-sided word." Yet his rendering is still too one-sided: "life as prolonged by nourishment" (section 1, a, β). The passage should have been quoted in his section 1, d: the soul as "the center of both the earthly (1a) and the supernatural (1c) life." For further discussion, see E. Schweizer, σῶμα, *TDNT* 7 (1964; Eng. trans., 1971), esp. 1058; ψυχή, *TDNT* 9 (1973; Eng. trans., 1974), esp. 637, 641–47; H.-Th. Wrege, *Die Überlieferungsgeschichte der Bergpredigt* (Tübingen: J. C. B. Mohr [Paul Siebeck], 1968), 119. See also below, n. 51.

33. The rhetorical structure of the pericope argues against the omission of the bracketed words. The three basic necessities of life, as stated in v. 31, presuppose the same sequence earlier in v. 25a. See the discussion below, and B. Metzger, *A Textual Commentary on the Greek New Testament* (New York and London: United Bible Societies, 1971), 17. In Greeven's revision of *Synopsis,* the disputed words are omitted.

34. In the SM the concept of σῶμα refers to the whole person (Matt. 5:29–30) and to the physical body as a container of the "inner light" (Matt. 6:22–23, see also above, 71–88). The context in Matt. 6:25 speaks of σῶμα in juxtaposition with "soul/ life" (ψυχή) as well as with clothing. Both juxtapositions suggest the concept of the body as the garment of the soul. At the same time, the text argues that the person is more than clothing and body. See for the background of this idea, A. Kehl, "Gewand (der Seele)," *RAC* 10 (1978): 945–1025.

35. The Greek οὐρανός stands for sky as well as heaven. Sky (v. 26) and field (v. 28) represent heaven and earth as the realm of the heavenly Father (vv. 26, 32).

    is able to add[36] one cubit[37] to his life?
v. 28 And why are you anxious about clothing?
    Learn from the lilies of the field, how they grow:
    they neither toil nor spin.[38]
v. 29 But I tell you, not even Solomon in all his splendor
    was clothed like one of these.
v. 30 But if God so clothes the grass of the field
    which today exists and tomorrow is thrown into the oven,
    will he not all the more clothe you, you men of little faith?
v. 31 Therefore, do not be anxious, saying, "What shall we eat?"
    or "What shall we drink?" or "What shall we wear?"
v. 32 For the pagans[39] strive for[40] all these things.[41]
    But your heavenly Father knows that you need all these
    things.[42]
v. 33 But seek[43] first the kingdom [of God][44] and his[45] righteous-
    ness,
    and all these things shall be provided for you as well.
v. 34 Therefore, do not worry about tomorrow,
    for tomorrow will worry about itself.
    Sufficient for the day is its own trouble.

36. The juxtaposition of human, προσθεῖναι, in v. 27 and divine, προστεθήσεται ("it shall be given in addition"), in v. 33 should not be overlooked.
37. The cubit, a measure of length, is used here as a metaphor for a short span of time. See Bauer, *Lexicon*, s.v. "πῆχυς."
38. For the textual evidence, see Metzger, *Textual Commentary*, 18.
39. The term τὰ ἔθνη is used throughout the SM in a distinctly negative sense. See also above, n. 22.
40. The term ἐπιζητέω is the negative counterpart to ζητέω, v. 33.
41. This expression (vv. 32 [twice], 33) refers to the three basic needs (vv. 25a, 31). See below, n. 90.
42. Concerning this doctrine, cf. Matt. 6:8; 7:11.
43. The notion of seeking (ζητέω) is positive throughout the SM. See also Matt. 7:7, 8; cf. 7:14.
44. The phrase τοῦ θεοῦ ("of God") cannot have been part of the original text: the SM always uses the expression "kingdom of the heavens" (ἡ βασιλεία τῶν οὐρανῶν, 5:3, 10, 19, 20; 7:21). Βασιλεία ("kingdom") alone occurs in the Lord's Prayer (6:10); its meaning was certainly clear without qualification (cf. Matt. 8:12; 9:35; 13:19, 38; 24:7, 14). T. Zahn, *Das Evangelium des Matthäus*, 4th ed. (Leipzig: Scholl, 1922), 299 n. 17, argues rightly that the modifiers are not needed, so that "kingdom" (βασιλεία) may be original.
45. Zahn, *Matthäus*, 299 n. 17, argues that even if the expression "of God" is not original, the pronoun "his" (αὐτοῦ) must be taken to refer to the "heavenly Father" in v. 32, and thus that it applies to both nouns in v. 33. He also recognizes that the reading of codex B is most fitting in the SM: "seek first righteousness and his kingdom" (cf. 5:20). So also E. Klostermann, *Das Matthäusevangelium*, 4th ed., HNT 4 (Tübingen: J. C. B. Mohr [Paul Siebeck], 1971).

Analysis of the Literary Composition

v. 25a   I. Introduction
         A. Connective: "therefore" (διὰ τοῦτο)
         B. Introductory formula (teaching formula): "I
            say to you" (λέγω ὑμῖν)
v. 25b   II. Exhortation
         A. Imperative (negative)
            1. Observation (presupposition)
               a. Anxiety as common human behavior
               b. Object in question: "soul" or "life" (τῇ
                  ψυχῇ)?
            2. Prohibition: "do not be anxious" (μὴ
               μεριμνᾶτε, cf. vv. 31a, 34a)
         B. Caricature of the behavior to be rejected
            1. Confusion of *care* for one's soul/life with
               the *procurement* of the necessities of life
               a. Eating
               b. Drinking
            2. Confusion of *care* for one's body/person
               with the *procurement* of clothing
vv. 25c–30   III. First Argument
         A. Theses (rhetorical questions)
            1. The soul/life is more than nourishment
            2. The body/person is more than clothing
         B. Conclusions (implied)
            1. It is foolish to confuse the procurement of
               food and clothing with care for one's soul/
               life
            2. It is prudent to care for one's soul/life and
               body/person
vv. 26–30   C. Proofs
vv. 26–27   1. The necessities of life: a comparison of
                  animals and humans
v. 26   a. The example of the birds
                  (1) Appeal to observe their behavior:
                     "look!" (ἐμβλέψατε, cf. v. 28b)
                  (2) The paradox to be observed in

98

respect to their behavior
(a) They do not sow
(b) They do not harvest
(c) They do not gather into barns
(d) And yet, they are fed

v. 26b   (3) Conclusion: God feeds them

v. 26c   (4) Consideration (rhetorical question in direct address)
(a) Presupposition: the traditional distinction between animals and humans in which humans are accorded a higher position
(b) Conclusion (*a minori ad maius*): if anxiety over food is unnecessary for animals, how much more so for humans

v. 27   b. An example from human life (rhetorical question in direct address)
(1) The paradox to be observed in respect to the future
(a) No one can add one cubit to his or her life
(b) Yet each day one's life is lengthened
(2) Conclusion (implied): God measures out one's life
(3) Consideration
(a) Presupposition: the future is measured by God, not by humans
(b) Conclusion (*a maiori ad minus*): if the future as a whole is under God's control, it is futile and improper for humans to worry about a part of the future as if it were under human control

vv. 28–30	2. Clothing: a comparison of plants and humans
v. 28a	a. Presentation of the problem (rhetorical question in direct address) (1) Reference to v. 25c (2) Reference to worry as common human behavior
v. 28b	b. The example of the lilies (1) Appeal to observe their behavior: "learn" (καταμάθετε) (2) The paradox to be observed in respect to their behavior (a) They do not toil (b) They do not spin (c) Nevertheless, they grow (3) Conclusion (implied): God causes them to grow
v. 29	(4) Consideration
v. 29a	(a) Introductory formula: "but I tell you" (λέγω δὲ ὑμῖν)
v. 29b	(b) Presupposition: the splendor of the royal robes of Solomon was thought to be unsurpassed (c) Conclusion: the clothing of the lilies, because a work of God, surpasses the human splendor of Solomon's garments
v. 30	c. An example from human life (rhetorical question in direct address)
v. 30a	(1) The paradox to be observed in respect to the future (a) The fate of the grass (i) Today it exists (ii) Tomorrow it is thrown into the oven as fuel (b) Yet God has arrayed them so splendidly

100

	(2) Conclusion (implied): God "wastes" the future on his creatures
v. 30b	(3) Consideration
	(a) Presupposition: God measures out the future without giving thought to the transitoriness of his creatures
v. 30c	(b) Conclusion (*a minori ad maius*): if God treats his lesser creatures in this way, how much more so his highest creation, humankind
v. 30d	(4) Address (at the same time the transition to the next argument): "you of little faith" (ὀλιγόπιστοι)

vv. 31–33 IV   Second Argument

v. 31a   A. Connective: "therefore" (οὖν)

          B. Repetition of the exhortation in v. 25b

            1. Imperative (negative)

              a. Observation (presupposition)

                (1) Anxiety as a common human disposition

                (2) Object: the future in general

              b. Prohibition: "do not be anxious" (μὴ μεριμνήσητε)

v. 31b   2. Caricature of the behavior to be rejected (dramatization)

              a. Eating

              b. Drinking

              c. Clothing

vv. 32–33   C. Proofs: comparison between pagans and Jews (Jewish Christians)

v. 32a   1. The example of the pagans

            a. Observation of their improper "striving" (ἐπιζητέω) for the goods of life

            b. Identification with the behavior rejected in v. 31

v. 32b	2. The traditional doctrine
	a. Of God's omniscience
	b. Of his provision of basic human needs
v. 33	D. Conclusions
v. 33a	1. Exhortation
	a. Imperative (positive)
	(1) The required behavior: "seeking" ($\zeta\eta\tau\acute{\epsilon}\omega$) rather than "worrying" (vv. 25b, 31a, 34a: $\mu\epsilon\rho\iota\mu\nu\acute{\alpha}\omega$) or "striving" (v. 32a: $\acute{\epsilon}\pi\iota\zeta\eta\tau\acute{\epsilon}\omega$)
	(2) Priority: "first" ($\pi\rho\hat{\omega}\tau o\nu$)
	(3) The proper object
	(a) Principal: the kingdom [of God]
	(b) Specific: God's righteousness ($\delta\iota\kappa\alpha\iota o\sigma\acute{\upsilon}\nu\eta$ $\alpha\acute{\upsilon}\tau o\hat{\upsilon}$)
v. 33b	2. Promise
	a. Condition: "and [only then]" ($\kappa\alpha\acute{\iota}$)
	b. Traditional doctrine of divine reward
	(1) Eschatological (presupposed)
	(2) Mundane (derived): "all these things" ($\tau\alpha\hat{\upsilon}\tau\alpha$ $\pi\acute{\alpha}\nu\tau\alpha$)
v. 34	V. Third Argument
v. 34a	A. Connective: "therefore" ($o\tilde{\upsilon}\nu$)
	B. Repetition of the exhortation in vv. 25b, 31a
	1. Imperative (negative)
	a. Observation (presupposition)
	(1) Worry as common human behavior
	(2) Object: tomorrow
	b. Prohibition: "do not worry" ($\mu\grave{\eta}$ $\mu\epsilon\rho\iota\mu\nu\acute{\eta}\sigma\eta\tau\epsilon$)
	[2. Abbreviation of the argument by omission of the description of the behavior to be rejected]
vv. 34b–c	C. Proofs
v. 34b	1. Maxim on tomorrow
v. 34c	2. Maxim on today

D. Conclusions (implied)

1. *A maiori ad minus:* if the future as a whole is under God's control, it is futile and improper for humans to worry about tomorrow, a part of that future

2. *E contrario:* If tomorrow is not under human control, then today's problems (its "trouble") must be dealt with by humans

3. *E contrario:* If it is futile and improper for humans to worry about the future, then the right way to deal with the problems of today is not by worrying about them, but by seeking in the "trouble" of each day the righteousness and thus the kingdom of God

As the above analysis makes clear, the pericope contains a continuous, carefully constructed argument. The care exercised in the composition may be attributed to the redactor of the SM, who derived his material from the Q-tradition, but not the composition as it now appears. The Lukan parallel (Luke 12:22–32) has its own nuances and is less tightly constructed. The same may be said of the remaining variants in *P. Oxy.* 655, the Coptic *Gospel of Thomas,* and Justin Martyr.[46] It is characteristic of the pericope in the SM that the Q material, whatever form it may have taken,[47] has been transformed into a theological argument[48] in keeping with the theology found in the SM.

As one may observe elsewhere in sayings-compositions in the SM, the pericope begins with an introductory paraenesis formulating the goal of the entire argument (vv. 25a–b). This is followed by three subsidiary arguments aimed at establishing the initial paraenesis of vv. 25a–b; (1) vv. 25c–30, (2) vv. 31–33, (3) v. 34. At the beginning of

---

46. For parallels, see K. Aland, *Synopsis Quattuor Evangeliorum,* 9th ed. (Stuttgart: Württembergische Bibelanstalt, 1976), 91.

47. The vexed problem of the Q-Vorlage need not be discussed here.

48. Similarly, S. Schulz, *Q. Die Spruchquelle der Evangelisten* (Zurich: Theologischer Verlag, 1972), 152–53.

each of these subsidiary arguments, the initial paraenesis (vv. 26a–b) is repeated in abbreviated form, with small but significant variations on each occasion (vv. 25a, 31a, 34a).

To comprehend the argument of the pericope in its entirety, the following problem must be kept in mind. An analysis that serves this purpose must deal with the text as it now stands. Yet the argument cannot be discerned from an analysis of the surface structure of the written text alone. The surface structure is designed to be a kind of auxiliary construction that serves to bring a far more complete, unwritten text to mind. Presuppositions and conclusions appear in this unwritten text that are sometimes explicitly observable in the surface structure, often merely implied. This form of argumentation is in keeping with the construction of the SM as a whole, as previously shown.[49] For this reason, the above analysis is not confined to the surface structure of the written text, but also attempts to discover the unwritten text and bring it to light, thus making the entire argument comprehensible.

A further matter is related to this unusual construction of the text. The initial paraenesis (v. 25b) exhibits an element of semantic obscurity which appears, nevertheless, to have been intentional: "Do not be anxious about your ψυχή." The word ψυχή can be variously translated: it can mean either "soul" or "life."[50] Recent scholarship has favored the translation "life,"[51] since the concept of the soul was long regarded as un-Jewish, and only a Semitic concept was felt to be compatible with the theology of Jesus.[52] Of course, neither argument

49. On this point, see also above, 41–42.
50. See above, nn. 32 and 34.
51. The translation of ψυχή as "life" is found in the standard translations as well (see above, n. 32). Martin Luther's *Die gantze Heilige Schrifft Deudsch 1545/Auffs new zugericht*, ed. H. Volz (Munich: Rogner & Bernhard, 1972), vol. 2, 1977, renders ψυχή as "Leben." The matter was discussed earlier by Augustine, *De sermone domini in monte* I, 15, 42, lines 1009–14, ed. A. Mutzenbecher, Corpus Christianorum 35 (Turnholti: Brepols, 1967), 47. He takes *anima* to refer to "this life" (*haec vita*) because of the food which sustains it. Cf. Chrysostom, according to J. A. Cramer, *Catenae Graecorum Patrum in Novum Testamentum* I (Oxford: At the Clarendon Press, 1840), 49.
52. This seems to be the reason for treating ψυχή as a Semitism, as is done by, for example, M. Black, *An Aramaic Approach to the Gospels and Acts*, 2d ed. (Oxford: Oxford University Press, 1954), 76; C. F. D. Moule, *An Idiom Book of New Testament Greek*, 2d ed. (Cambridge: At the University Press, 1959), 185; BDR, § 283 n. 8; BDF, §283 (4).

is correct. The concept of the soul[53] was widespread in Judaism of the first century A.D., and there are a number of sayings belonging to the Jesus-tradition that speak unambiguously of the "soul." Furthermore, one always has to reckon with the theological concepts of Jewish Christianity in the context of the SM. Finally, the contrast of σῶμα (body) with ψυχή makes the translation "soul" unavoidable. Yet it must at once be added that what seems to the modern reader to be a problem in translation has an intentional function in the argument of the passage.

The initial paraenesis begins with an observation about human behavior in general. For the prohibition of anxiety assumes that anxiety is typical of human behavior. People, and above all, the religious people of the Hellenistic age, were tormented by anxiety.[54] No doubt there were enough reasons for care. The political disasters and socioeconomic unrest of the period have often been described. What is less widely known is that for centuries, men and women had been regularly brought up on care. The literature, Jewish and non-Jewish, of the Hellenistic age is full of admonitions and exhortations of the most varied kinds that have anxiety as their subject.[55]

For what reason were people anxious? One worried over all sorts of things without being clear which worries were justified and which

---

53. The concept of the soul is itself rather complicated and must not be standardized as "the immortal soul." See J. Bremmer, *The Early Greek Concept of the Soul* (Princeton, N.J.: Princeton University Press, 1983).

54. Cf. R. Bultmann, μεριμνάω, *TDNT* 4 (1942; Eng. trans., 1967), 589–93; H. D. Betz, "The Mithras Inscriptions of Santa Prisca and the New Testament," *NT* 10 (1968): 69–71.

55. The primary reason for anxiety was found in humanity's fragile natural condition, demonstrated at birth, when the body was set out naked and helpless in a world full of dangers and enemies. This topos on the *conditio humana* is widely attested in ancient literature. See especially the summaries in Lucretius, *De rer. nat.* 3.1046–75; 5.222–34; Pliny, *NH* 7, praefatio 1–5. The discussion originates with Hesiod's myths of Pandora and Cronus (*Op.* 80, 105, 110–201) and Protagoras's myth of Prometheus and Epimetheus (Plato, *Prot.* 320c–322a); Ps.-Plato (Philip of Opus), *Epinomis*, 973d–947a (see L. Tarán, *Academica: Plato, Philip of Opus, and the Pseudo-Platonic Epinomis* [Philadelphia: The American Philosophical Society, 1975], 209–11); Ps.-Plato, *Axiochus*, 366d–367a. For the Hellenistic-Jewish literature, see Wis. 7:1–6 (cf. 6:2–20; 8:9; 15:9); Sir. 40:1–11 (cf. 30:21–25; 31:1–4); Tobit 5:17–21; 10:1–7; Philo, *Praem. poen.* 98–126; *virt.* 1–6. See on the whole topic also E. Pöhlmann, "Der Mensch—das Mängelwesen? Zum Nachwirken antiker Anthropologie bei Arnold Gehlen," *Archiv für Kulturgeschichte* 52 (1970): 297–312.

were uncalled for. It has been typical of the common person in all eras to be anxious about all sorts of things without knowing why. By contrast, the wise man or woman was one who knew how to make distinctions, who concerned him- or herself about important things and left out of account what was unimportant.

So might the ancients have answered, on the whole, had they been asked whether people were anxious about their souls. This anxiety had been enjoined upon them for centuries by various religions and philosophical schools.[56] In the Greek world since Socrates "care for the soul" ($\dot{\eta}$ $\dot{\epsilon}\pi\iota\mu\dot{\epsilon}\lambda\epsilon\iota\alpha$ $\tau\hat{\eta}s$ $\psi\upsilon\chi\hat{\eta}s$) had been declared the paramount task of the philosophic and religious person.[57] Not only the philosophers, but in increasing measure the religious as well, began to address themselves to this anxiety.

But the description of human anxiety in vv. 26a–b exhibits, in the form of a caricature, a strange contradiction. Concern for the soul or life is confused with concern for the necessities of life, that is, for food and drink. Similarly, concern for the $\sigma\hat{\omega}\mu\alpha$ is confused with the acquisition of clothing.

A problem presents itself again in relation to the translation of $\sigma\hat{\omega}\mu\alpha$: the term can designate the "body," but also the "person."[58] What the text aims at, no doubt, are the basic anthropological concepts of body and soul; but the tension between concern for the acquisition of clothing and concern for the body indicates that more is concealed in the concept $\sigma\hat{\omega}\mu\alpha$ than "body" in the superficial sense. People purport, it is observed, to obtain clothing for the protection of the body. But ancient humanity already knew that clothing had a much wider function in relation to the person. "Clothes make the man" was already a familiar proverb in those days.

Thus it seems that by emphasizing the ambiguity of the words $\psi\upsilon\chi\dot{\eta}$ ("soul, life") and $\sigma\hat{\omega}\mu\alpha$ ("body, person"), the introductory paraenesis

---

56. Before long, various types of worriers began to be represented in literature. Plato mentions "the quibbling worriers" (οἱ λεπτῶς μεριμνῶντες), *Resp.* 10.607c. Religion was acquainted with the overly scrupulous person, δεισιδαίμων. See for this character, Theophrastus, *Char.* 16; Plutarch, *De superstitione,* with the commentary by M. Smith, in H. D. Betz, ed., *Plutarch's Theological Writings and Early Christian Literature,* SCHNT 3 (Leiden: E. J. Brill, 1975), 1–35.
57. According to Plato, *Apol.* 30b; *Alc.* I. 128e–135e.
58. See above, n. 34.

makes the confusion prevailing among people its theme.[59] If this is so, then the translator is faced with the problem of concealing the point at issue in the text and disguising it for the reader by an unambiguous translation, whether as "soul" or "life," "body" or "person." But on the other hand, the entire argument presented in vv. 25–34 leads one to a conclusion on what is justified and what is unjustified anxiety. After careful consideration, the reader knows how the paraenesis is to be understood. But this insight is not simply told to him or her. What is communicated, on the contrary, is the situation that has given rise to the problem, that is to say, confusion over the basic questions of human life. For this reason, at the very beginning the reader is confronted with the fundamental problem of human existence, which is precisely this confusion. The problematic is preserved in the ambiguity of the terminology. The reader must arrive at a decision about what is warranted and unwarranted anxiety upon reflection. The proper choice is written nowhere on the page, and thus must not be interpolated into the text by translation. Here one clearly stands on the boundary of the translatability of the SM. The text is truly translatable only by carrying out the argument that it presents.

The first of the three subsidiary arguments embraces vv. 25c–30. It begins (v. 25c) with a thesis in the form of a rhetorical question, to which a positive answer is expected. It is obvious, so runs the common assumption, that soul/life and body/person are of greater value than food and clothing. If this assumption is accepted, and everyone in the ancient world accepted it, then one who confuses these values is a fool. In contrast to such a person, a prudent individual is one who is able to avoid confusion, one who lives in keeping with the aims of the SM.[60]

Following the introductory thesis in v. 25c, two proofs are presented in vv. 26–30 with respect to food and clothing. First, anxiety over food is dealt with (vv. 26–27), then anxiety over clothing (vv. 28–

---

59. Such confusion is the mark of the fool. See esp. Luke 12:16–21, where this character is depicted. On this passage, see the study by E. W. Seng, "Der reiche Tor. Eine Untersuchung von Lk. xii 16–21 unter besonderer Berücksichtigung form- und motivgeschichtlicher Aspekte," *NT* 20 (1978): 136–55.

60. See the "prudent man" in Matt. 7:24–25 and the discussion above, 3–7. Cf. also A. S. Pease, *M. Tulli Ciceronis De natura deorum libri III* (Darmstadt: Wissenschaftliche Buchgesellschaft, 1968), vol. II, 1035–40.

30). The proof with respect to food is provided by a comparison of animals and humans, that with respect to clothing by a comparison of plants and humans. The proof relating to anxiety over nourishment opens with a summons to observe the behavior of the birds.[61] In this call to observation of nature, a paradox that has already been identified may be confirmed. Once again, the text does not deprive the reader of his or her own judgment; rather, one must verify what the text claims by personal observation and judgment. Paradoxically, the birds behave differently from people: they do not sow, they do not reap, they do not gather into barns. And yet they are fed! How is this possible? The answer takes the form of an inference from the creation theology held by the text: God feeds the birds, as we would say, by means of nature.

Then in v. 26c a thought is derived from the above-mentioned observation in the form of a rhetorical question which again awaits a positive response. The question states the presupposition: traditionally the animal kingdom is distinguished from that of human beings, and a higher rank is conferred upon human beings in the hierarchy of creation. But the conclusion is left open: if concern for food is unnecessary among the animals, how much more so for humans.

To comprehend this conclusion one must, of course, make several other presuppositions clear. The proof presupposes a concept of the origin of culture in which human culture and civilization emerged from the animal kingdom.[62] According to this theory, the behavior of

---

61. This method is not so naive as one might think at first sight. The Greek philosophers called it "proof based on analogy"; see *Philodemus, On Methods of Inference,* ed. with a trans. and commentary by P. H. De Lacy and E. A. De Lacy, 2d ed. (Naples: Bibliopolis, 1978); also H. Diller, "ὄψις ἀδήλων τὰ φαινόμενα," *Hermes* 67 (1932): 14–42, reprinted in his *Kleine Schriften zur Literatur* (Munich: Beck, 1971), 119–42; G. R. E. Lloyd, *Magic, Reason and Experience. Studies in the Origins and Development of Greek Science* (Cambridge: At the University Press, 1979).

62. For ancient views on the origin and development of human culture, see W. Spoerri, *Späthellenistische Berichte über Welt, Kultur und Götter,* Schweizerische Beiträge zur Altertumswissenschaft 9 (Basel: Reinhardt, 1959); F. Lämmli, *Vom Chaos zum Kosmos. Zur Geschichte einer Idee,* Schweizerische Beiträge zur Altertumswissenschaft 10 (Basel: Reinhardt, 1962); B. Gatz, *Weltalter, Goldene Zeit und sinnverwandte Vorstellungen,* Spudasmata 16 (Hildesheim: Olms, 1967); J. Ebach, *Weltentstehung und Kulturentwicklung bei Philo von Byblos. Ein Beitrag zur Überlieferung der biblischen Urgeschichte im Rahmen des altorientalischen und antiken Schöpfungsglaubens,* BWANT 108 (Stuttgart: Kohlhammer, 1979); U.

the animals has not changed, but still conforms today to the primeval order of creation. Humankind, however, has changed; its conduct no longer corresponds to the original order, but is "degenerate."[63] The animals need not concern themselves over food because they limit themselves to the satisfaction of their basic needs.[64] Animals have only "natural" needs, and these can be satisfied by the provisions of nature. Humanity, on the other hand, has developed "artificial" needs which cannot be met by the divinely established order of creation and nature. These artificial needs (luxuries) arose as a consequence of agricultural inventions by people (sowing, reaping, gathering into barns). Not only were human needs changed by agriculture, but as a result, anxiety arose. Had human beings remained embedded in the animal kingdom, there would have been no concern for food; anxiety would have remained unknown and unnecessary. The distinction between humans and the animals is, however, secondary in nature and can be reversed. Humanity only needs to return to the order of nature by the conscious renunciation of "unnatural" desires,

Dierauer, *Tier und Mensch im Denken der Antike. Ideengeschichtliche Studien zur Tierpsychologie, Anthropologie und Ethik*, Studien zur antiken Philosophie 6 (Amsterdam: Grüner, 1977); B. Manuwald, *Der Aufbau der lukrezischen Kulturentstehungslehre (De rerum natura 5, 925–1457)*, Abhandlungen der Akademie der Wissenschaften und der Literatur in Mainz, geistes- und sozialwissenschaftliche Klasse 1980: 3 (Wiesbaden: Steiner, 1980); A. Kehl and H.-I. Marrou, "Geschichtsphilosophie," *RAC* 10 (1978): 703–79, esp. 710.

63. This comes close to the critique of civilization by the Cynics; see on this point, Dierauer, *Tier und Mensch*, 180–93. Cf. the expulsion of Adam and Eve from paradise, Genesis 1–3, esp. 1:29–30; 2:15, 3:17–19, and later interpretations in Jub. 3:9–35; Josephus, *Ant.* 1:46–49; for Rabbinic texts, see Billerbeck, vol. 1, 435–37.

64. This view has interesting parallels in some Greek philosophical traditions. For Epicurus's teachings on necessary and unnecessary desires, see frag. 469, ed. Usener, trans. according to C. Bailey, *Epicurus: The Extant Remains* (Oxford: At the Clarendon Press, 1926), 137 n. 67: "Thanks be to blessed Nature because she has made what is necessary easy to supply, and what is not easy unnecessary." See also *Ep. ad Menoeceum*, 127; 131; *Kyriai Doxai*, 26; 29; and the treatment by R. Müller, *Die epikureische Gesellschaftstheorie*, Schriften zur Geschichte und Kultur der Antike 5 (Berlin: Akademie-Verlag, 1972), 22–28. The problem is how Epicurus's "asceticism" is to be related to the older ideal of the simple life, especially in its development in Cynic philosophy. See R. Vischer, *Das einfache Leben. Wort- und motivgeschichtliche Untersuchungen zu einem Wertbegriff der antiken Literatur* (Göttingen: Vandenhoeck & Ruprecht, 1965); K. Döring, *Exemplum Socratis. Studien zur Sokratesnachwirkung in der kynisch-stoischen Popularphilosophie der frühen Kaiserzeit und im frühen Christentum*, Hermes-Einzelschriften 42 (Wiesbaden: Steiner, 1979).

and it is free from anxiety over nourishment.[65] So long as humanity confines itself to the basic necessities of food and drink, it is amply supplied by nature. To be sure, it is never suggested that people renounce civilization as such, only the false expectations and desires which it calls forth. This step is illustrated by the second proof (vv. 28–30).

But first the behavior of animals is contrasted with that of humans in v. 27, and this again in the form of a rhetorical question, to which a negative answer must be given. The paradox that may be observed in the behavior of animals is contrasted with the absurdity characterizing the actions of humans. A person who is anxious about food is at the same time anxious about his or her future. Yet he or she is unable to add a single span to his or her life. But with each new day a further span is added.

So much can be inferred from the written text of v. 27. But the reader is meant to reflect more deeply. First, the inference: if a person who is concerned about the future is unable to add a single new day to his or her life, and if precisely this happens day by day nevertheless, then it is God who calls each new day into existence. So it is God—not human beings—who measures out the period of one's life—a commonly held belief in antiquity which finds confirmation here. A further conclusion follows from this: if the future lies in God's hands, then it is foolish and unwarranted when people are worried about a part of the future, as if it were under their control.[66] Thus human anxiety over the future is improper and unwise because it is part of divine creation, the *creatio continua*. In respect to the future, therefore, human life is not fundamentally different from that of the animals; yet unlike the animals, humanity does not entrust itself to the future that is continually being called into existence by God.[67]

---

65. Cf. *Gnomologium Vaticanum Epicureum* 44 (trans. according to Bailey, *Epicurus*, 113): "The wise man when he has accommodated to straits knows better how to give than to receive: so great is the treasure of self-sufficiency which he has discovered."

66. The conclusion *a minori ad maius* is implicit in v. 27 but explicit in the parallel in Luke 12:26: "If then you are incapable (of doing) even the smallest (thing), why do you worry about the rest?"

67. This concept of the future is rooted in Jewish Wisdom, for which many parallels could be adduced. See, esp. LXX Ps. 36:28–40; Prov. 23:17–18; 24:13–20; Eccles. 8:5–8; Wis. 7:18; 8:1; 19:1; Sir. 38:20–23; 40:1–17. From the New Testa-

The proof in respect to clothing (vv. 28–30) is made by a comparison of plants with human beings.[68] The argument is introduced by a reference to v. 25 in the form of a rhetorical question. The readers are addressed directly as if they were themselves among those who are anxious about clothing (v. 28a). Again there is a call to the observation of nature (v. 28b)—to learn from the plants. In comparison with v. 26, it assumes a heightened form.[69] Again, a paradox is observed in nature: the lilies[70] of the field neither toil nor spin, and yet they grow. Just as in v. 26, the conclusion is inferred: God causes them to grow.[71]

But what does this have to say about human clothing? Verses 29–30 are devoted to this question, again introduced (cf. v. 25a) by the question, "But I tell you." It is not only a matter of the growth of the lilies, but also of the beauty of their appearance.[72] God not only causes the lilies to grow, but gives the flowers a beauty that surpasses even the proverbial splendor of Solomon's garments. To comprehend the argument one must understand that the ancient world was of the opinion that the beauty of nature always surpasses human beauty—even the beauty of humanity's greatest creations—because it is a work of God. Human artistry can at best imitate the divine beauty of nature, but can never equal it. This aesthetic view, common to antiquity, underlies vv. 28–30.

ment, see esp. Luke 12:19-20; Acts 14:17; 17:26, 30. Cf. also Epicurus, *Ep. ad Menoeceum* (Diog. Laert. 10. 127): "We must remember that the future is neither wholly ours nor wholly not ours, so that neither must we count upon it as quite certain to come nor despair of it as quite certain not to come." Trans. is according to R. D. Hicks's edition of *Diogenes Laertius, Lives of Eminent Philosophers*, LCL (Cambridge: Harvard University Press; London: William Heinemann, 1925), vol. II, 653.

68. No attention is paid here to physiological differences between animals and plants, an important topic in the origin of science. Cf., however, LXX Wis. 7:20. See Dierauer, *Tier und Mensch*, esp. 44, 47, 109-16, 142-43.

69. The climax is reached only at Matt. 6:26a, 28b; Luke has κατανοήσατε ("contemplate") in both instances (12:24a, 27a).

70. The lily (Greek τὸ κρίνον; Hebrew *šūšan, šōšān, šōšannā*) plays an important role in the aesthetics of the Old Testament; its beauty was proverbial and is often compared with human beauty. See J. C. Trever, "Lily," *IDB* 3 (1962), 133-34; Bauer, *Lexicon*, s.v. "κρίνον"; J. Feliks, "Lilie," *BHH* 2 (1964): 1093.

71. The conclusion is implicit. Cf. 1 Cor. 3:7: ὁ αὐξάνων θεός ("the God who makes things grow"); 2 Cor. 9:10. See H. D. Betz, *2 Corinthians 8 and 9: Two Administrative Letters of the Apostle Paul* (Philadelphia: Fortress Press, 1985), on 2 Cor. 9:10.

72. The emphasis is on "how" (πῶς).

The next thought in v. 30 takes up the matter of the future, and in analogy to v. 27. Here, too, a paradox is discovered: today the grass grows in the field in all its glory, but tomorrow it will be cast into the oven as fuel.[73] If God nevertheless clothes the grass, one must conclude that he actually wastes the future on it. This conclusion seems to invite the observation that God measures out the future without regard for the transitoriness of his creatures. And if God deals with even the lowliest of his creatures in this manner, how much more so with humankind.

Consequently, it is senseless to worry about clothing. Whoever nevertheless persists in anxiety is a person of little faith. The address "you men of little faith" (v. 30d)[74] states unequivocally that all who are worried about what they will wear in the future are of little faith. If they only trusted in God, they would be free of care.

A problem arises at this point in relation to the history of culture. In the view of antiquity, human clothing was fundamentally different from the covering of the other creatures in that it was artificial. This helps to explain why clothing is dealt with separately from food: in the view of antiquity, nature had not, in fact, clothed humanity but had sent it into the world naked.[75]

The address, "you men of little faith," assumes that God's care is not limited to what is provided by nature. The problem of human nakedness is already discussed in Genesis 3.[76] After their fall into sin, Adam and Eve discover that they are naked. They attempt to remedy this situation by sewing fig leaves together: "Then the eyes of both were opened, they knew that they were naked; and they sewed fig leaves together and made themselves aprons" (Gen. 3:7, RSV). Of course, this primitive attempt is rejected as inadequate. God himself

73. Cf. LXX Eccles. 3:2b: "A time to plant and a time to pull up what is planted."
74. The address, "O men of little faith" (ὀλιγόπιστοι), occurs in the parallel in Luke 12:28 as well and must therefore be interpreted in a pre-Matthean sense as "men of little trust in God." For Rabbinic parallels, see Billerbeck, vol. 1, 438–39; cf. Schürer, *History*, vol. 2, 487. Cf. for Matthean interpretation, G. Strecker, *Der Weg der Gerechtigkeit. Untersuchung zur Theologie des Matthäus*, 3d ed., FRLANT 82 (Göttingen: Vandenhoeck & Ruprecht, 1971), 233–34.
75. See on the history of culture, Ebach, *Weltentstehung* (see above, n. 62), 287–90, with references and literature; cf. K. Thraede, "Erfinder II (geistesgeschichtlich)," *RAC* 5 (1965): 1191–1278, esp. 1241.
76. See Gen. 2:15; 3:7, 10, 11; Job 1:21; Eccles. 5:15.

must come and instruct the first humans in how they can obtain better clothes: "And the Lord God made for Adam and for his wife garments of skins, and clothed them" (Gen. 3:21, RSV). Certainly these instructions carry us beyond the realm of nature. Here God acts forthrightly as the bringer and inventor of culture. The person who trusts in God knows that God also fulfills human needs through culture, so long as those needs remain "natural" and ethically justifiable.

The second argument (vv. 31–33) presupposes the first (vv. 26–30). This is indicated by the conjunction οὖν in v. 31a. That it is a new argument may be seen from the fact that the initial paraenesis of v. 25b is repeated with minor changes (v. 31a). The imperative is now reformulated as an aorist imperative:[77] "Therefore, do not be anxious." The depiction of anxiety is now heightened and dramatized by self-caricature: "'What shall we eat?' or 'What shall we drink?' or 'What shall we wear?'" (v. 31b).[78]

The second argument now addresses itself to the problem of anxiety in a positive sense: how then shall people care for their soul/life and body/person in the right manner? The two proofs, which are adduced for the sake of clarification, are not derived from nature or history in this instance, but are theological arguments in the narrower sense. Both proofs in vv. 32a and 32b take the form of a comparison between pagans and Jews. First the conduct of the pagans is described. From the Jewish standpoint,[79] their conduct deserves to be identified with the false anxiety rejected in the preceding argument. The pagans are distinguished from the Jews by "seeking" after the things of this life: the verb ἐπιζητέω is thus chosen deliberately. Were Jews to engage in such behavior, it would amount to forbidden assimilation.[80] The orthodox Jew, as presented in the SM, proceeds on the assumption

77. See BDF §337 (3); BDR §337 n. 3.
78. See a similar dramatization in Epictetus, *Diss.* I.9.8, 12, 19–20; III.26.37. It is found even in a Babylonian incantation against toothache, cited in S. N. Kramer, *Mythologies of the Ancient World* (Garden City, N.Y.: Doubleday & Co., 1961), 123–24: "After Anu had created heaven, heaven had created earth, earth had created rivers, rivers had created canals, canals had created marsh, marsh had created worm—the worm came weeping before Shamash, his tears before Ea: 'What will you give me to eat? What will you give me to drink?'"
79. The parallel Luke 12:30 (RSV) reads differently: "all the nations of the world" (πάντα τὰ ἔθνη τοῦ κόσμου), which presupposes a Gentile Christian perspective.
80. See the passages referred to above, n. 23.

that the heavenly Father knows that people need "all these things," that is, the basic necessities of life (v. 32b).[81]

What conclusion is to be drawn from this observation? How can people be anxious in the right manner? The answer to this question is found in a key sentence in v. 33 which encapsulates the theology of the entire SM. Here the paraenesis is formulated in a positive way. The positive expression "to seek" ($\zeta\eta\tau\acute{\epsilon}\omega$) replaces "to be anxious" ($\mu\epsilon\rho\iota\mu\nu\acute{a}\omega$) or "to seek after" ($\dot{\epsilon}\pi\iota\zeta\eta\tau\acute{\epsilon}\omega$) as the decisive verb.

The person of the SM is, therefore, no quietist who merely waits upon what God gives through the resources of nature, like an animal. On the contrary, the person who has learned to be properly anxious in the sense of the SM is necessarily a seeker,[82] not after the things of this life, to be sure, but "first" ($\pi\rho\hat{\omega}\tau o\nu$) after the kingdom of God.[83] He or she is found upon the hard way and seeks the narrow gate to the city of heaven (Matt. 7:13–14).[84] But how does one go about seeking the kingdom of God? The answer to this question is embodied in a brief phrase which is nevertheless of decisive importance: "and his righteousness" ($\kappa\alpha\grave{\iota}$ $\tau\grave{\eta}\nu$ $\delta\iota\kappa\alpha\iota\sigma\sigma\acute{\nu}\nu\eta\nu$ $\alpha\grave{\upsilon}\tau o\hat{\upsilon}$). The duty of Jesus' disciples in this life, according to the SM, is to seek and find the righteousness of God.[85] This is what is meant by the search for the kingdom of God. But while such seeking remains the principal task ($\pi\rho\hat{\omega}\tau o\nu$),[86] it is not the complete answer to the question of the proper anxiety.

To be sure, the search for the kingdom of God has an eschatological orientation and leads to eternal life in the hereafter (Matt. 7:13–14); thus it seems at first to overlook worldly affairs. But these are by no means forgotten or thrust aside by pious preoccupation with the hereafter.

Alongside the paraenesis of v. 33a stands the promise of v. 32b: it is not eternal life in the hereafter alone that is held out as a reward to the earnest seeker but, in anticipation of eternal life, the guarantee of the

---

81. Cf. esp. Matt. 6:7–8, followed by the Lord's Prayer 6:9–13, in which the elementary needs are defined from a somewhat different perspective.
82. The term "seek" ($\zeta\eta\tau\acute{\epsilon}\omega$) also occurs in Matt. 7:7–8.
83. See on this concept above, n. 44.
84. See on this passage above, nn. 6 and 7.
85. See also Matt. 5:6, 10, 20; 6:1; cf. 5:45.
86. See Matt. 5:24; 7:5.

necessities of earthly existence[87] —the seeker is promised that every-thing necessary for life "shall be provided" ($\pi\rho\sigma\tau\epsilon\theta\dot{\eta}\sigma\epsilon\tau\alpha\iota$).[88] According to the SM, the disciple of Jesus is one who at once both seeks and finds. Neither is this person needlessly worried like a fool, nor does he or she seek after the things of this life, like a pagan. But, rather, he or she is devoted entirely to the search for God's right-eousness, trusting that God will also give what is necessary for this life as a "bonus." In principle, therefore, one has no right to expect that he or she will be given what is necessary for life.[89] Even when people limit themselves to the basic necessities (food, drink, clothing),[90] they cannot expect that nature or human civilization will satisfy these needs. The gifts of God remain just that, and are bestowed as a reward. The search for God's kingdom and righteousness is a pre-requisite, and the gifts of God's *creatio continua* remain gifts *in addition* to the eschatological reward. This doctrine is presented in a striking manner in the SM, but it was nothing new to Judaism of the period. Rather, it is part of the Jewish notion of reward and the doc-trine of divine providence. Moreover, it harmonizes without difficulty with other expressions of the concept of reward attributed to Jesus in the New Testament.[91]

The third argument is found in v. 34. To be sure, it is more con-cisely worded than the preceding arguments, but it presupposes the

---

87. See also v. 32; cf. Luke 21:34: $\mu\epsilon\rho\iota\mu\nu\alpha\iota$ $\beta\iota\omega\tau\iota\kappa\alpha\iota$ ("worries of daily life").
88. For the term $\pi\rho\sigma\tau\dot{\iota}\theta\eta\mu\iota$, see above, n. 36.
89. The doctrine presupposes the *theologumenon* of divine benevolence which takes many different forms in ancient religion and philosophy. For example, cf. *Ps. Sol.* 4:25; Rom. 8:28, 37; 1 Cor. 2:9; 8:3; James 1:12; 2:5. For Rabbinic texts, see Billerbeck, vol. 1, 439–40.
90. The matter of what constitutes the necessities of life was widely discussed in antiquity. See, for example, Sir. 29:21 (RSV): "The essentials for life are water and bread and clothing and a house to cover one's nakedness." Cf. Epictetus, *Ench.* 33.7: "In things that pertain to the body take only as much as your base need requires, I mean such things as food, drink, clothing, shelter and household-slaves; but cut down everything which is for outward show or luxury." For a collection of passages, see Pease, *M. Tulli Ciceronis,* vol. II, 690–91 on *De nat. deor.* 2:60. To this should be added the magical gem inscription given in C. Bonner, *Studies in Magical Amulets Chiefly Graeco-Egyptian* (Ann Arbor: University of Michigan Press, 1950), 182 (Brit. Mus. 56260): "Water for thirst, bread for hunger, fire for cold." See furthermore A. R. Hands, *Charities and Social Aid in Greece and Rome* (Ithaca, N.Y.: Cornell University Press, 1968), 89–115: "The provision of basic com-modities."
91. See on this point Braun, *Radikalismus,* II, 54 n. 1.

same train of thought. Characteristically, the three arguments are so artfully constructed that only the first (vv. 26–30) appears in the written text in its entirety, while the second (vv. 31–33) and third (v. 34) appear shortened in ever-increasing measure, though the arguments themselves remain unabridged.[92] What has been omitted from the written text can easily be supplied in the unwritten text by the intelligent reader. The conjunction οὖν in v. 34a permits us to recognize the transition to the third argument without difficulty. A new thought is brought forward here, which is nonetheless connected to what has gone before. Again (cf. 31a) reference is made to the initial paraenesis in v. 25a. The prohibition is repeated, but the cause of anxiety is now said to be "tomorrow." That anxiety as a phenomenon implies a certain concept of time was already demonstrated in v. 30. Again it is assumed that humanity is customarily anxious about tomorrow. But a more detailed account of the attitude being criticized is omitted; one can imagine it easily enough for oneself. Again, two arguments are supplied, but this time they take the form of independent maxims (vv. 34b–c) which are merely arranged alongside one another without apparent connection: "Tomorrow will worry about itself,"[93] and "Sufficient for the day is its own trouble."[94] The

92. This was first pointed out to me by Bernard Lategan.

93. The *gnome* in v. 34a has no precise parallel elsewhere in the New Testament, but there are many *sententiae* of similar form and content in ancient gnomological literature. For collections of parallels, see J. J. Wettstein, *Novum Testamentum Graecum* (Amsterdam: Dommer, 1752), I, 336–37; M. Dibelius, *James* (Philadelphia: Fortress Press, 1976), 232–33; Billerbeck, vol. 1, 441; P. W. van der Horst, *The Sentences of Pseudo-Phocylides*, Studia in Veteris Testamenti Pseudepigrapha 4 (Leiden: E. J. Brill, 1978), 195–98, on *Sent.* 116–21; J. G. Griffiths, "Wisdom about Tomorrow," *HThR* 53 (1960): 219–21, with parallels from Egyptian sources. See esp. 1 Cor. 15:32 (Isa. 22:13); James 4:13–14; Prov. 1:27; Sir. 10:10; 11:18; 20:15; *Abot* 2:14; Epicurus, Frag. 492, ed. Usener, as quoted by Plutarch, *De tranquillitate animi* 16, 474C (see H. D. Betz, ed., *Plutarch's Ethical Writings and Early Christian Literature*, SCHNT 4 [Leiden: E. J. Brill, 1978]: 223, with note, 222); *Gnomologium Vaticanum Epicureum* 14, ed. P. von der Mühll, *Epicuri epistulae tres et ratae sententiae a Laertio Diogene servatae*, BT (Leipzig: Teubner, 1922), 61; Teles, Frags. V and VI, ed. O. Hense; Horace, *Od.* I.11.8; Stobaeus, *Ecl.* III. XVI. 28.

94. The second maxim in v. 34b is also unique in the New Testament. Many parallels could be adduced from the same sources mentioned in n. 93 above. See esp. Eccles. 7:14; 12:1; Epictetus, *Diss.* 3.24.25–26; 4:12.20–21. Billerbeck, vol. 1, 441, refers to a Rabbinic parallel (*Berakhot* 9ᵇ). See also G. Heinrici, *Die Bergpredigt (Matth. 5–7; Luk. 6, 20–49) begriffsgeschichtlich untersucht* (Leipzig: Edelmann, 1905), 78–79.

conclusions are left unexpressed; the sympathetic reader must draw them for him- or herself.

In the interpretation of both maxims, which may be assumed to have been taken over from the popular gnomic tradition, it is necessary to keep their literary character in view. They are half-philosophical statements in which observations on the affairs of daily life combine with practical conclusions to be drawn from them. The maxims themselves do no more than give expression to the facts; practical conclusions are hinted at, but are finally left to the reader or hearer. It would be wrong, and hardly in keeping with the sense of the SM, if one were to draw pessimistic conclusions from the situations described. The maxims are characterized by extreme realism, as is often the case in gnomic literature; but they do not tend to that pessimism which exclaims, "There is no purpose to it all!" And in any event the context demands that the maxims be interpreted in relation to the theology of the SM.

In this context the maxims must be taken to refer to anxiety about the future. The sayings rightly observe that in so-called everyday life people have to deal with existence as it confronts them day by day. This means that the general concept of "the future" is resolved into its practical components of tomorrow and today. People are foolish to be concerned about tomorrow since, as v. 27 has shown, it is not under human control. Therefore worrying about tomorrow is excluded, and along with it, anxiety about the future in general. This first conclusion *a maiori ad minus* does not really introduce anything new, but only reiterates what has already been said in vv. 27 and 30.

This clearly suggests a second conclusion: if, in fact, people have no power over the coming day, they nevertheless have power over the present. Today is always there, relentlessly confronting people with its "trouble" (κακία).[95] This trouble must always be overcome in the present if one wishes to attain tomorrow. It lies in the realm of human possibility to accomplish this, but it demands one's entire strength and vigilance. This kind of concern is commanded. The second conclusion is, therefore, *e contrario,* reversing the form of the first conclusion.

95. Thus, rightly, Klostermann, *Matthäusevangelium* 65, who follows Chrysostom.

The third conclusion is once again *e contrario:* if it is wrong to be anxious on account of the future, and particularly on account of tomorrow, then the right way to care for today is not by *being anxious* (μεριμνάω), but by *seeking* after the kingdom and righteousness of God (v. 33) in the trouble of each day. This conclusion is, in fact, identical with the ethics of the SM as a whole.[96]

Thus the third proof presents a very practical way of mastering the future: the future is a temporal concept that may be analyzed into today and tomorrow. So long as one gazes anxiously at tomorrow—whose problems may neither be known nor overcome until tomorrow has become today—one fails to lay hold of the problems of today, with which one is always confronted. Only if one is freed from this pointless anxiety can one concern oneself with today and its troubles. These troubles are always concrete necessities whose conquest lies in the realm of human possibility.

For Jesus' disciples in the SM, the search for the kingdom and righteousness of God (v. 33) means freedom for the practical conquest of the problems of the present. Such a conquest occurs when the disciple of Jesus seeks after the kingdom and righteousness of God in the face of the plague of the present day.

III. SOTERIOLOGY AND ETHICS IN THE SERMON ON THE MOUNT

How then are soteriology and ethics related in the SM as a whole, on the basis of the pericope in Matt. 6:25-34? In what follows, we shall

---

96. A collection of parallel sayings employing the concept of "seeking first . . ." would serve to substantiate the central role of v. 33 in the SM. The goals of the search vary, of course, with the different religious or philosophical systems. In the Old Testament, the goal is to seek God and his will (see S. Wagner, "דָּרַשׁ *dāraš*," *TDOT* 3 [1978]: 293-307, with further bibliography); in the New Testament, seeking after the kingdom is soon interpreted in new ways (cf. Rom. 3:11; 1 Thess. 4:1; Col. 3:1; Heb. 13:14, etc. (see E. Larsson, "ζητέω," *EWNT* 2 [1980], 253-56). In Rabbinic Judaism, preoccupation with the Torah is the first priority (see *Abot* 3.5; 4.9-10, etc.). In Greek philosophy, from which many parallels could be drawn, the search for philosophical wisdom is the primary concern (see, for example, Socrates according to Plato, *Apol.* 20d-21e, and passim; Epicurus, *Ep. ad Menoeceum* [Diog. Laert. 10.122]; *Gnomologium Vaticanum Epicureum* 78; Epictetus, *Diss.* 3.20.12; 15; 3.22.44; Frag. 3; Philo, *fuga* 38; *Praem. Poen.* 104).

attempt to come nearer to an answer to this question, at least in rough outline. It must first be said that the position that the SM takes on this matter appears to have resulted from a profound crisis of faith in providence.[97] This crisis of faith in divine providence was by no means confined to early Christianity, but was spread over the whole of the ancient world. The titles of numerous works of the period testify that anyone who wished to be taken seriously as a philosopher or theologian had to address him- or herself to this matter and offer suggestions for overcoming the crisis.[98] The position taken by the SM must be seen in the context of this problem of antiquity for its peculiar character to be made clear in comparison with competing views. For on this issue, the SM goes its own way.

Within contemporary Judaism, the SM moves in the realm of Jewish Wisdom literature, from which part of the material in Matt. 6:25–34 appears to be derived. But at a decisive point the SM turns away from the Wisdom tradition: v. 33 with its concept of seeking after the kingdom and righteousness of God is foreign to Wisdom. It is found nowhere else in contemporary Jewish literature, and thus appears to be an aspect peculiar to the teaching of Jesus.

97. Though the term does not occur in the SM, Matt. 6:25–34 amounts to an apology for divine providence. This has long been recognized by commentators. See, for example, Augustine, De sermone domini in monte II, 15, 51, lines 1103–4, ed. Mutzenbecher, 141; Zahn, Matthäus, 296ff.; Klostermann, Matthäusevangelium, 62; R. Bultmann, Jesus and the Word (New York: Charles Scribner's Sons, 1958), 160 (however, the statement concerning a "childlike belief in providence and a naive optimism in his view of nature and the world" does not apply to Matt. 6:25–34. Bultmann omits vv. 33 and 34). Another view is held by W. Grundmann, Das Evangelium nach Matthäus, 2d ed. (Berlin: Evangelische Verlagsanstalt, 1971), 214: "Lehrgedicht vom Sorgen," and again by Schulz, Q, 152: apocalyptic "Warnrede."

98. For the principal sources, see Pease, M. Tulli Ciceronis, vol. II, 740–42, 839, 879, 1175), with notes; J. Behm, "προνοέω, πρόνοια," TDNT 4 (1942; Eng. trans., 1967): 1013–16. For Judaism, see M. Hengel, Judaism and Hellenism (Philadelphia: Fortress Press, 1974), vol. I, 141, 158, 312; II, 92 n. 228; E. E. Urbach, The Sages (Jerusalem: Magnes, 1975), 225–85; Schürer, History, vol. 2, 393. Close parallels between Matt. 6:25–34 and several of Epictetus's diatribes point to a common tradition. Diss. 1:9 develops the concept of a philosophic way of life based on imitation of the deity, "our maker, father and guardian" (1.9.7; see also the quotation below, n. 103). Diss. 1.16 is entitled "On Providence" (περὶ προνοίας) and exhorts to a life in harmony with nature by learning from the behavior of animals. Diss. 3.26 is aimed at those who fear running out of the necessities of life. The first priority in dealing with such fear is acquisition of the logos (3:26.15). See also 3.9.15–22; 3.20.12, 15; 3.24; 4.6.22–24; 4.10.

How then does the SM attempt to solve the crisis of faith in divine providence? It reaches back to earlier traditions of Jewish thought, which are then reinterpreted in a new context. The principal theological concept in the SM is that of "the kingdom of heaven" (ἡ βασιλεία τῶν οὐρανῶν). God does not rule over his kingdom like an absolute monarch, in keeping with contemporary political theory and practice, but as a cosmic Father. This concept was widespread in the ancient world, even outside Judaism. The SM has derived the notion from the theology of Jesus in which the idea of the heavenly Father played a paramount role, as we learn from other texts.[99]

But the treatment of the *theologumenon* of the heavenly Father has its own characteristics in the SM. The fatherhood of God has a cosmic character and manifests itself in the *creatio continua* on the one hand, and in the relationship to the disciples of Jesus on the other.

In its account of the *creatio continua,* the SM is not reluctant to draw upon archaic, mythological traditions. According to Matt. 5:45, God "makes his sun rise on the evil and the good, and sends rain upon the just and the unjust." This mythical description of the cosmic fatherhood of God is a commonplace throughout the whole of antiquity.[100] But that it recurs in the New Testament is startling. In Matt. 7:11, human fatherhood is compared with the fatherhood of God in a manner that seems deliberately provocative: both fathers give good things to those who ask of them. Thus the SM is not afraid to speak of God in a mythical-personal manner, in contrast to the Hellenistic tendency to depersonalize the deity.[101]

99. The oldest passage in the SM is in the Lord's Prayer, Matt. 6:9; then SM has it in 5:16, 45, 48; 6:1, 4, 6, 8, 14, 15, 18, 26, 32; 7:11, 21. See J. Jeremias, *New Testament Theology* (London: SCM Press, 1971), vol. I, 61–68; cf. Braun, *Radikalismus,* vol. 2, 127 n. 3. Cf. Matt. 5:35, where God is given the title "the great King" (ὁ μέγας βασιλεύς).
100. For the Old Testament, see LXX Gen. 2:5; Job 28:28a; Amos 4:7; cf. Isa. 5:6; Ezra 22:24; for the New Testament, cf. James 5:17–18; Rev. 11:6, where anthropomorphism is avoided. See Bauer, *Lexicon,* s.v. "βρέχω," 2; BDR, §129 n. 1; §309 n. 3; BDF, §129; §309 (2). See W. Speyer, "Die Zeugungskraft des himmlischen Feuers in Antike und Urchristentum," *Antike und Abendland* 24 (1978): 57–75; idem, "Gewitter," *RAC* 10 (1978): 1107–72.
101. One must, however, take care with this aspect of the matter: there are indications that personal belief in God as Father continued in the Hellenistic and Roman era. See, for example, Marcus Aurelius, *Ad se ipsum* 5.7: "A prayer of the Athenians: 'Rain, Rain, O dear Zeus, upon the corn-land of the Athenians and their

Equally surprising is the positive manner in which the natural order is treated in the SM, a subject in which the New Testament otherwise shows little interest. But the goodness of nature is not demonstrated by reference to the creation account in Genesis. Skepticism was obviously so great in respect to this story that a simple appeal to it was no longer convincing. In their own way, apocalyptic and Jewish apologetic bear witness to this skepticism as well. But the SM has recourse neither to apocalyptic visions nor the cosmologies of Hellenistic philosophy in stating the meaning of the creation story. Rather, the approach of the SM is to take this skepticism seriously. It concludes: that alone is convincing which stands immediately before one's eyes and which can be verified critically. The goodness of the created order is thus grounded in daily experience: sunrise and sunset, rain, daily bread, etc. If our skepticism will only allow us to believe that which we perceive with our senses—so much the better! Precisely these experiences testify to the goodness of nature. And anyone who understands this can bear witness to it.[102]

 Needless to say, this view does not lead to the romanticizing of

meads.' Either pray not at all, or in this simple and frank fashion." Trans. according to the LCL ed. by C. R. Haines (Cambridge: Harvard University Press; London: William Heinemann, 1916). I owe the reference to W. Burkert, *Griechische Religion der archaischen und klassischen Epoche* (Stuttgart: Kohlhammer, 1977), 200. See also Pausanias's interpretation of a statue (1.24.3); for passages from the Greek Magical Papyri, see A. J. Festugière, *La révélation d'Hermès Trismégiste*, 4th ed., vol. IV (Paris: Société d'Édition "Les Belles-Lettres," 1981), 186 n. 6 (listing *PGM* IV.1160–66; XII.60–61). To these some hymnic fragments should be added: *PGM* V.151–53; XII.241–44; XII.766; XXI.2, 5–10. The edition cited is that of K. Preisendanz, *Papyri Graecae Magicae. Die griechischen Zauberpapyri*, 2 vols., rev. ed. by A. Henrichs (Stuttgart: Teubner, 1973, 1974); Eng. trans., see H. D. Betz, ed., *The Greek Magical Papyri in Translation, Including the Demotic Spells* (Chicago and London: University of Chicago Press, [forthcoming]). On the background of these texts, see J. Assmann, "Primat und Transzendenz: Struktur und Genese der ägyptischen Vorstellung eines höchsten Wesens," in *Aspekte der ägyptischen Religion*, ed. W. Westendorf, *Göttinger Orientforschungen*, 4th series (Wiesbaden: Harrassowitz, 1979), vol. 9, 7–42.

102. Cf. on this point, Philo, *De sacr.* 34: "For this cause and because, as I said before, things holy in virtue and of their essential goodness cannot but through their nature have speech for us, though we pass them by in silence, I say no more about them. For neither do sun and moon need an interpreter, because their rising by day or by night fills the whole world with light. Their shining is a proof that needs no further witness, established by the evidence of the eyes, an evidence clearer than the ears can give." Eng. trans. by F. H. Colson and G. H. Whitaker in the LCL ed. (Cambridge: Harvard University Press; London: William Heinemann, 1929), vol. II, 121.

nature. The SM takes the world seriously. The Beatitudes impress us from the very beginning with its daily troubles: poverty, sorrow, brutality, injustice, unmercifulness, impurity of heart, war, persecution of the righteous, repression of the community of Jesus, and at last martyrdom. In contrast with this stands the double-parable of the builders who built their houses—the first upon rock, the second upon sand—at the end of the SM (Matt. 7:24–27). The images of torrential rain, flood, and storm are traditional and symbolize the turbulent and unforeseeable powers of nature and history. But above all, what makes the world so dangerous is human folly and sin. On the other hand, it is to be attributed to the fatherhood of God that the world endures despite evil, and that there is always a possibility for conversion and repentance. Thanks to the fatherhood of God, the prudent have a chance for survival (7:25).

The heavenly Father treats Jesus' disciples as his own sons (and daughters)[103] and they in turn understand themselves as sons (and daughters) of God.[104] Like all children, the disciples of Jesus must mature. To provide the necessary guidance in this respect is the task and aim of the SM. It teaches them to imitate their heavenly Father in daily life, that is, to live in such manner as befits children of God.[105]

In this doctrine, the central concept of the newly won faith in providence is attained. Accordingly, faith in providence can no longer be maintained in its traditional form, but only in a reconstituted

103. Notably, the SM is addressed to male disciples ("sons") only. One wonders why women seem to be excluded, since we know that Jesus had women among his disciples.

104. On the title "sons of God," see Matt. 5:9, 45; 7:9–11. The title is, of course, traditional in Judaism. See P. Wülfing von Martitz, "$\upsilon i \acute{o}\varsigma$," *TDNT* 8 (1969; Eng. trans. 1972), esp. sections B.5.c; C.I.1.c; II.3; D.IV.1–2. Cf. also Epictetus, *Diss.* 1.9.4–6, a passage based on Poseidonius: "Well, then, anyone who has attentively studied the administration of the universe and has learned that 'the greatest and most authoritative and most comprehensive of all governments is this one, which is composed of men and God, and that from Him have descended the seeds of being, not merely to my father or to my grandfather, but to all things that are begotten and that grow upon earth, and chiefly to rational beings, seeing that by nature it is theirs alone to have communion in the society of God, being intertwined with him through the reason'—why should not such a man call himself a citizen of the universe? Why should he not call himself a son of God?" Eng. trans. by W. A. Oldfather in the LCL ed. (Cambridge: Harvard University Press; London: William Heinemann, 1961). For the background and history of the concept, see also C. Colpe, "Gottessohn," *RAC* 12 (1981): 19–58.

105. Matt. 5:45, 48.

manner. This newly established faith in providence is rooted in a special relationship to God. Those who belong to the community of the SM come to understand themselves as "sons (and daughters) of the heavenly Father." Since the heavenly Father regards them as his offspring and treats them as such, they act as sons (and daughters) of God on earth.

Thus the ethics of the SM is at home in the context of Jewish piety and theology. Like all Jewish ethics, it is an ethic of obedience to the Torah. But this ethics maintains throughout its own very distinct characteristics. This is above all the case with respect to the connection between ethics and the notion of the *creatio continua* of God, understood as Father of the cosmos. To seek the kingdom and righteousness of God is the duty of God's children, and this is accomplished by imitating the daily experience of God's kingdom. Thus for the SM, ethics is not based upon speculative cosmology, as in Greek philosophy, or on creation myths, like that of Genesis, or on certain prescribed rituals. All these options are implicitly rejected by the SM. Ethical behavior consists, on the contrary, in learning the way and manner in which God loves and preserves his creation. Therein one must seek the righteousness of God, who day by day makes his sun to rise upon the evil and the good, and sends rain on the just and the unjust.

7

An Episode in the
Last Judgment (Matt. 7:21-23)

The passage Matt. 7:21-23 is important in more than one respect for an understanding of the Sermon on the Mount. The following investigation aims at winning further insight into the literary origin and the ideological context of the Christology and eschatology of the SM. Finally, these observations should help to demonstrate, through the weight of cumulative evidence, the pre-Matthean origin of the SM.[1]

I. LITERARY COMPOSITION

This clearly marked-off section begins with a sentence that, from a formal point of view, belongs to two categories of sayings at the same time, the so-called sentence of holy law[2] and the saying regarding entrance into the kingdom of God[3] (v. 21): "Not everyone who says to me, 'Lord, Lord,' shall enter into the kingdom of heaven, but he who

1. The present essay supplements earlier works, all now in this volume: H. D. Betz, "Eine judenchristliche Kult-Didache in Matthäus 6:1–18" in *Jesus Christus in Historie und Theologie, Festschrift für H. Conzelmann* (1975), 445–57; idem, "Die Makarismen der Bergpredigt (Matthäus 5,3–12). Beobachtungen zur literarischen Form und theologischen Bedeutung," *ZThK* 75 (1978): 3–19; idem, "Matthew VI.22f and Ancient Greek Theories of Vision," in *Text and Interpretation: Studies in the New Testament Presented to M. Black* (Cambridge: At the University Press, 1978), 43–56; idem, "The Sermon on the Mount (Matt. 5:3–7:27): Its Literary Genre and Function," *JR* 59 (1979): 285–97.

2. On these sayings see E. Käsemann, "Sentences of Holy Law in the New Testament" in *New Testament Questions of Today* (Philadelphia: Fortress Press, 1969), 66–81. Käsemann does not deal with Matt. 7:21, but with analogous sayings in Rom. 10:11, 13 (p. 76).

3. Cf. H. Windisch, "Die Sprüche vom Eingehen in das Reich Gottes," *ZNW* 27 (1928): 163–92; J. Schneider, *TDNT* 2, 676–78; H.-Th. Wrege, *Die Überlieferungsgeschichte der Bergpredigt* (Tübingen: J. C. B. Mohr [Paul Siebeck], 1968), 147.

does the will of my Father who is in heaven" (Οὐ πᾶς ὁ λέγων μοι· κύριε, κύριε, εἰσελεύσεται εἰς τὴν βασιλείαν τῶν οὐρανῶν, ἀλλ᾽ ὁ ποιῶν τὸ θέλημα τοῦ πατρός μου τοῦ ἐν τοῖς οὐρανοῖς).

Yet on closer examination it is clear that while the above-mentioned types of sayings are regarded as literary and employed as such, they have been reworked into a new maxim that corresponds to neither of these types of sayings in a real sense. The first part of the sentence (v. 21a) appears to be formulated as a sentence of holy law, but as indicated by the negative οὐ prefixed to the phrase, the maxim thus created is to be regarded as false and therefore rejected. Of course a saying of Jesus can never have been transmitted seriously which read: "Whoever says to me, 'Lord, Lord,' shall enter into the kingdom of heaven." Like the false Jesus-saying in Matt. 5:17,[4] this saying can only have been formulated artificially, in imitation of the form, and for the sole purpose of being rejected. As v. 22 shows, this formulation, which is supplemented and replaced by the second part of the sentence (v. 21b), results from satirical-paraenetic intent. This second part is formulated elliptically,[5] contrasted positively with the preceding negative clause (ἀλλά); it is completely in keeping with the theology of the SM. The positive maxim must therefore have run: "Whoever does the will of my Father who is in heaven shall enter into the kingdom of heaven."

But what, then, is so objectionable, one asks oneself, about the first part of the sentence? The answer to this question is provided by vv. 22–23: mere speech (λέγειν) cannot replace the doing (ποιεῖν) of God's will, even if what is involved in such speaking is the acclamation of Jesus as *kyrios*. The mere acclamation of Jesus as *kyrios*, as programmatically set forth here, does not suffice as a condition for admission into the kingdom of God.[6] Thus the maxim in v. 21 summarizes the result of vv. 22–23.

---

4. On this verse, see "The Beatitudes of the Sermon on the Mount (Matt. 5:3–12)," in this volume, 39–43.

5. There seems to be little possibility of misunderstanding, but several manuscripts felt it necessary to make a small addition for the sake of clarification: αὐτὸς (οὗτος C² 33 pc) εἰσελεύσεται εἰς τὴν βασιλείαν τῶν οὐρανῶν C² W θ 33. 1241 pc lat syᶜ; Cyprian, Theodoretus. Thus according to Nestle-Aland, 26th ed. (Stuttgart: Deutsche Bibelstiftung, 1981).

6. Cf. Rom. 10:9; Phil. 2:11; 1 Cor. 12:3; 2 Cor. 4:5; further, Rom. 10:11, 13; Acts 2:21; 7:59; 9:14, 21; 22:16; 1 Cor. 1:2; 2 Tim. 2:22. On Kyrios-acclamations see

The episode in vv. 22–23 depicts in briefest scope proceedings at the last judgment, indicated by the familiar phrase "on that day" (ἐν ἐκείνῃ τῇ ἡμέρα, v. 22a).[7] To understand this episode, one must recall what the narrator could assume to have been known to his reader or hearer. That is to say, it is not only assumed that the reader or hearer is familiar with the theme of the last judgment in a general sense, but that he or she also knows the course of events in detail, so that the story can be restricted to the most important scenes.[8]

It is regarded as common knowledge that in the last judgment God will sit upon the judgment seat and humankind will appear before him in groups[9] to hear his verdict. One of these groups is brought into sharper focus, a large group of people (πολλοί)[10] who seek entrance into the kingdom of God by appealing to the name of Jesus. Jesus, who speaks in the first person in the text and who paints the picture of the last judgment, is himself on hand at the proceedings. But his function in the judgment scene must be indirectly inferred from the text. It is further assumed that the proceedings have already reached an advanced stage. That is, the nature of the statements made by the group in v. 22b makes it necessary for us to assume that two events have already taken place. In terms of the story, the condemnation must already have been pronounced over the group, and the appeal, which will then have been made, must already have been rejected.[11] For what the group submits in v. 22b is a frightened appeal, indeed a protest against the words of condemnation already pronounced by Jesus, and thus an attempt to call into question the verdict which has been passed:

K. Wengst, *Christologische Formeln und Lieder des Urchristentums* (Gütersloh: Gerd Mohn, 1972), 131ff.; H. Conzelmann, *Theologie als Schriftauslegung* (Munich: Chr. Kaiser, 1974), 109–10, 112–13; P. Vielhauer, *Geschichte der urchristlichen Literatur* (New York and Berlin: Walter De Gruyter, 1975), 13–14, 23ff.

7. On this eschatological concept see P. Volz, *Die Eschatologie der jüdischen Gemeinde im neutestamentlichen Zeitalter* (Tübingen: J. C. B. Mohr [Paul Siebeck], 1934), 163ff.; G. Delling, *TDNT* 2, 948–53; Bauer, *Lexicon*, s.v. "ἡμέρα," 3, b, β.

8. On this point see Volz, *Die Eschatologie*, 272ff.

9. On this concept, see below, 135–36.

10. While πολλοί in 7:13 designates the masses of humankind on their way to destruction, the πολλοί of 7:22 are the majority of Gentile Christians, in comparison with whom the Christians of the SM feel themselves to be in the minority (cf. 7:14: οἱ ὀλίγοι).

11. On the repeated rejection, see below, 148–49.

Many will say to me in that day,
"Lord, Lord!
Did we not prophesy in your name,
and in your name cast out demons,
and in your name perform many miracles?"
πολλοὶ ἐροῦσίν μοι ἐν ἐκείνῃ τῇ ἡμέρᾳ·
κύριε, κύριε,
οὐ τῷ σῷ ὀνόματι ἐπροφητεύσαμεν,
καὶ τῷ σῷ ὀνόματι δαιμόνια ἐξεβάλομεν,
καὶ τῷ σῷ ὀνόματι δυνάμεις πολλὰς ἐποιήσαμεν;

Now it is remarkable that the group does not, as one would expect, turn to the judge—that is, to God himself—with an appeal for mercy, but to Jesus as the advocate whom they clearly believe to be responsible for their case. But Jesus refuses to represent the group or to speak on its behalf:

And then I will declare to them:
I never knew you;
depart from me, you who work iniquity.
καὶ τότε ὁμολογήσω αὐτοῖς ὅτι
οὐδέποτε ἔγνων ὑμᾶς·
ἀποχωρεῖτε ἀπ᾽ ἐμοῦ οἱ ἐργαζόμενοι τὴν ἀνομίαν.

This statement (ὁμολογεῖν), which is made in a very official manner,[12] can only be understood as the emphatic confirmation of a rejection which has already been expressed. The three questions introduced by the phrase "Have we not in your name . . . ?" only make sense if they are brought forward as objections against an initial rejection by Jesus. The protest seeks to demonstrate by a kind of proof of their qualifications and legitimacy[13] that Jesus is obligated to defend the group, and moreover, in keeping with their implicit plea of not guilty,[14] to seek to overturn the verdict. But by reiterating his

12. On the forensic meaning of ὁμολογέω, see O. Michel, *TDNT* 5, 201–2, 207ff.; Wengst, *Christologische Formeln,* 107ff.
13. In Pauline terms it is a matter of illegitimate καυχᾶσθαι. On this point, see R. Bultmann, *TDNT* 3, 645ff.; H. D. Betz, *Der Apostel Paulus und die sokratische Tradition* (Tübingen: J. C. B. Mohr [Paul Siebeck], 1972), 73; idem, *Plutarch's Ethical Writings and Early Christian Literature* (Leiden: E. J. Brill, 1978), 381ff.; idem, *Galatians* (Philadelphia: Fortress Press, 1979), 317ff.
14. Protestations of innocence before the divine tribunal have a long literary history, at the beginning of which stands the 125th chapter of the Egyptian *Book of the Dead.* Here the dead person enters a judgment hall where Osiris holds court,

rejection of the group, Jesus makes clear that their protest rests upon a total misunderstanding and thus misses the mark. Consequently, Jesus' statement in v. 23 contains two points.[15] First, he declares that he is not responsible for the group: "I never knew you." This formulaic statement rests upon the legal principle that one ought not appear in court as advocate, bailsman, or witness for one who is a total stranger.[16] Then Jesus utters a repudiation of the group in the words of Ps. 6:8:[17] "Depart from me, you who work iniquity."[18] Within the context of the story, this "lawlessness" or "iniquity" must have been the cause of the verdict that has already been delivered. In keeping with literary parallels[19] yet to be discussed, the group has been questioned in the preceding episode about their obedience to

---

surrounded by forty-two judges of the dead, representing the districts of the land. Before entering the hall, the dead person makes a deposition in which he or she enumerates his or her deeds in a long list in a positive sense, and protests negatively his or her innocence; see the critical edition by T. G. Allen, *The Book of the Dead* (Chicago and London: University of Chicago Press, 1974), 97–98, and C. Maystre, *Les déclarations d'innocence (Livre des morts, chapître 125)* (Cairo: Institut français d'archéologie orientale, 1937). One also encounters in this context the notion of the substitute (*uschebti*); see S. Morenz, *Religion und Geschichte des alten Ägypten* (Cologne and Vienna: Böhlau, 1975), 198ff. Protestations of innocence are also found in Egyptian priestly oaths; see R. Merkelbach, "Der Eid der Isismysten," *ZPE* 1 (1967): 55–73; idem, "Ein ägyptischer Priestereid," *ZPE* 2 (1968): 7–30; L. Koenen, "Die Unschuldsbeteuerungen des Priestereides und die römische Elegie," *ZPE* 2 (1968): 31–38. Literary connections are also to be found within the Old Testament, for example, in Job 31 and in several of the Psalms (5; 7; 17; 26); see P. Humbert, *Recherches sur les sources égyptiennes de la littérature sapientale d'Israël* (Neuchâtel: Secrétariat de l'Université, 1924), 91ff.; cf. C. Westermann, "Unschuld" in *BHH* 3 (1966): 2054–55.

15. Appealing to Billerbeck, vol. 1, 469, the formula is often designated a "synagogal excommunication formula" (*"synagogale Bannformel"*); see W. Doskocil, *Der Bann in der Urkirche* (Munich: Zink, 1958), 28–29; O. Michel, *TDNT* 5, 207; Wrege, *Die Überlieferungsgeschichte*, 149 n. 3. But this designation is highly misleading. Rather we have to do with two formulas, a renunciation formula and an expulsion formula, which appear in early Christian literature together (Matt. 7:️; Luke 13:27; 2 *Clem.* 4:5), or separately (renunciation formula alone: Matt. 25:12; Luke 13:25; expulsion formula alone: Justin, *Apol.* I, 16, 11; idem, *Dial.* 76,5; cf. also 2 *Clem.* 4:5 [see below, 145]).

16. Cf. the formula in the passion narrative in Mark 14:71 par., as well as 2 Cor. 5:16.

17. Cf. also Pss. 119:115; 139:19; Job 21:14; 22:17.

18. On the expulsion formula, cf. Matt. 4:10; Mark 8:33//Matt. 16:23; 2 *Clem.* 4:5; Luke 10:16; 1 Cor. 1:19; 9:27; Rom. 11:1ff.; Clemens Alex., *Strom.* 3, 18, p. 246, 31: ἀποκηρύκτους εἶναι τῆς βασιλείας τοῦ θεοῦ ("cut off from the kingdom of God").

19. See below, 135–36.

the Torah. Because they had nothing of the kind to produce, they were condemned.[20] In this case, not doing "the will of the Father who is in heaven" is the same as practicing lawlessness.[21]

The foregoing overview of the literary structure of vv. 21–23 may be taken to have demonstrated the unity of the pericope.[22] It consists of two parts, neither of which could have had independent existence: the depiction of an episode in the last judgment (vv. 22–23) and a statement summarizing the results of the episode (v. 21). Thus the analysis of the passage may be presented as follows:

vv. 21–23   A warning against self-deception[23]

v. 21   I. A sentence of holy law in the form of a statement of the condition for admission into the kingdom of God

v. 21a   A. Negative: rejection of a satirically formulated, false definition

     1. Pointed negation, preceded by οὐ

     2. False definition

       a. Description of the required conduct

         (1) Action: "speaking" (λέγειν)

         (2) Nature of the action: the *kyrios*-acclamation, twice-repeated[24]

       b. Promise

---

20. Cf. Matt. 25:41, 46; Justin, *Dial.* 76, 5; further Gal. 1:8–9 and Betz, *Galatians,* 50ff.

21. Matt. 7:21.

22. Unfortunately, R. Bultmann confounded the question of the "originality," the source question, and the composition with one another in his discussion of the pericope in his *History of the Synoptic Tradition,* 2d ed. (New York: Harper & Row, 1968), 116–17. Cf. also the *Ergänzungsheft,* 4th ed. (Göttingen: Vandenhoeck & Ruprecht, 1971), 44; W. L. Knox, *The Sources of the Synoptic Gospels,* vol. II (Cambridge: At the University Press, 1957), 32; Wrege, *Die Überlieferungsgeschichte,* 149; differently, E. Klostermann, *Das Matthäusevangelium,* 4th ed. (Tübingen: J. C. B. Mohr [Paul Siebeck], 1971), 70–71; S. Schulz, *Q* (Zurich: Theologischer Verlag, 1972), 424ff.

23. See on this point below, 154ff.

24. The double acclamation "Lord, Lord" (κύριε, κύριε) is often falsely designated as a Semitic characteristic, though it corresponds to the common rhetorical figure of *geminatio.* Cf. H. Lausberg, *Elemente der literarischen Rhetorik,* 3d ed. (Munich: Hueber, 1976), §§244–49; J. Martin, *Antike Rhetorik: Technik und Methode* (Munich: Beck, 1974), 301–2; BDR, §491, 1. F. Hahn, *Christologische Hoheitstitel. Ihre Geschichte im frühen Christentum* (Göttingen: Vandenhoeck & Ruprecht,

v. 21b   B. Positive: presentation of the proper definition (elliptically)
         1. Adversative particle: ἀλλά
         2. Proper definition
             a. Description of the required conduct
                 (1) Action: "doing" (ποιεῖν)
                 (2) Nature of the action
             [b. Promise: to be inferred from v. 21a]

vv. 22–23   II. Preview of a scene in the last judgment

v. 22a   A. General description of the situation
         1. The persons involved
             a. Jesus as the attorney
             b. A large group of clients
         2. Time

v. 22b   B. The scene in sharper focus: the decisive episode in the course of the trial
         1. Protest of the clients against their prior rejection by Jesus
             a. Address to Jesus: *kyrios*-acclamation, twice-repeated
             b. Presentation of proof of legitimacy on three grounds in the form of a question
                 (1) Prophetic discourse in the name of Jesus
                 (2) Exorcisms in the name of Jesus
                 (3) Miracles in the name of Jesus

v. 23   2. Statement of the attorney: repeated and final rejection

v. 23a   a. Time
             b. Nature of the statement: ὁμολογεῖν

vv. 23b–c   c. Recitation of legal formulas
                 (1) Indication of citation: ὅτι

v. 23b   (2) Formula of renunciation

v. 23c   (3) Formula of repudiation (Ps. 6:8)

1963), 96, referring to W. Foerster, *TDNT* 3, 1086, argues for a "typically Semitic character"; cf. also G. Dalman, *Die Worte Jesu*, 3d ed. (Leipzig: Hinrichs, 1930), 168, 186, 353. See also John 13:13; Matt. 23:8, 10.

II. THE PROBLEM OF THE SOURCES

The question of the probable sources of the pericope at once raises difficult methodological problems. A glance at the synopsis shows that Luke 6:46 must be considered as a possible source: "Why do you call me, 'Lord, Lord!' but do not the things that I say?" Though many exegetes are inclined to see the source of Matt. 7:21–23 in Luke 6:46,[25] the literary support for such dependency is completely wanting. Even if the redactor of the SM knew the saying in Luke 6:46, it would still be necessary to explain how the literary transformation of a simple rhetorical question into a far more complicated narrative took place. Luke 6:46 is part of the so-called Sermon on the Plain in Luke 6:20b–49, a section which has much in common with the SM, but which is also very different from it. The literary relationship between the Sermon on the Plain and the SM in general is still completely unsettled,[26] so that the hypothesis of literary dependency cannot be established. It is true that Luke 6:46 stands near the end of the Sermon on the Plain, at approximately the same place occupied by Matt. 7:21–23 in the SM. But what does this really mean in view of the major differences in form and content between the two texts?[27] The origin of the rhetorical question in Luke 6:46 is obscure, even if one assumes, with Bultmann, that the saying derives from the historical Jesus.[28] Of course, even this derivation cannot be proven. The saying does not make reference to the last judgment, but presupposes a simple teacher-student relationship. The address, "Lord, Lord!" is not found in a cultic-eschatological context, as in Matt. 7:21–23,[29] but

---

25. Thus W. Bousset, *Kyrios Christos*, Eng. trans. J. Steely (Nashville: Abingdon Press, 1970); Bultmann, *History*, 120–21; Klostermann, *Das Matthäusevangelium*, 70–71.

26. Thus also Hahn, *Christologische Hoheitstitel*, 97; Wrege, *Die Überlieferungsgeschichte*, 147.

27. Cf. Wrege, *Die Überlieferungsgeschichte*, 147: "Although Matthew's interest in the judgment-paraenesis is prominent, one cannot designate 7:21 any longer as a Matthaean form of a source such as Luke 6:46; for what is claimed for Matthew as redactor may already be said here of the tradition. A common written source for Matt. 7:21//Luke 6:46 must be excluded in accordance with observations on the tradition-history of the preceding tree-fruit material."

28. Bultmann, *History*, 122–23, 135, 163.

29. Bousset's observation is certainly correct (*Kyrios Christos*, 90–91), as over

represents the students' respectful address to their teacher.[30] By repeating the address, Jesus seems to make fun of the conduct of his disciples. He points to the contrast between the disciples' submissiveness, manifest in their polite address, and their failure to carry out his teaching. What is condemned is the contradiction between formal gestures of loyalty and inner faithlessness, a contradiction upon which their whole discipleship founders.

There is no straight path which leads from the saying in Luke 6:46 to Matt. 7:23. Even if Luke 6:46 is taken as the point of departure for Matt. 7:21–23, other factors must be called on to account for the literary creation, and the entire concept of the source must be understood in a wider sense.

First one must call attention to the literary originality of the SM, which is not only evident here but throughout. Clearly the redactor did not shrink from presenting his own understanding of the course of events in the last judgment in the name of Jesus. In fact, Matt. 7:21–23 presents us with a greatly abbreviated but complete picture of the judgment. The episode which is of decisive importance to the redactor of the SM is narrated so masterfully that the reader or hearer can supply the episodes which have preceded and followed from his or her own imagination, and thus obtain a general idea of the entire scene. Thus the reader or hearer enters into the events of the tale and becomes, unaware, a conarrator who is naturally led to take sides against those rejected by Jesus. What is demonstrated in this story to the reader and hearer is the justice of Jesus and the righteousness of God.

Of course, one must add immediately that the literary originality of the SM is nourished by sources of a special kind. To judge from the extant witnesses, the depiction of eschatological judgment scenes constituted a literary genre in its own right. In regard to Matt. 7:21–23, the branch of this genre found in the Jewish tradition is of primary

---

against Bultmann, *History*, 116 n. 2, that Matt. 7:21 is "already stylized in comparison with the simple Lukan saying in 6:46 in respect to the Christian cult and the liturgy." Cf. also 133 n. 50 in regard to 1 Cor. 12:1–3.

30. Thus with Bultmann, *History*, 116 n. 2; Hahn, *Christologische Hoheitstitel*, 97–98.

importance.[31] But there are also connections[32] to the rich Egyptian[33] and Greek[34] traditions. The Jewish stream of tradition of such eschatological judgment scenes is widely branched and saturated with interpolations and allusions. Thus if the most extensive stories are of a relatively late date, one may still assume that the genre itself is older and that only part of the previously extant literature has been preserved. Naturally, Matt. 7:21–23 is in no way dependent on this later literature, but must be seen and interpreted in the context of earlier expressions of this narrative tradition. But at the same time, the later texts give some indication of what was typical, and thus serve to illuminate Matt. 7:21–23.

Here we shall take as our example the greatly elaborated story from *b. Abodah Zarah*.[35] The Gemara is attributed by some to R. Ḥanina b. Papa (Palestine, c. 300), by others to R. Šimlai (Palestine, c. 250). If this information is correct it provides evidence, nevertheless, for no more than a particular form of the material, but not for the beginning of the tradition itself. The story in question deals with the theme of God's judgment of the nations, and in particular with the evidence submitted by the various peoples in their own defense. The reason for

31. On the Jewish material see Billerbeck, vol. 4, part 2, excursus 33: "Judgment-scenes from ancient Jewish Literature" (1199–1212); Volz, *Die Eschatologie*, 89ff., 272ff.; G. W. E. Nickelsburg, *Resurrection, Immortality, and Eternal Life in Intertestamental Judaism*, HTS 26 (Cambridge: Harvard University Press, 1972); H. C. C. Cavallin, *Life After Death* I, CB.NT 7.1 (Lund, 1974); G. W. E. Nickelsburg, ed., *Studies on the Testament of Abraham*, SCSt 6 (Missoula, Mont.: Scholars Press, 1976); J. J. Collins, ed., *Apocalypse: The Morphology of a Genre*, Semeia 14 (Missoula, Mont.: Scholars Press, 1979).
32. Cf. A. Dieterich, *Nekyia*, 3d. ed. (Darmstadt: Wissenschaftliche Buchgesellschaft, 1969), passim; E. Wüst, "Die Seelenwägung in Ägypten und Griechenland," *ARW* 36 (1939): 162–71; G. W. Macurdy, "Platonic Orphism in the Testament of Abraham," *JBL* 61 (1942): 213–26; cf. also Nickelsburg, *Studies*, 27ff. with further literature.
33. On the Egyptian material see in addition to n. 14 above: H. Kees, *Totenglauben und Jenseitsvorstellungen der Alten Ägypter*, 3d ed. (Berlin: Akademie-Verlag, 1975); R. Grieshammer, *Das Jenseitsgericht in den Sargtexten* (Wiesbaden: Harassowitz, 1970); Morenz, *Religion und Geschichte*, 173ff.
34. On this Greek material see L. Ruhl, *De mortuorum iudicio*, RVV 2/2 (Giessen: Töpelmann, 1903); R. Ganszyniec, "Katabasis," *PRE* 20 (1919): 2359–2449, 2413ff.; E. Norden, *P. Vergilius Maro Aeneis Buch VI*, 3d ed. (Leipzig: Teubner, 1926), 3ff.; H. D. Betz, *Lukian von Samosata und das Neue Testament* (Berlin: Akademie-Verlag, 1961), 81ff.; W. Burkert, *Griechische Religion der archaischen und klassischen Epoche* (Stuttgart: Kohlhammer, 1977), 436ff.
35. Cited according to the translation of I. Epstein, *The Babylonian Talmud. Seder Nezikin* (London: Soncino Press, 1935), 2ff.

the inclusion of this material in the Gemara was obviously the word "witnesses," for the Gemara proceeds to discuss whether אֵידֵיהֶן or עִידֵיהֶן is to be read in the phrase from Mishnah "before the feasts." The problem goes back to oral tradition, in which both terms circulated. With the help of Scripture, the attempt is made to account for the variant readings. Isa. 43:9 is appealed to in support of עִידֵיהֶן: "Let them bring their witnesses (עֵדֵיהֶם) to justify them." In accordance with Rabbinic conception, this passage refers to the last judgment. Thus the point of contact of the material in the story is given. It is clear that the Gemara reaches back into oral tradition[36] and subsequently appeals to already existing material: "In times to come, the Holy One, blessed be He, will take a scroll of the law in His embrace and proclaim: 'Let him who has occupied himself herewith come and take his reward'."[37]

Then the nations of the world assemble themselves before the throne of God in accordance with Isa. 43:9. But first God must bring order into chaos and confusion: "'Come not before Me in confusion, but let each nation come in with its scribes'; as it is said, *and let the peoples be gathered together;* and the word *le'om* [used here] means a kingdom, as it is written, *and one kingdom* [*u-leom*] shall be stronger than the other kingdom."[38] The great assembly begins with the Romans because they are superior to all the other nations, as evidenced by scriptural citations and the sayings of famous rabbis. Then the text returns to the story:

The Holy One, blessed be He, will then say to them: "Wherewith have you occupied yourselves?" They will reply: "O Lord of the Universe, we have established many market-places, we have erected many baths, we have accumulated much gold and silver, and all this we did only for the sake of Israel, that they might [have leisure] for occupying themselves with the study of the Torah." The Holy One, blessed be He, will say in reply: "You foolish ones among peoples, all that which you have done,

36. Thus L. Goldschmidt, *Der Babylonische Talmud* (Berlin: Jüdischer Verlag, 1967), vol. IX, 433 n. 3.
37. Epstein, *Babylonian Talmud,* 2.
38. Ibid.; the scriptural passages are Isa. 43:9; Gen. 25:33—The concept has an interesting parallel in Greek myths of the afterlife. According to Plato, *Gorgias* 523A–524A, Rhadamanthys shall judge the Asiatics and Aiakos the Europeans, while Minos decides the issue when the votes are evenly split. For the reference I thank Jan Bergman.

you have only done to satisfy your own desires. You have established market-places to place courtesans therein; baths, to revel in them; [as to the distribution of] silver and gold, that is mine, as it is written: *Mine is the silver and mine is the gold, saith the Lord of Hosts;* are there any among you who have been declaring *this?*" And *"this"* is nought else than the Torah, as it is said: *And* this *is the Law which Moses set before the children of* Israel. They will then depart crushed in spirit.[39]

After the Romans have withdrawn, the Persian kingdom enters. Its status and character are again determined by the citation and interpretation of Scripture. The Persians receive the same treatment as the Romans:

> The Holy One, blessed be He, will ask of them: "Wherewith have ye occupied yourselves?"; and they will reply, "Sovereign of the Universe, we have built many bridges, we have captured many cities, we have waged many wars, and all this for the sake of Israel, that they might engage in the study of Torah." Then the Holy One, blessed be He, will say to them: "You foolish ones among peoples, you have built bridges in order to extract toll, you have subdued cities, so as to impose forced labor; as to waging war, *I* am the Lord of battles, as it is said: *The Lord is a man of war;* are there any amongst you who have been declaring *this?*" And *"this"* means nought else than the Torah, as it is said: *And* this *is the* law *which Moses set before the Children of Israel.* They, too, will then depart crushed in spirit.[40]

Before the text turns to the next nation, there is a passage to explain why the Persian nation comes forward at all when they have seen how it went with the Romans, and to explain, in addition, why only the Romans and the Persians appear:

> But why should the Persians, having seen that the Romans achieved nought, step forward at all? They will say to themselves: "The Romans have destroyed the Temple, whereas we have built it." And so will every nation fare in turn. But why should the other nations come forth,seeing that those who preceded them had achieved nought. They will say to themselves: "The others have oppressed Israel, but we have not." And why are these [two] nations singled out as important, and not the others? Because their reign will last till the coming of the Messiah.[41]

---

39. Epstein, *Babylonian Talmud,* 39; the scriptural passages are Hag. 2:8; Deut. 4:44.
40. Ibid., 3–4; the scriptural passages are Exod. 15:3; Isa. 43:9.
41. Ibid., 4.

In what follows, the text passes abruptly to another scene in which the heathen nations offer resistance against God's rejection of them and present arguments in their defense: "The nations will then contend: 'Lord of the Universe, hast Thou given us the Torah, and have we declined to accept it?'"[42] The answer that is expected is that God has not given the Torah to the nations and that they could not, therefore, reject it. Since no one must submit to a law to which he or she is not bound, God's condemnation of them is shown to be unjust. Apologetic interpolations then attempt to prove the opposite from Scripture in order to safeguard the righteousness of God. Then the text proceeds: "Their contention will be this: 'Did we accept it and fail to observe it?' But surely the obvious rejoinder to their plea would be: 'Then why did you not accept it?'"[43] The argument presupposes what has preceded: even if God had offered the Gentiles the Torah, they would not have accepted it, and thus they are not obliged to keep it. But the conclusion is false, because God's offer ought not to have been refused! A lawless person does not go unpunished because he or she refuses to accept the obligation of the law. "This, then, will be their contention: 'Lord of the Universe, didst Thou suspend the mountain over us like a vault as Thou hast done unto Israel and did we still decline to accept it?'"[44]

This argument presupposes a tradition which is traced back to a certain R. Dimi b. Ḥama (or R. Abdeni b. Ḥama b. Ḥasa).[45] According to this tradition, God had to force the people of Israel to accept the Torah. This tradition is confirmed by interpretation of Exod. 19:17—*and they took their stand at the foot of the mountain.* The interpretation explains what is meant by the expression "at the foot of": "This teaches us that the Holy One, blessed be He, suspended the mountain over Israel like a vault, and said unto them: 'If ye accept the Torah, it will be well with you, but if not, there will ye find your grave'."[46]

If therefore God compelled Israel to accept the Torah, but employed no force in dealing with the Gentiles, this shows a certain

---

42. Ibid.
43. Ibid., 4–5.
44. Ibid., 5.
45. Thus according to J. Jeremias and K. Adolph in Billerbeck, vol. 6 (2d ed., 1963), 148 n. 1.
46. Epstein, *Babylonian Talmud*, 5.

partiality on the part of God toward Israel. This can be no grounds for the condemnation of the Gentiles. Again God's integrity seems to be called into question. Surprisingly, God enters into the dispute and brings forward a piece of evidence from history: "Thereupon the Holy One, blessed be He, will say to them: 'Let us then consider the happenings of old,' as it is said, *Let them announce to us former things:* 'there are seven commandments which you did accept, did you observe them?'"[47] In other words: the argument offered by the Gentiles in their defense does not succeed, because they have accepted, as God reminds them, the seven commandments of the Noachic covenant, but have failed to keep them. How much less would they have observed the entire law! But first of all the question is whence we know that the Gentiles have not observed the seven Noachic commandments. The answer is supplied by R. Joseph through the interpretation of Hab. 3:6: *He stood and measured the earth; he looked and shook the nations:* "What did He see? He saw that the nations did not observe even the seven precepts which the sons of Noah had taken upon themselves, and seeing that they did not observe them, He stood up and released them therefrom."[48]

Secondary interpolation at this point seeks to negate the obvious conclusion: "Then they benefited by it; according to this it pays to be a sinner!"[49] In addition, some decision must be reached in the case of an individual non-Jew who keeps the law after the Gentiles are released from the Noachic covenant. Can such a one receive his or her reward? The opinion of the rabbis is divided; but the final decision is negative:

> Said Mar the son of Rabina: "The release from these commands only means that even if they observed them they would not be rewarded." But why should they not? Is it not taught: R. Meir used to say, "Whence do we know that even an idolator who studies the Torah is equal to a High Priest?" From the following verse: *Ye shall therefore keep my statutes and my ordinances which, if a man do, he shall live by them.* It does not say "If a Priest, Levite, or Israelite do, he shall live by them," but "a man"; here, then, you can learn that even a heathen who studies the Torah is equal to

47. Ibid., 5; Isa. 43:9 is cited.
48. Ibid.
49. Ibid.; cf. Paul's argument in Rom. 3:5-8; 6:1-2.

a High Priest! What is meant, then, is that they are rewarded not as greatly as one who does a thing which he is bidden to do, but as one who does a thing unbidden. For, R. Ḥanina said: "He who is commanded and does stands higher than he who is not commanded and does."[50]

At the conclusion of this discussion, the text returns to the narrative: "The nations will then say, 'Sovereign of the Universe, has Israel, who accepted the Torah, observed it?'"[51] Thus the Gentile nations offer as new grounds for their exoneration the fact that the people of Israel have, indeed, accepted the Torah, but have not observed it. This fact is so obvious that God must admit it; the conclusion cannot be avoided that the Israelites are no better than the Gentiles.[52] "The Holy One, blessed be He, will reply, 'I can give evidence that they observe the Torah'."[53] But such a biased character witness cannot be accepted as evidence by the court: "'O Lord of the Universe,' they will argue, 'can a father give evidence in favor of his son? For it is written, *Israel is My son, My firstborn'*."[54] God appears to be getting himself deeper and deeper into trouble and seeks a new way out. But this expedient as well is rejected as legally invalid. "Then will the Holy One, blessed be He, say: 'Heaven and Earth can bear witness that Israel has fulfilled the entire Torah.' But they will [object], saying: 'Lord of the Universe, Heaven and Earth are partial witnesses, for it is said. . . .'"[55]

After the partiality of heaven and earth is proven by the citation of Scripture and Rabbinic interpretation, God produces a new group of witnesses from the Gentile world itself:

Then the Holy One, blessed be He, will say, "Some of yourselves shall testify that Israel observed the entire Torah. Let Nimrod come and

50. Ibid., 5–6; cf. Rom. 4:4–5 as well as the interpretation of Lev. 18:5 in Gal. 3:12; Rom. 10:5.
51. Ibid., 6.
52. The accusation against Israel is already dealt with in the parallel texts. The teaching attributed to Eleazar of Modiim (born c. 135 C.E.), that Israel actually deserves no better reward than the heathen, is unusual. God passes judgment that all the nations together with their gods must descend into Gehenna, including Israel with Yahweh, in order to be punished (*Midr. Cant. Cant.* 2,1,95ᵃ with the parallel in *Midr. Ps.* 1, 20, 11ᵃ). Are gnostic influences at work here?
53. Epstein, *The Babylonian Talmud*, 6.
54. Ibid.
55. Ibid.

testify that Abraham did not [consent to] worship idols; let Laban come and testify that Jacob could not be suspected of theft; let Potiphar's wife testify that Joseph was above suspicion of immorality; let Nebuchadnezzar come and testify that Hanania, Mishael and Azariah did not bow down to an image; let Darius come and testify that Daniel never neglected the [statutory] prayers; let Bildad the Shuite, and Zophar the Naamathite, and Eliphaz the Temanite [and Elihu the son of Barachel the Buzite] testify that Israel has observed the whole Torah; as it is said, *Let them [the nations] bring their [own] witnesses, that they [Israel] may be justified.*"[56]

Now the heathen admit their defeat and resort to supplications and prayers: "The nations will then plead, 'Offer us the Torah anew and we shall obey it'." Such a request is obviously ridiculous, for no one can turn back the wheels of time in the hour of judgment and begin again from the beginning. And yet the judge is prepared to accept their suggestion and put it to the test:

But the Holy One, blessed be He, will say to them, "You foolish ones among the peoples, he who took trouble [to prepare] on the eve of the Sabbath can eat on the Sabbath, but he who has not troubled on the eve of the Sabbath, what shall he eat on the Sabbath? Nevertheless I have an easy command which is called *Sukkah;* go and carry it out."[57]

Again there follow interpolations that seek to justify the incomprehensible and seemingly arbitrary exception which God makes for the Gentiles. The story continues, and we see the Gentile nations again returned to the earth where they have been given yet another chance to pass the test by observing the feast of Sukkoth:

Straightaway will everyone of them betake himself and go and make a booth on top of his roof; but the Holy One, blessed be He, will cause the sun to blaze forth over them as at the summer solstice, and every one of them will trample down his booth and go away, as *it is said, Let us break their bands asunder, and cast away their cords from us.*[58]

Further interpolations bring forward additional arguments, which must first be refuted, for dismissing the case: namely, that God deals

56. Ibid., 6–7.
57. Ibid., 7.
58. Ibid., 8; Ps. 2:3 is cited.

with his creation imperiously by sending the heat of the summer solstice, a thing which is not in keeping with his nature, that Israel is granted relief in such great heat, etc. Then the long story comes to a close: "Thereupon the Holy One, blessed be He, will laugh at them, as it is said, *He that sitteth in heaven laugheth.*"[59] That God's laughter borders on the macabre did not go unnoticed by the tradition, for R. Issac adds immediately: "Only on that day is there laughter for the Holy One, blessed be He!"[60]

The Rabbinic story has been presented at such great length because only thus does light fall on its proximity to and distance from Matt. 7:21–23. Common to both stories is the literary genre of the judgment scene—with the appearance of groups of persons, rather than individuals; God's willingness to enter into protracted dealings with the Gentile nations; and the admission of objections and grounds for defense, petitions, and the calling of witnesses. The events described here and in the SM imitate the legal proceedings of an earthly court in general. In both instances the proceedings conclude with the confirmation of the original verdict. It remains to be asked whether in the Rabbinic tale an implicit debate is being carried on with the Christian notion of the justification of the Gentiles.

What distinguishes the two stories, on the other hand, are the differences in theological context, length, and complexity: in contrast to the broad Rabbinic tale enriched by numerous interpolations, Matt. 7:21–23 is extremely brief, the work of a single hand, and Jewish-Christian in outlook. Matt. 7:21–23 portrays only a single episode in the last judgment, albeit the most decisive. God does not appear; one must assume that he observes the events in silence, as a judge might watch an insignificant interruption of the business of the court. But the SM and the Rabbinic tale are in agreement as to their general tendency: having failed to obey the Torah, the Gentiles are lost in the last judgment.

If our eyes are now trained to recognize the literary genre, other New Testament texts may be taken into account as sources or as parallel constructions in the interpretation of Matt. 7:21–23.

59. Ibid.; Ps. 2:4 is cited.
60. Ibid.

The christological concept in accordance with which Jesus appears in the last judgment as advocate and witness for his own followers is preserved in important sayings in the Q-tradition. Among these sayings, Matt. 10:32-33//Luke 12:8-9[61] is unique in many respects:

Therefore everyone who confesses me before men,
I will also confess him before my Father who is in heaven;
but whoever denies me before men,
him will I also deny before my Father who is in heaven.
Πᾶς οὖν ὅστις ὁμολογήσει ἐν ἐμοὶ ἔμπροσθεν τῶν ἀνθρώπων,
ὁμολογήσω κἀγὼ ἐν αὐτῷ ἔμπροσθεν τοῦ πατρός μου τοῦ ἐν [τοῖς] οὐρ]ανοῖς,
ὅστις δ᾽ ἂν ἀρνήσηταί με ἔμπροσθεν τῶν ἀνθρώπων,
ἀρνήσομαι κἀγὼ αὐτὸν ἔμπροσθεν τοῦ πατρός μου τοῦ ἐν [τοῖς] οὐρανοῖς.

The version in Matthew 10 cited here is found in a source which Matthew has taken up into his Gospel, the great Mission Discourse of Matt. 10:1-42, a work that resembles the pre-Matthean SM in many respects.[62] This primitive saying, found only here in the synoptic tradition, has been dealt with repeatedly by the exegetes.[63] Peculiar to the Matthean version is the fact that Jesus functions as an advocate for his disciples before the throne of the heavenly Father in the last judgment, and not as judge or Son of man. The Lukan version (12:8-9), on the other hand, speaks of the Son of man standing opposite the angels of God who make up the divine tribunal.[64] The act of acknowledgment is mutual:[65] whoever confesses him- or herself as a disciple

61. On this Q-saying see Bultmann, *History*, 112, 126, 150; *Ergänzungsheft*, 41-42; H. Braun, *Spätjüdisch-häretischer und frühchristlicher Radikalismus*, 2d ed. (Tübingen: J. C. B. Mohr [Paul Siebeck], 1969), vol. 2, 101 n. 6; G. Bornkamm, "Jesu Wort vom Bekennen," in *Geschichte und Glaube*, vol. I [*Gesammelte Aufsätze*, vol. II] (Munich: Chr. Kaiser, 1968), 25-36; Schulz, *Q*, 66ff. Cf. also the Beatitudes in Matt. 11:6//Luke 7:23.

62. In analogy to the SM, the question must also be raised with respect to the mission instruction whether it represents a Matthean or a pre-Matthean composition. Cf. D. Lührmann, *Die Redaktion der Logienquelle* (Neukirchen-Vluyn: Neukirchener Verlag, 1969), 49ff.; S. Brown, "The Mission to Israel in Matthew's Central Section (Matt 9:35-11:1)," *ZNW* 69 (1978): 73-90.

63. The expression "to confess someone" (ὁμολογέω ἔν τινι) is to be regarded as semiticizing; see Bauer, *Lexicon*, s.v.; BDR, §220, 2.

64. "Before the angels of God" (ἔμπροσθεν τῶν ἀγγέλων τοῦ θεοῦ). Cf. the obviously dogmatic conjectures in the *var. lect.*

65. It is, therefore, one of the statements which Käsemann designated a "sentence of holy law" (see n. 2). Bornkamm, "Jesu Wort," 65 is in agreement; as Lührmann, *Die Redaktion*, 51.

142

of Jesus before others in this life, Jesus (Matthew) or the Son of man (Luke) will acknowledge such a one as his advocate in the last judgment. The same is true of the opposite situation, that of denial.[66] What is at stake in such ὁμολογεῖν or ἀρνεῖν is clear from the episode in Matt. 7:21-23, where Jesus' ὁμολογεῖν amounts, in fact, to the ἀρνεῖν of the denial formula.[67]

The kinship between Matt. 10:32-33 par. and Matt. 7:21-23 is further evidenced by the unusual sayings-tradition cited in 2 Clement 3-4.[68] The entire group of sayings found there, together perhaps with their paraenetic explanations, has been taken over from Jewish-Christian writings. The section is closely akin theologically to the SM, though not simply derived from it. Thus it belongs to the same Jewish-Christian milieu as the SM, and has access to sayings-material handed down as a part of this tradition, while not being *literally* dependent upon the SM. One of these Jesus sayings runs as follows (2 Clem. 3:2):

And he himself also says:
"Whoever confesses me before men,
I will confess him before my Father."

λέγει δὲ καὶ αὐτός·
Τὸν ὁμολογήσαντά με ἐνώπιον τῶν ἀνθρώπων,
ὁμολογήσω αὐτὸν ἐνώπιον τοῦ πατρός μου.

As R. Knopf[69] rightly observed in his commentary, the wording of the saying follows "Matthew more closely than Luke, but does not appear to have been taken directly from Matthew. . . . That the preacher actually had the text of Matthew in mind and reworked it freely is hardly imaginable, since the motives for such a transforma-

66. Thus, correctly Billerbeck, vol. 1, 469; Bauer, *Lexicon*, s.v. "ἀρνέω"; H. Schlier, *TDNT* 1, 469.
67. See above n. 16; Bornkamm, "Jesu Wort," 30ff., 34ff.
68. Cf. Bornkamm, "Jesu Wort," 34 n. 7; H. Köster, *Synoptische Überlieferung bei den Apostolischen Vätern* (Berlin: Akademie-Verlag, 1957), 71ff., 79ff.; K. P. Donfried, *The Setting of Second Clement in Early Christianity* (Leiden: E. J. Brill, 1974), 60ff.; M. Mees, "Ausserkanonische Parallelstellen zu den Gerichtsworten Mt. 7:21-23; Lk 6,46; 13,26-28 und ihre Bedeutung für die Formung der Jesusworte," *VetChr* 10 (1973): 79-102; idem, *Ausserkanonische Parallelen zu den Herrenworten und ihre Bedeutung* (Bari: Instituto di letteratura cristiana antica, 1975), 87ff.
69. Cf. R. Knopf, *Die Apostolischen Väter* I (Tübingen: J. C. B. Mohr [Paul Siebeck], 1920), 157-58; similarly Donfried, *Setting of Second Clement*, 60-61; differently Köster, *Synoptische Überlieferung*, 71ff.

tion are lacking. ... Thus the only remaining alternative is that he knew the saying from another tradition, whether written or oral." The interpretation of Jesus' saying which follows is also near to the SM theologically, but makes use of material that surfaces elsewhere in the synoptic and apocryphal traditions:[70]

> This then is our reward,[71] if we confess him through whom we were saved. But in what manner do we confess him? By doing what he says,[72] and not disobeying his commandments,[73] and by honoring him not only with our lips, but "with our whole heart and with our whole mind."[74] For he also says in Isaiah: "This people honors me with their lips, but their heart is far from me."[75]

Then in the very next paragraph is found the allusion to Matt. 7:21–23: "Let us not, then, merely call him Lord, for this will not save us. For he says: 'Not everyone who says to me, "Lord, Lord!" will be saved, but he who does righteousness'."[76] This quotation as well cannot have been derived word for word directly from the SM, yet it corresponds in essence to Matt. 7:21–23 and is hardly imaginable apart from a knowledge of it.[77] The same may also be said of the interpretation (2 Clem. 4:3):

> So then, brothers, let us confess him in deeds,[78] by loving one another, by neither committing adultery, nor slandering one another, nor being jealous, but by being self-controlled, merciful, good;[79] and we ought to share one another's lot, and not be lovers of money.[80] By such deeds we confess him and not by those of the opposite kind.[81]

70. 2 Clem. 3:3–5; the translation is that of Laurence Welborn.
71. μισθός. On this concept in the SM see Matt. 5:12, 46; 6:1, 2, 5, 16; cf. also 10:41ff.
72. Cf. Matt. 7:24–27.
73. μὴ παρακούειν αὐτοῦ τῶν ἐντολῶν (3:4) makes reference to the commandments of Jesus; cf. Matt. 5:19: the ἐντολαί are the commandments of Jesus in the SM, esp. 5:21ff.
74. Deut. 6:5, cited in Mark 12:30 par.
75. Isa. 29:13, cited in Mark 7:6; Matt. 15:8.
76. 2 Clem. 4:2.
77. Cf. Matt. 5:7, 10, 20; 6:1, 33.
78. ἐν τοῖς ἔργοις αὐτὸν ὁμολογῶμεν. Cf. Matt. 5:16.
79. On ἀγαπᾶν cf. Matt. 5:43, 46; μοιχᾶσθαι, 5:32; καταλαλεῖν is not found in the SM, cf., however, 5:11; 7:1; James 4:11; ζηλοῦν and ἐγκρατής are lacking in the SM; ἐλεήμων, Matt. 5:7 (cf. 6:2); ἀγαθός, 5:45.
80. συμπάσχειν and φιλαργυρεῖν are lacking in the SM.
81. μὴ ἐν τοῖς ἐναντίοις (ἔργοις) is noteworthy; in the background is the Two

The conclusion of the section in *2 Clem.* 4:4-5 manifests, once again, a close relationship theologically to the SM, though it is impossible to demonstrate literal dependence on Matthew 5-7:[82]

> And we must not fear men rather than God.[83] For this reason, if you do these things, the Lord said, "If you are with me, gathered into my bosom, but do not keep my commandments, I shall cast you out, and I shall say to you, 'Depart from me, I do not know you, whence you are, you workers of iniquity'."[84]

How the tradition found in *2 Clement* 3-4 is literarily related to the SM is difficult to say. It is not simply a matter of choosing between literal dependence and the canonical Gospel of Matthew and familiarity with the oral tradition. It is wholly possible that *2 Clement* 3-4 is acquainted with the pre-Matthean SM which, as a piece of literature, aims at being appropriated contemplatively. Such an appropriation and interpretation in the form of commentary may have been undertaken here; but if so the SM is only one source among many. *Second Clement* 3-4 belongs to the literature of commentary in which Jesus' sayings are subsequently interpreted, here in the context of Jewish-Christian theology. Thus we can conclude that the tradition preserved in *2 Clement* 3-4 comes from the same literary milieu as the SM, that is, from Jewish Christianity. No doubt other sources, apart from the SM, were in circulation which originated in this milieu, but which have not otherwise been preserved. They surface at widely scattered points in later traditions.[85] A saying from one such work

---

Ways teaching. Cf. J. Bergman, "Zum Zwei-Wege-Motiv. Religionsgeschichtliche und exegetische Bemerkungen," *SEA* 41-42 (1976-77), 27-56; Betz, "The Sermon on the Mount," 286 and in this volume, 1-16.

82. The translation is that of L. Welborn; on this passage cf. Knopf, *Die Apostolischen Väter*, 159.

83. Cf. Matt. 6:25-34, as well as 10:26-33.

84. On the derivation of this citation from an apocryphal gospel manuscript, see Knopf, *Die Apostolischen Väter*, 159; cf. also HSW, *NT Apocrypha* I, 113. A similar saying is found in the *Gospel of the Nazarenes*, see A. Schmidtke, *Neue Fragmente und Untersuchungen zu den judenchristlichen Evangelien* (Leipzig: Hinrichs, 1911), 39 no. 42, 297ff.; HSW, *NT Apocrypha* I, 95; Wrege, *Die Überlieferungsgeschichte*, 148ff.

85. A similar situation exists with respect to another cluster of citations: cf. *1 Clem.* 13:2 (with par. to Matt. 5:7; 6:14, 15; 7:1, 2, 12); *2 Clem.* 6:1 (Matt. 6:24); *Polycarp* 2:3 (Matt. 7:1, 2; 5:3, 10); 6:2 (Matt. 6:12, 14, 15)—not to speak of the *Didache*. Cf. Köster, *Synoptische Überlieferung*, passim.

seems to have been preserved in Rev. 3:5:[86] "and I will confess his name before my Father and before his angels" (καὶ ὁμολογήσω τὸ ὄνομα αὐτοῦ ἐνώπιον τοῦ πατρός μου καὶ ἐνώπιον τῶν ἀγγέλων αὐτοῦ). As is well known, the wording of Jesus' promise here cannot simply be derived from the synoptic sayings-material. The saying makes an archaic impression within the Apocalypse of John, for the notion of Jesus as advocate for his disciples is clearly in tension with the Christology of the Apocalypse itself. Besides Matt. 10:32–33 pars. from which we began, there is still another saying of Jesus that must be taken into consideration in interpreting Matt. 7:21–23, a saying intimately connected to the entire complex: Mark 8:38//Luke 9:26,[87] cited here in the Markan version:

> For whoever is ashamed of me and my words in this adulterous and
> sinful generation,
> the Son of man will also be ashamed of him, when he comes
> in the glory of his Father with the holy angels.
>
> ὃς γὰρ ἐὰν ἐπαισχυνθῇ με καὶ τοὺς ἐμοὺς λόγους ἐν τῇ γενεᾷ ταύτῃ τῇ
> μοιχαλίδι καὶ ἁμαρτωλῷ,
> καὶ ὁ υἱὸς τοῦ ἀνθρώπου ἐπαισχυνθήσεται αὐτόν, ὅταν ἔλθῃ ἐν τῇ
> δόξῃ τοῦ πατρὸς αὐτοῦ μετὰ τῶν ἀγγέλων τῶν ἁγίων.

The expression of shame here corresponds to failure to confess or denial in Matt. 10:32–33 pars. and Jesus' refusal to testify on behalf of those condemned in Matt. 7:21–23. Furthermore, all these sayings exhibit an eschatological principle of reciprocity: the disciple's conduct in this life entails the corresponding experience in the afterlife.[88]

86. Cf. also 2 Tim. 2:12 within a group of sayings. Cf. Bornkamm, "Jesu Wort," 26–27.

87. The literature on this saying is immense, but is mostly concerned with the problem of the Son of man. Cf. Bultmann, History, 112, 126, 150; Ergänzungsheft, 41–42; H. E. Tödt, Der Menschensohn in der synoptischen Überlieferung, 2d ed. (Gütersloh: Gerd Mohn, 1963), 37ff., 50ff.; Käsemann, "Sentences," 78–79; Hahn, Christologische Hoheitstitel, 32ff., 321; P. Vielhauer, Aufsätze zum Neuen Testament (Munich: Chr. Kaiser, 1965), 76ff.; Braun, Spätjüdisch-häretischer, 17 n. 3; 46 n. 1; 101 n. 6; Schulz, Q, 66ff.; W. G. Kümmel, "Das Verhältnis Jesus gegenüber und das Verhalten des Menschensohnes. Markus 8,38 par. and Lukas 12,8f. par. Matthäus 10,32f.," in Heilsgeschehen und Geschichte, vol. II (Marburg: Elwert, 1978), 201–14.

88. For Käsemann, "Sentences," 78, this saying too belongs to the sentences of holy law; cf. also Bornkamm, "Jesu Wort," 29–30; Vielhauer, Aufsätze zum Neuen Testament, 78; Lührmann, Die Redaktion, 51; for considerations which weigh against Käsemann's thesis see, with additional literature, Kümmel, "Das Verhältnis

In addition, Mark 8:38 pars. is less concerned with the last judgment than with the Parousia of the Son of man, a tendency which culminates in Matt. 16:27 with the redactional insertion of Ps. 62:13. This brings its Christology into agreement with the Matthean notion of Jesus as the Son of man–Judge.[89] Thus, in comparison with Matt. 10:32–33 pars. and Matt. 7:21–23, Mark 8:38 pars. represents another Christology, in which Jesus appears on earth as the herald of the coming Son of man. The Son of man, then, takes up the cause of Jesus in the Parousia.

In respect to the sources of Matt. 7:21–23, we may conclude that sayings such as Matt. 10:32–33 pars. and Mark 8:38 pars. are literarily related to the story found in Matt. 7:21–23. But on account of the various Christologies found in those sayings, which cannot be reduced to a common denominator, it is impossible to state whether these sayings served as the source for Matt. 7:21–23. So much may at least be said with regard to their relationship: the sayings embody the episode portrayed in the story in condensed form, the narrative only serving to expand what is there presented didactically. Literarily speaking, the sayings-form presupposes the story-form, while the story presupposes the sayings discussed above in a general, mythical sense. Thus in the present instance the following sequence may be postulated: the didactic content of sayings such as Matt. 10:32–33 pars. and Mark 8:38 pars. was made into a story in Matt. 7:22–23, which was again reduced to a sentence in Matt. 7:21.

What follows from this for an understanding of the relationship of Luke 6:46 and Matt. 7:21–23? If one assumes that Luke 6:46 must somehow have formed the basis for Matt. 7:21–23, then the transformation of the sayings-material might have taken place in the following way: Jesus' warning with regard to his disciples' conduct in this life, "Why do you call me 'Lord, Lord!' but do not the things that I say?" was later thought out in terms of its eschatological implications. In keeping with the eschatological *ius talionis*, Jesus is made to draw the eschatological consequence of the saying that he uttered while on earth in Luke 6:46. The paraenetical intention of the

Jesus," 211–12.
89. Cf. Matt. 16:28; 19:28; 24:30–31; 25:31.

situation portrayed in Matt. 7:22–23 is then summarized in the admonition in 7:21. The entire composition (7:21–23) should thus be understood as an answer to the question asked in Luke 6:46. It gives the reason why it is absurd to call Jesus "Lord, Lord!" on earth, but disregard his commandments: because in the last judgment only doing of God's will, that is the will of God as interpreted by the commands of Jesus, will be accounted as righteousness.

In a broader, literary sense, the form of the story that depicts scenes from the last judgment must also be considered a source for the episode described in Matt 7:21–23. A number of passages in the New Testament and in extracanonical literature indicate that this narrative form was used elsewhere in early Christian literature.

Luke 13:23–28 contains one of Jesus' eschatological discourses given in answer to his disciples' question. Interestingly, the question is formulated in an oracular style:[90] "Lord, will those who are saved be few?" In other words: will only a few be saved in the last judgment? Jesus answers their question affirmatively:

> And he said to them, "Strive to enter in through the narrow door; for many, I tell you, will seek to enter and will not be able."[91] When once the master of the house has arisen and shut the door, you will begin to stand outside and knock upon the door, saying, "Lord, open to us!"[92] And he will answer you, "I do not know you, whence you are." Then you will begin to say, "We ate and drank before you, and you taught in our streets."[93] But he will say to you, "I do not know [you], whence you are; depart from me all you workers of iniquity!" There will be weeping and gnashing of teeth when you see Abraham and Isaac and Jacob and all the prophets in the kingdom of God and you yourselves cast out.

The source of this discourse, preserved only in Luke, remains an unsolved problem.[94] But it contains so many seemingly archaic elements that Grundmann's verdict carries weight: "It is probable

90. "Lord, are those saved going to be few?" (κύριε, εἰ ὀλίγοι οἱ σῳζόμενοι;) Cf. Bauer, *Lexicon*, s.v. "εἰ," V, 1; BDR, §440, 3. See in addition Matt. 9:37//Luke 10:2; Matt. 22:14 par.; Mark 10:26–27 par.
91. Cf. Matt. 7:13–14.
92. Cf. Matt. 7:7–11.
93. This version of the proof of innocence has in part influenced the transmission of the text of Matt. 7:22; cf. Nestle-Aland, 26th ed.; Köster, *Synoptische Überlieferung*, 86ff. on this passage.
94. Thus rightly Lührmann, *Die Redaktion*, 55 n. 2.

that Luke took the discourse from a special tradition, where he found it already composed."[95] The similarity of the pericope to Matt. 7:21–23 is obvious: here too we have an episode with eschatological character, in which a group of Christians address Jesus as Lord. Interestingly, one finds stated explicitly here the double rejection that is only implied in Matt. 7:21–23: Jesus' initial rejection followed by a speech in their defense by those who seek admission; then follows a second rejection, heightened by citation of Ps. 6:8.[96] But in contrast to Matt. 7:21–23, the episode in Luke 13:23–28 is not played out at the last judgment, but before the entrance to the kingdom of God. Thus it bears comparison with Matt. 7:13–14, yet goes far beyond the notions employed there, in that Jesus as master of the house and doorkeeper is given free rein to deny entrance to a group who call on his name. The group is only permitted to gaze into paradise from the outside, to see there Abraham, Isaac, and Jacob, along with all the prophets. They see, moreover, all those who have come from the four corners of the earth to sit at table in the kingdom of God (v. 29).

A literarily similar phenomenon is found in Matt. 25:1–13.[97] The allegorical Parable of the Ten Virgins depicts a heavenly scene in which the foolish maidens are turned away by Jesus with the following words (vv. 11–12, RSV): "Afterward the other maidens came also, saying, 'Lord, Lord, open to us.' But he replied, 'Truly, I say to you, I do not know you'."

That this narrative form was perpetuated in the apocryphal gospel tradition is clear from the passage in 2 Clement 4 discussed above, at the end of which Jesus once again rejects those who do not obey his commands: "If you are gathered together with me in my bosom, and do not my commandments, I will cast you out, and will say to you: 'Depart from me, I do not know you, whence you are, you workers of

---

95. W. Grundmann, *Das Evangelium nach Lukas* (Berlin: Evangelische Verlagsanstalt, 1961), 284; thus also Wrege, *Die Überlieferungsgeschichte,* 150–51; differently Bultmann, *History,* 116–17, 130, who holds the piece to be a Lukan composition on the basis of Q; so also Schulz, *Q,* 310.

96. The citations from Ps. 6:8 (LXX:9) in Luke 13:27; Matt. 7:23; 25:41; 2 *Clem.* 4:5; Justin, *Apol.* I, 16, 11; *Dial.* 76, 5 follow different versions of the LXX in part, and thus can hardly be dependent upon one another.

97. For literature see Bultmann, *History,* 417, n. to 176; *Ergänzungsheft,* 71; W. Grundmann, *Das Evangelium nach Matthäus* (Berlin: Evangelische Verlagsanstalt, 1968), 514ff.

iniquity'."[98] Attempts to derive this saying from the *Gospel of the Egyptians* have not proven convincing, but we can hardly go amiss with the assumption that the saying comes from a Jewish-Christian gospel[99] no longer extant, or from a sayings-collection of this sort, and that its similarity to the SM can be accounted for in this way.

Closely related to the material in the SM is a saying of Jesus twice cited by Justin (*Apol.* I, 16, 9-11):

> For he spoke thus:
> Not everyone who says to me, "Lord, Lord" shall enter into the kingdom of heaven,
> but he who does the will of my Father in heaven.
> For whoever hears me and does the things that I say hears him who sent me.
> But many will say to me:
> "Lord, Lord,
> have we not eaten and drunk in your name and worked miracles?"
> And then I will say to them, "Depart from me, you workers of iniquity."
> Εἶπε γὰρ οὕτως·
> Οὐχὶ πᾶς ὁ λέγων μοι· κύριε, κύριε εἰσελεύσεται εἰς τὴν βασιλείαν τῶν οὐρανῶν,
> ἀλλ᾽ ὁ ποιῶν τὸ θέλημα τοῦ πατρός μου ἐν τοῖς οὐρανοῖς.
> ῞Ος γὰρ ἀκούει μου καὶ ποιεῖ ἃ λέγω, ἀκούει τοῦ ἀποστείλαντός με.
> Πολλοὶ δὲ ἐροῦσί μοι·
> Κύριε, κύριε,
> οὐ τῷ σῷ ὀνόματι ἐφάγομεν καὶ ἐπίομεν καὶ δυνάμεις ἐποιήσαμεν;
> καὶ τότε ἐρῶ αὐτοῖς· ᾽Αποχωρεῖτε ἀπ᾽ ἐμοῦ, ἐργάται τῆς ἀνομίας.

The saying seems to presuppose knowledge of the SM, but there are important differences that counsel caution. The inclusion of a new saying in I, 16, 10, cited again with a slightly different wording in I, 63, 5, is reminiscent of Matt. 10:40, and indicates dependence upon another tradition.[100] Moreover, the attempt of those rejected to justify

98. The translation is that of L. Welborn.
99. See the conjectures in HSW, *NT Apocrypha* I, 112ff.; cf. also the *Gospel of the Nazarenes*, ibid., I, 95, no. 6: "The Jewish gospel reads here as follows: If you are in my breast and do not do the will of my Father in heaven, I will thrust you away from my breast." For discussion, see ibid., 93-94; Köster, *Synoptische Überlieferung*, 92ff.; Wrege, *Die Überlieferungsgeschichte*, 148ff.
100. Cf. also the parallels in Luke 10:16; John 13:20; Gal. 4:14; *Didache* 11:4; *Ign. Eph.* 16:1. For discussion see Köster, *Synoptische Überlieferung*, 87ff.; A. J. Bellinzoni, *The Sayings of Jesus in the Writings of Justin Martyr* (Leiden: E. J. Brill, 1967), 22ff.

their actions has been altered by mention of the eucharistic celebration. Eating and drinking in the name of Jesus has been given new significance as a false appeal to the sacrament.[101] The episode has therefore been brought up to date paraenetically. The rejected, however, no longer represent competing Gentile Christianity, but the "lapsed" within the community of the church itself. When Justin quotes the same saying in *Dial.* 76, 5, the wording is strongly different, though he adds no explanation for the change:

Many will say to me in that day:
"Lord, Lord,
have we not eaten and drunk and prophesied and cast out demons in
your name?
And I will say to them, 'Depart from me'."

Πολλοὶ ἐροῦσί μοι τῇ ἡμέρᾳ ἐκείνῃ·
Κύριε, κύριε,
οὐ τῷ ὀνόματι ἐφάγομεν καὶ ἐπίομεν καὶ προεφητεύσαμεν καὶ δαιμόνια
ἐξεβάλομεν;
καὶ ἐρῶ αὐτοῖς· Ἀναχωρεῖτε ἀπ᾽ ἐμοῦ.

However the differences in these citations are to be explained, they demonstrate that the literary creation of stories such as that in Matt. 7:21-23 was carried on up to the middle of the second century.

III. THE CHRISTOLOGICAL PROBLEM

Although the SM elsewhere contains only indirect statements about Jesus, Matt. 7:21-23 comes nearest to an explicit Christology. To be sure, it is a Christology that is wholly embedded in eschatology. Moreover, one might ask whether the view of Jesus expressed here merits the name of "Christology" at all.[102] At this point it is particularly important to avoid the frequently encountered methodological error of reading other and better-known christological concepts—that, for example of the Son of man and Judge of the last days[103] —into Matt. 7:21-23.[104]

101. Cf. Luke 13:26 (see above, 148-49).
102. I am obliged to thank Jan Bergman for critical observations at this point.
103. On this point see above all E. Lohse, "Christus als Weltenrichter," in *Jesus Christus in Historie und Theologie*, 475-86.
104. I have myself made this mistake ("Die Makarismen der Bergpredigt," 6, and

The eschatology of the SM consists in the hope that Jesus will appear as advocate for his faithful followers, that is, for those who have done the will of his Father in heaven, in accordance with his teaching, in the last judgment.[105] This view of Jesus as the Paraclete remains entirely within the context of Jewish eschatology, which holds that God will entrust not only angelic beings, but certain holy and wise men with this task.[106] In the context of Jewish thought, the Paraclete is not necessarily to be understood as a mediator of salvation. This fits well with the Jewish-Christian view found in the SM, in which the eschatological advocacy of Jesus is motivated neither by his atoning death nor by his crucifixion and resurrection. Jesus has no salvific function in the SM, apart from obedience to the Torah that he teaches. Not even in those passages where martyrdom is discussed is his death regarded as an example (cf. Matt. 5:11, 12, 44). Jesus' eschatological function is thus restricted to bearing witness to the fact that the disciples who have been faithful in following the interpretation of the Torah he taught have fulfilled the will of the Father in heaven.

One can rightly ask whether a belief about Jesus that is so disposed merits being called a "Christology" at all. On the other hand, Pauline and Johannine texts illustrate the capacity of such a conception of Jesus as Paraclete to expand, so that it may be regarded, at least, as the starting point for the development of higher Christologies, above all the conception of Jesus as Judge and Son of man.[107]

In Paul one is reminded of the notion of the Paraclete only at Rom. 8:34[108] where, however, it is combined with a Redeemer Christology:

It is Christ [Jesus] who died, but was raised,

n. 15), following Bultmann, *History,* 122 n. 1. See in this volume 21 and n. 15.

105. Thus rightly Lohse, "Christus," 479–81.

106. On this point see esp. N. Johansson, *Parakletoi. Vorstellungen von Fürsprechern für die Menschen vor Gott in der alttestamentlichen Religion, im Spätjudentum und im Urchristentum* (Lund: C. W. K. Gleerup, 1940); on the current state of research see R. Schnackenburg, *Das Johannesevangelium* (Freiburg: Herder, 1975), vol. III, 156ff.

107. In Lohse's judgment, in "Christus," the pre-Pauline statement in 1 Thess. 1:9–10, that Jesus frees us from the coming wrath, stands on the border between the concept of Jesus as witness and as judge.

108. So also Lohse, "Christus," 480, who also refers to 1 John 2:1 and Heb. 7:25. Cf. also 1 Thess. 2:19; 3:13; 4:15–17; 5:23; Heb. 9:24; *1 Clem.* 36:1, etc.

who is at the right hand of God,
who also intercedes for us.
Χριστὸς ['Ιησοῦς] ὁ ἀποθανών, μᾶλλον δὲ ἐγερθείς,
ὃς καί ἐστιν ἐν δεξιᾷ τοῦ θεοῦ,
ὃς καὶ ἐντυγχάνει ὑπὲρ ἡμῶν.

It is interesting, moreover, that the notion of the last judgment plays an important role throughout the Epistle to the Romans. The first mention of the theme in 1:16 (RSV) already points in this direction:[109] "for I am not ashamed of the gospel" (οὐ γὰρ ἐπαισχύνομαι τὸ εὐαγγέλιον)—a statement that gives shape to the entire argument of the epistle, and that reaches its climax in 8:31-39. Paul's defense of the gospel in the Epistle to the Romans may well be compared with that of Matt. 7:21-23. Paul would agree entirely with the SM that any attempt at justification by appealing in Jesus' name to prophecy, exorcism, and miracles is bound to fail, since all who wish to enter into the kingdom of God must be found blameless.[110] Yet according to Paul, this righteousness is the fruit of the obedience of faith, and not obedience to the Torah. But even Paul must impress on his communities time and again that the obedience of faith is a matter of doing, that it is in works of love that the demands of the Torah are practically fulfilled, and that in the last judgment only such works count.[111] On the other hand, the SM[112] agrees with Paul[113] that the conventional understanding of the Torah leads not to justification, but only obedience to the Torah as understood by Jesus, which Paul, like the SM, sees epitomized in the love-commandment.[114] With regard to the notion of the Paraclete, it is clear that it may still be detected in Paul though overlain and displaced by the Redeemer Christology, the Parousia and judgeship of Christ.[115]

109. See on this point above all C. K. Barrett, "I am not Ashamed of the Gospel" in *New Testament Essays* (London: SPCK, 1972), 116–43; E. Käsemann, *Commentary on Romans,* Eng. trans. G. Bromiley (Grand Rapids: Wm. B. Eerdmans, 1980), 16–17.
110. Under this sign stand above all the Corinthian epistles; see esp. 1 Cor. 1:7–8; 3:10–17; 15:58; 2 Cor. 1:14; 5:10; 11:2, 15.
111. See esp. Gal. 5:14–6:10 and Betz, *Galatians,* 309ff.
112. Cf. esp. Matt. 5:17–48; 6:1–18.
113. Cf. in Paul esp. Gal. 2:15–16; 5:14 and Betz, *Galatians,* 69ff., 274ff.
114. Cf. Matt. 5:43–48; Gal. 5:14; 6:2 and Betz, *Galatians,* 274ff., 298ff.
115. The concept of the Spirit-Paraclete, which plays so great a role in the Gospel of John, is also found in Paul (Rom. 8:27; Gal. 4:6). Cf. Johansson,

The concept of the Paraclete in the Gospel of John has been dealt with more often and is thus better known. When the Johannine Jesus promises that he will send the Spirit as "another paraclete" (ἄλλος παράκλητος) after his return to his Father, he makes clear in the first place that he himself was regarded as a Paraclete.[116] Thus Jesus' prayer in John 17 represents nothing other than a plea, or intercession, for his own before the Father, in which the differences between the judgment of the end time and the earthly present are transcended in a manner characteristic of the Fourth Gospel. In 1 John 2:1 one discovers, to one's surprise, that this primitive notion of the Paraclete lies behind the Johannine conception,[117] though formulated certainly from a later point of view: "My children, I am writing these things to you so that you may not sin. But if anyone does sin, we have an advocate with the Father, Jesus Christ the righteous" (Τεκνία μου, ταῦτα γράφω ὑμῖν ἵνα μὴ ἁμάρτητε. καὶ ἐάν τις ἁμάρτῃ, παράκλητον ἔχομεν πρὸς τὸν πατέρα, Ἰησοῦν Χριστὸν δίκαιον).

In conclusion, one may say that Matt. 7:21-23 puts forward an eschatological concept of Jesus as advocate for his disciples in the last judgment. This belief, which appears in other passages in the New Testament only as an archaic relic, represents a very ancient "Christology" that originated in Jewish Christianity, if in fact it deserves to be termed a Christology at all.

IV. THE FUNCTION OF THE PERICOPE
WITHIN THE
SERMON ON THE MOUNT

Within the SM, Matt. 7:21-23 is found embedded in the context of eschatological warnings (7:13-23). These warnings are introduced by the figure of the Two Ways and the two gates leading into the city of

Parakletoi, 268ff.; Betz, *Galatians*, 211 n. 94.

116. Cf. John 14:16-17, 26; 15:26; 16:5-11, 12-15, as well as G. Bornkamm, "Der Paraklet im Johannesevangelium," in *Gesammelte Aufsätze*, vol. III, 68-89.

117. The origin of the Johannine title "paraclete" in the history of religions remains disputed. Cf. Bornkamm's remarks "Der Paraklet," 70 n. 10. One must distinguish more precisely in this matter between the specifically Johannine form and its religious-historical roots. To the latter certainly belongs the concept of the advocate or intercessor, as we find it in Judaism. See above all R. Bultmann, *The Gospel of John: A Commentary*, Eng. trans. G. Beasley Murray (Philadephia:

heaven (7:13-14). While the many travel toward eternal destruction on the wide and easy way and through the broad gate, it is the arduous path that is characterized as the way of salvation proclaimed by the SM.[118] Only a few have chosen to struggle upon this way, and only they have found the narrow gate leading to eternal life.

There follows in Matt. 7:15-20 a special warning with regard to false prophets or wandering missionaries of rival Christian groups. Matt. 7:21-23 is independent of this section and brings the eschatological portion of the SM to a close, followed only by the double parable in 7:24-27 as a kind of epilogue. Taken together, the eschatological images employed here are out of balance: the Two Ways motif does not really correspond to the image of the heavenly city with its two gates, one of which leads to hell, the other to paradise.[119] According to 7:21-23, the last judgment must take place in the heavenly city; but 7:13-14 prepares us as little for 7:21-23 as the latter pericope presupposes the first. The section 7:15-20 is inserted between these two scenes, but is related to them only by virtue of the context. To the information provided in 7:13-14, 7:15-20 adds only that among the multitudes on their way to perdition are Christians as well who were deceived by false prophets. Section 7:21-23 then relates how these misguided Christians fare in the last judgment. Just as they have misjudged the bad fruits of the false prophets on earth, they now misunderstand their true situation in the last judgment. Because they have followed false prophets, they now find themselves forsaken in the judgment.

In the course of the eschatological section 7:13-23, the broad and easy road that leads to destruction is made progressively more concrete. Section 7:15-23 specifies the inner-Christian dimension of the general paraenesis in 7:13-14. The false prophets mentioned in 7:15-20 are those who have taught that Jesus came in order to destroy the law and the prophets; now they must face the consequences of their

Westminster Press, 1971), 205, 437ff. (excursus: the paraclete); *Ergänzungsheft*, 41-42.

118. See on this point Betz, "The Sermon on the Mount," 286ff., and this volume, 1-16.

119. Cf. J. Jeremias, *TDNT* 6, 922; Grundmann, *Das Evangelium*, 230ff.; Betz, "The Sermon on the Mount," 286, and this volume, 2.

teaching.[120] They are the ones who are responsible for the fact that the group depicted in 7:21-23 appeals to such "rotten fruit," while lacking the good fruit of obedience to the will of God. There can be no doubt that these false prophets are Gentile Christian missionaries like Paul, who proclaim the gospel apart from the law. Of course Paul's own letters indicate that the apostle had to struggle repeatedly against enemies who attempted to lure the communities grounded upon his kerygma onto the path of false "boasting" ($\kappa\alpha\acute{\nu}\chi\eta\sigma\iota\varsigma$).[121] Thus Paul's defense of his Gospel and the anti-Pauline polemic of the SM are not simply in opposition to one another. Far from being a simple "misunderstanding" of Paul's doctrine, this polemic assaults the Pauline Gospel at its most vulnerable point, that is, at the point where Paul himself is constrained to take up weapons in his own defense. The polemic of the still-quite-puzzling Epistle of James points in a similar direction.[122]

Yet the inner-Christian polemic is not an end in itself, but serves the paraenetic attempt to label the competition as "heretical."[123] Thus the concluding section provides a defense against Gentile Christianity free of the law, whose seductive powers had been clearly recognized. Matt. 7:21-23 warns in particular against allowing oneself to be blinded by supposed religious "attainments," such as prophecy, exorcism, and miracles. Such religious achievements foster nothing other than the assertion of false claims in the last judgment, and end necessarily in tremendous disillusionment, as shown in 7:22-23.[124] From all this there results a rather confusing situation. How is

120. Cf. Betz, "Die Makarismen der Bergpredigt," 5-6, and this volume, 19-20.
121. Cf. Betz, *Paulus,* 70ff.; H. Braun, *Jesus of Nazareth: The Man and His Time,* Eng. trans. E. R. Kalin (Philadelphia: Fortress Press, 1979), 126; E. Schweizer, "Gesetz und Enthusiasmus bei Matthäus" in *Beiträge zur Theologie des Neuen Testaments* (Zurich: Zwingli Verlag, 1970), 49-70.
122. We can only mention here in passing the completely open problem of the relationship of the SM to the Epistle of James.
123. In this tendency the SM agrees with what I have attempted to show is an anti-Pauline fragment in 2 Cor. 6:14-7:1, but otherwise these texts cannot be reduced to a common denominator (see H. D. Betz, "2 Cor. 6:14-7:1: An Anti-Pauline Fragment?" *JBL* 92 [1973]: 88-108; idem, *Galatians,* 329-30).
124. Is there a connection between the SM and the Epistle to the Galatians here? Was the intention of the Galatians to turn away from the Pauline Gospel and to accept the Jewish-Christian kerygma a reaction to warnings such as those in Matt. 7:21-23? Cf. on the intentions of the Galatians, Betz, *Galatians,* 5ff.

the anti-Paulinism of the SM related to that of Paul's opponents? They are neither to be simply equated, nor is Paul simply opposed to them. Both warn in their own ways against the illusions cherished by the Gentile-Christian circle in respect to the demands of God. Thus the aims of the paraenesis of the SM run parallel to those of Paul in part. Jesus' teaching about the law had led to the false doctrine of the abrogation of the law and made necessary the composition of the SM as an epitome of the teaching of Jesus;[125] in a similar way, Paul saw himself confronted in his communities with the fact that consequences had been drawn from his preaching which in the last analysis destroyed the eschatological hopes of his churches. It was such developments, in fact, that led to the composition of Paul's epistles. Needless to say, the texts cannot be harmonized on this account. There can be no doubt that Matt. 7:21-23 does not merely criticize the misunderstanding embodied in the Gentile-Christian kerygma, but holds this kerygma itself responsible for the illusions cherished by the rejected group.[126] What, in a certain sense, constitutes the opposed eschatological scene is sketched by Paul at the end of Romans 8. In this scene, the gospel of the love of God in Christ triumphs in the last judgment as well. The prosecutor will fail; God will waive the negative verdict and accept those who are beloved of him in Christ as righteous. Here, too, Jesus appears as the defender of his own before God; but he stands there as the one who has been crucified and risen, as the son offered by his Father, as the redeemer of the lost. Thus in conclusion we must raise the important question of whether the paraenesis of the SM and Paul's argument in defense of his Gospel are related to one another in such a manner that they reflect the dialogue so fervently pursued in early Christianity over the meaning of the message of Jesus.

125. See on the point Betz, "Die Makarismen der Bergpr edigt," 6–7, and 20–21 in this volume; "The Sermon on the Mount," 285ff., and this volume, 1–16.

126. Cf. on this point the differing views of W. D. Davies, *The Setting of the Sermon on the Mount* (Cambridge: At the University Press, 1966), 334ff.; A. Lindemann, *Paulus im ältesten Christentum* (Göttingen: Vandenhoeck & Ruprecht, 1979), 155–56.

Index of Authors

Index of Passages

165

JEWISH WRITINGS

EARLY CHRISTIAN LITERATURE

INDEX OF PASSAGES

GREEK AND LATIN AUTHORS

Apuleius, *Met.*
XI, 16, 22-23—28

Cicero

De fin.
II, 7, 20—12

De nat. deor.
I, 30, 85—12
II, 60—115

Diog. L.
X, 27—12
X, 31—12
X, 35—12, 14
X, 36—14
X, 37—12
X, 82—14
X, 83—14
X, 85—12, 14
X, 116 11
X, 122—118
X, 123—14
X, 127—111
X, 129—11
X, 135—14
X, 139-54—11

Diogenes of Oenoanda
Frag. 23—12

Epictetus

Diss.
I, 1, 21—8
I, 1, 21-25—8
I, 1, 22—8
I, 9, 4-6—122
I, 9, 7—119
I, 9, 8—113
I, 9, 12—113
I, 9, 19-20—113

I, 16—119
I, 28, 28—11
I, 28, 30—11
I, 30, 5—9
II, 1, 29—8
II, 1, 30-33—9
II, 1, 38—9
II, 2, 21-26—9
II, 6, 14—9
II, 11, 13-25—11
II, 13, 4—9
II, 16, 2-3—9
II, 16, 15—9
II, 16, 27—8
II, 20, 21—11
II, 23, 21—11
III, 3, 14—11
III, 3, 15—11
III, 3, 20-22—74
III, 7, 17-18—9
III, 9, 15-22—119
III, 12, 8 8
III, 20, 12—118-19
III, 20, 15—118-19
III, 22, 44—118
III, 24—119
III, 24, 25-26—116
III, 26, 15—119
III, 26, 37—113
IV, 1, 83—8
IV, 1, 111—8
IV, 1, 132—8
IV, 1, 170—8
IV, 6, 16—8
IV, 6, 22-24—119
IV, 10—119
IV, 12, 20-21—116

Ench.
I, 1-3—11
I, 5—11

XVI—11
XXXIII, 7—115
LII, 2—11
LIII, 1—11

Epicurus

Ep. ad Men.
127—109
131—109

Frag.
469—109
492—116

Kyriai Doxai
I-XXXVIII—15
XXIX—109

Herodotus
1, 30-32—31

Homeric *Hymn to
Demeter*
480-83—26, 32, 34

Horace

Ep.
I, 4—15

Od.
I, 11, 8—116

Jamblichus, *Vit. Pyth.*
84—75

Lucian, *Alex.*
47—12

Lucretius, *De rer. nat.*
III, 1046-75—105
V, 222-34—105

169

Marcus Aurelius
5, 7—120

PGM
IV, 1160–66—121
V, 151–53—121
XII, 60–61—121
XII, 241–44—121
XII, 766—121
XXI, 2—121
XXI, 5–10—121

Pausanias
1, 24, 3—121

Pindar
Frag. 121—27

Plato

Alc.
128e–135e—106

Apol.
20d–21e—118
30b—106

Gorg.
523a–524a—135

Prot.
320c–322a—105

Rep.
VI, 507b—80
VI, 507b–509c—79
VI, 507d–e—80
VI, 508b—80
VI, 508c—80
VI, 508d—80
VI, 508e–509a—81
VI, 510b–511b—79
VII, 514a–518b—79
VII, 515c—81
VII, 515d—81
VII, 516e–517a—82
VII, 517b—82
VII, 517c—82
VII, 518a—81, 83
VII, 518c—83
VII, 518d—83
VII, 518e—83
VII, 519a—83

Tim.
45a—83
45c–d—84
54d—84

Pliny, *N. H.*
7, 1–5—105

Plutarch, *De tranquil.*
animi
16, 474c—116

Ps.-Plato, *Axioch.*
366d–367a—105
371d—27

Ps.-Plato, *Epinom.*
943d–947a—105

Stobaeus, *Ecl.*
III, 16, 28—116

Theophrastus

De sens.
1–2—74, 78

Char.
16—106

Xenophon, *Mem.*
1, 5, 6—31